# Thicker Than Blood

# Thicker Than Blood

## How Racial Statistics Lie

Tukufu Zuberi

*University of Minnesota Press*
*Minneapolis*
*London*

Published by the University of Minnesota Press
111 Third Avenue South, Suite 290
Minneapolis, MN 55401-2520
http://www.upress.umn.edu

Library of Congress Cataloging-in-Publication Data

Zuberi, Tukufu.
        Thicker than blood : how racial statistics lie / Tukufu Zuberi.
            p.      cm.
        Includes bibliographical references and index.
        ISBN 0-8166-3908-6 (acid-free paper)
            1. United States—Race relations—Research—Statistical methods.
        2. Ethnology—United States—Research—Statistical methods.    3. United
        States—Population—Research—Statistical methods.    4. African
        Americans—Research—Statistical methods.    5. Eugenics—United States.
        I. Title.
        E184.A1 Z83    2001
        305.8'007'27—dc21                                                        2001000925

Printed in the United States of America on acid-free paper

The University of Minnesota is an equal-opportunity educator and employer.


12  11  10  09  08  07  06  05  04  03  02  01      10 9 8 7 6 5 4 3 2 1

To Willie McDaniel and Annie E. Franklin

# Contents

# Prologue

For years we have understood that race is, biologically speaking, an exceedingly complex matter and that preconceived biases much more than biology govern the way people think about it. The statistics that are publicized these days in which race is prominent treat it as an objectively determined collection of discrete categories. Because the premises about race are false, the conclusions must be also; as the saying goes, *garbage in, garbage out*. Moreover, adding to this problem, many researchers—who should know better—argue that race causes a person to be in a certain condition or state, when the most that has been demonstrated is that race involves an association of undetermined causes. These errors in racial statistics are endemic and subvert even the most sympathetic attempts to address questions about race quantitatively.

We should not commit the error of accepting a research result because of its political or social implications unless such implications have a methodological impact on the subject being studied. In the case of racial statistics, policy-oriented research requires that the researcher consider the side effects of the findings. We cannot discredit an argument by demonstrating that it leads to unwanted political conclusions unless those conclusions imply a methodological error. Arguments based on racial statistics too often relate to a general misunderstanding of the foundations of statistical analysis.

These problems should not be misconstrued as being of merely academic significance. Statistical conceptions of race are more likely to be noticed in the sciences, but they play a critical role in guiding and justifying both private belief and public policy. For example, almost all of the federally sponsored studies of racial statistics conducted in the social sciences deal with causal inferences.

With racial statistics, one can "quantify" what one subjectively perceives as a problem to be studied using objective methods. Because such statistics look and sound scientific and are usually promulgated by reputable scholars, great weight is accorded them, even if their import is in fact distorted by subjective predispositions. If the statistics are misleading, inappropriate, or false or if the methodology incorporates false assumptions, few scholars or public officials are in a position to detect it. Analysis of racial statistics has helped justify harm to large groups of people.

Current statistical methodologies were developed as part of the eugenics movement and continue to reflect the racist ideologies that gave rise to them. Of course, racial statistics have not been used exclusively by supporters of racist policies. Social scientists, particularly in more recent times, have regularly resorted to using racial statistics in an effort to refute racist arguments or vindicate past misdeeds. However, by employing racial statistics they have actually legitimated the use of methodologies that perpetuate the problems they seek to overcome.

I will argue in this book that statistical analysis can and must be deracialized. However, I will suggest that this deracialization must be part of a process that recognizes the importance of history and the goal of achieving racial justice for all. Appeals to causality where none has been demonstrated, or can be demonstrated using statistical methods, should be loudly challenged. Studies relying on assumptions that impose a decontextualized racial identity in a social stratum should be replaced by better studies that incorporate more accurate assumptions. Social science must strive to develop a true human science where the dimensions of all population experiences are investigated within the broader social context in which we find ourselves.

Demographic and statistical methodologies tend to be rather mathematical and in some cases prohibitive for the uninitiated. I have tried to describe these mathematical concepts without resorting to equations, but inevitably, a few equations do rear their ugly heads in chapter 7. When equations do appear, I have endeavored to provide sufficient explanation such that even readers with no background in social statistics or mathematics will be able to understand their significance. For those readers with a slightly deeper knowledge of social statistics, I have provided several more technical notes with references to more technical research.

I begin with the history of the idea of race and its relationship to racial classification and evolutionary theory. First, I sketch the background of racial stratification to help set the stage for understanding the analysis of race in the twentieth century. This sketch is followed by a historical outline of evolutieth ideas used to describe and justify racial classification.

By tracing the history of inferential statistics from the evolutionary theory of Francis Galton to modern social statistics, I discuss how social scientists have helped reify notions of racial stratification. I also trace the history of descriptive statistics from the introduction of the social survey by Charles Booth in London and W. E. B. Du Bois in the United States to modern sociologists; I discuss racial statistics as numerical descriptions of various aspects of racial stratification. Next I extend this discussion to eugenics in demographic research. I conclude this part of the book with a critical evaluation of the current practice of inferential racial statistics in apparently "antiracist" research.

Finally, I return to statistical methodology. My purpose in this part of the manuscript is twofold. First, the section offers a critical evaluation of the process of racial classification; second, I offer a corrective to the faulty logic involved in the analysis of racial statistics. In order to accomplish this task, I focus on two areas that have impacted racial statistics: the population perspective in genetics, and demography. I discuss how these undermine the scientific basis for racial statistics and what they suggest about racially classifying data. A perspective is suggested on the basis of the principle of race-conscious social justice.

Social scientists have regularly resorted to racial statistics in an effort to present and refute racist arguments. By employing a causal framework in their racial statistics, both groups of scholars have legitimated the use of methodologies that justify racial stratification. On the basis of my readings between the evolutionary origin of social statistics and the reflexive discourse among statisticians as we embrace the twenty-first century, I propose that we need a new perspective.

# Acknowledgments

This book is an expansion of ideas that have developed over the years as I have taught at the University of Pennsylvania. I would like to thank the hundreds of students in two of my courses at the University of Pennsylvania, Race and Ethnic Relations and the Demography of Race, for providing the intellectual discourse and context for the ideas that eventually found their way into this book. Akil K. Khalfani, Linda J. Mamoun, Amson Sibanda, Jenifer Bratter, Shasta Jones, and Quincy Stewart read parts of the book at various stages of its development and made invaluable comments. I am also grateful for comments received from my colleagues Kenneth L. Shropshire, Elijah Anderson, Farah J. Griffin, Guthrie P. Ramsey Jr., Oscar H. Gandy Jr., Herbert L. Smith, Samuel H. Preston, and Douglas Ewbank. Angela James, Hayward Derrick Horton, Geoffrey J. Huck, and Howard Winant carefully read the entire manuscript and helped prevent many errors of fact and analysis. Several anonymous reviewers also provided helpful comments.

Vivian L. Gadsden read the first draft of the manuscript and advised me to expand the first chapter into a book. I followed her advice, and thanks to her the book is much improved. During the summer of 2000, Etienne van de Walle and I spent a week discussing the book. Etienne and I share a love for uncompromising scholarship; however, we come from two very different perspectives. I am sure that I have not captured or addressed all of his suggestions, but Etienne's critical reading of the manuscript and our discussions improved the manuscript in numerous ways.

My thanks to Carrie Mullen and the editorial staff at the University of Minnesota Press for scrupulous editing and good judgment and to Robin Whitaker for copyediting the manuscript with enlightened precision. Finally, I would like to thank my family for support during the time that it took to write this book.

In doing the research on which this book draws, I had support from the National Institute of Mental Health (1R01MH58009-01).

# INTRODUCTION

## Racial Statistics

> The problem of the twentieth century is the problem of the colour line, the question as to how far differences of race, which show themselves chiefly in the colour of the skin and the texture of the hair, are going to be made, hereafter, the basis of denying to over half the world the right of sharing to their utmost ability the opportunities and privileges of modern civilization.
> —Alexander Walters, Henry B. Brown, H. Sylvester Williams, and W. E. B. Du Bois, "To the Nations of the World" (1900)

At the dawn of the twenty-first century the problem of the color line remains with us. Since Du Bois's declaration almost one hundred years ago, there has been a flood of writings about racial classification and the meaning of race. Some writers deconstruct race as a social concept with no physical basis, while others see in race the biological differences of humans. My aim in writing *Thicker Than Blood* is to point objectively to the problems related to the statistical analysis of race, which lies at the heart of racial formation and classification.[1] I will attempt to demonstrate how the study of social statistics in racially structured or dominated situations could be positively illuminated by the examination of its foundation.

Routine racial classification started at the same time as the national census, which categorized the population by occupation, religion, place of birth, citizenship, and race, among other characteristics. The census has facilitated the development and public awareness of social statistics and demography, and now the public is served a steady diet of statistical and demographic analyses. It is not unusual for these analyses to grab the headlines; the morning paper and evening news continually provide the latest counts of unemployment, teenage pregnancy, crime, divorce, and life expectancy—all differentiated by race. These findings are accepted as the result of scientific methods of data collection and analysis and believed to be politically neutral. Federal governments spend millions of dollars for the collection of racial data and the analysis of racial statistics.

The numbers of mathematics and the numbers of statistics (including those of economics, sociology, and demography) are quite different. Mathematics is a system of statements that are accepted as true.[2] Mathematical statements follow one another in a definite order according to certain principles and are accompanied by proofs. The numbers from mathematics are the result of logical calculations. In mathematics the numbers are either exact or have a known or estimable error. Statistics is a system of estimation based on uncertainty. Statistics is a form of applied mathematics. Often in statistics, the numbers are no more than the axioms applied and may have little to do with the conditions of the correct applicability in the real world.

It is these conditions of applicability to race that are the concern of this book. Statistical interpretation of racial differences has taken on an almost deceptive quality. As a result, social statisticians have forgotten (or perhaps some have never realized) that the social concept of race affects how we interpret racial statistics.[3] Moreover, many racial statistics fail to be considered in a social context, thus allowing the faulty assumption that the existence of race relations could be benign. *Thicker Than Blood* represents my ongoing struggle to counter this view by critically evaluating the analysis of racial data.

At the root of statistical research is, of course, empirical social science, which was developed in response to the need for measured accounts of social changes. For example, the end of African enslavement and the establishment of settler states in the Americas, Asia, and Africa accompanied the transition to modern society. From its beginnings, the social science discipline has been handicapped by intellectual limitations whereby meaningful discussion about social change is restricted. An example of these intellectual limitations can be seen in the study of race.

Race has been defined statistically, genetically, and demographically.[4] In statistical analysis a race consists of an observational record of a particular attribute that indicates or "measures" an individual's racial identity. Genetic "races" consist of a group of individuals of a species living in a certain area. Demographic "races" consist of individuals coexisting at a given time and space and defined according to various criteria. Each of these disciplines has, under the influence of eugenics, contributed to the reification of race in social statistics or more specifically to the development of racial statistics.[5] My purpose is to show how race is neither a genetic nor a demographic characteristic. For me, race is a biological notion of physical difference grounded in ideology. To understand this ideology, we must take a social and historical approach.

In the beginning of the twentieth century, empirical social scientists took an evolutionary perspective toward race. Among them, Du Bois voiced an exception to the accepted view of race. He formulated the first empirical refutation of the evolutionary-based justification of racial differences in *The Philadelphia Negro*. After conducting an empirical study of African American life in a modern city, Du Bois illustrated how biological notions of African inferiority were grounded only in ideology.

Since the Enlightenment, conceptions of identity have defined the very core of questions about human difference in the Western world.[6] Sociology, for example, was founded by intellectuals who believed that "the world" (i.e., Europe or the West) was changing; social theorists such as Karl Marx, Max Weber, and Émile Durkheim examined the ways in which individual identity was shaped by the transformation of "traditional" societies into "modern" ones. Traditional preindustrial societies were seen as the embodiment of a collective identity in which the individual was aware of who she is and why she exists.

The clarity of traditional identities is blurred by the transition to the modern division of labor. As modern capitalism develops and rational behaviors dominate, the problems of identity are left behind. Yet the same social theorists who founded sociology had little to say about the role of race in modern society.[7] Marx treated racial inequality as a problem secondary to the class struggle. Weber treated race as an unsubstantiated category with marginal significance for understanding national identity, which he defined in opposition to ethnicity and race.[8] Du Bois recognized the importance of identity for the modern worldview, and he developed a critique of the theories of modern society in his thesis of the color line. He emphasized the importance of racial stratification:[9] one could not understand the impact of the modern division of labor, he argued, unless one understood African enslavement in the Americas, "on which modern commerce and industry was founded."[10] Du Bois's formulation of the problem presents race and class as significant, twin aspects of the modern division of labor.

At the heart of any statistical analysis of race are discussions of identity and the process of racial stratification. It is important that we recognize the role of racial statistics in enshrining and upholding racial hierarchies. In this book I consider the history of the statistical analysis of race, critically describe the logic of analysis of racialized data, and prescribe a method of interpreting these data without racial reasoning. To accomplish this task, one must go back to the foundations of racial statistics both historically and methodologically. The story of racial statistics has to begin with the original problem or else it does not make sense. I hope to provide a clarification across rival methodologies and point the way to improvements.

Here is what race means. Race is a socially constructed process that produces subordinate and superordinate groups.[11] Racial stratification is the key social process behind racial classifications. The meaning of race depends on the social conditions in which it exists.[12] In this work I ask the skeptic who does not believe in the physical existence of race to confront the social reality of race in the same way as the believer in the physical existence of race. The person who does not bring to the study of race some belief in the existence of race cannot speak about the subject. There cannot be a rational interpretation of race that fundamentally denies the existence of race. But I ask the believer in physical race, without becoming a disbeliever, to forget it provisionally, reserving the right to return to it later. I ask both the believer and the disbeliever to consider that race exists socially because human beings exist socially in a world shaped, in part, by human beings. As a social concept, race is not a material thing, but it does exist in a different way from the way material things exist. Race is, above all, a system of ideas by which men and women imagine the human body and their relationships within society. My definition of racial identity rests on the experience of shared social relations rather than on unitary shared subjective characteristics.

Race expresses and symbolizes two aspects of social identity. It is the outward form of socially salient physical difference; it is also the flag of the population, the sign by which each racial group is distinguished from others, a visible mark of distinctiveness that is borne by everything that emanates from the race. For example, some people talk about race as if it were culture; others talk about race as if it were a biological identity. Race is the symbol of both stratification and population identity, because racial stratification and identity are both aspects of society and, in fact, are both the same. Race is an emblem of a population within racially stratified societies. The identity of a group in a racially stratified society, its history and culture, is the mechanism by which the group is socially stratified, but the group transfigured and imagined in the physical form of skin color, facial features, ancestral origins—in a word, racialized—is what appears as race. Yet even this transfiguration hides the social reality of race.

When I approach the study of race, it is with the certainty that it is grounded in social reality. Social statistics are part of a discourse with which social questions are open to debate. Statistics are both descriptive and inferential.[13] Most social statistics are numerical descriptions of various aspects of the social world. Inferential statistics summarize data using mathematical tools. The development of the system of statistical reasoning cannot be separated from the political and social processes that motivated the articulation of the variables, or objects, employed as a reference for debate and discussion—the discourse.

Statistical analysis makes sense only in a context of a common language, marked by some level of agreement about the technical and social purpose. The variables and conventions that serve as the basis of statistics follow political, social, and mathematical developments.[14] Public debate that uses statistical reasoning is limited by how we define statistics and by our ideas about how society should operate.

Alain Desrosières notes that the existence of statistics "allows a certain type of public sphere to develop, but its vocabulary and syntax can themselves be debated: debate on the referent of the debate, and the words used to conduct it, is an essential aspect of any controversy."[15] I question the space within which race is debated as well as the use, vocabulary, and syntax of social statistical analysis.

Since its inception, social statistics has been concerned with difference. Critical to understanding social difference is the issue of individual and group identity. The identities that provided stability in past societies are being contested, giving rise to new identities and calling into question the process of identity formation itself. In part, our identities arise from our membership in a distinctive historical, linguistic, religious, and political culture. This group membership leads to our interest in how people are represented and how they represent themselves within a historically specific social context.

Many contemporary social statisticians tend to remove racial signifiers, like black and white, from their social and political context. This decontextualization has led many researchers to present racial categories as biologically constituted realities. Several scholars have reintroduced critical evaluations of the use of race as a variable in quantitative research; however, these critics have lacked the methodological rigor presented in this text.[16] I focus on the intersection of racial biases and the application of statistical science in various social science disciplines. Although some disciplines have questioned the nature and use of race, the intersection of race and methodology has not been sufficiently examined.

Different disciplines approach the study of race differently. For example, cultural studies (in history, literary criticism, sociology, and philosophy) have questioned the concept of race, yet they generally accept the race counts of uncritical social scientists and institutions. In part, this is clearly a result of how disciplinary lines are drawn. Most empirical social science is written in ways that exclude nonspecialists and scholars in cultural studies, who, like the general public, lack the training that allows them to critically read quantitative research in general and racial statistics in particular.

Power and domination are a regular part of the analysis in cultural studies; however, empirical social scientists tend to treat them as programmatic.[17] Whereas cultural studies question the legitimacy of power and domination, quantitative social scientists tend to accept the authority and rarely anticipate significant social change. The meaning of race has been transformed in the humanities and in cultural studies, yet most scholars continue to depend on empirical results produced by scholars who have not seriously questioned racial statistics.

I reject the belief that race is a stable underlying aspect of human difference; instead, race relations are better understood as racial stratification. The story of racial statistics must discuss how scholars attempting to understand race have misused statistical methods intentionally and unintentionally.

The recent increase of research on the history of statistics and probability makes it possible to undertake an interpretation of the sociology of knowledge of racial statistics. My sociology is both historical and comparative. I have selected two regions as examples: Africa and the Americas. They were chosen because of the available documentation and because significant episodes of the development of empirical analysis of race occurred in these regions.

Demographic and statistical research tend to confound race with ethnicity,[18] although recent theoretical understandings of the racialization of identity tend to distinguish race and ethnicity when physical characteristics, especially skin color, are a principal factor in identity formation. Therefore, before we discuss racial statistics and population analysis, we must revisit the meaning of race.

At the population level my analysis examines how the development of modern society helps naturalize racial differences. I focus on the social analysis by humans, without which there is no human history. I argue that different historical and social contexts have imposed different constraints on the ways in which we have defined and studied race. These constraints have structured the relations between racial groups and have produced dissimilar contexts not only for the manifestations of racial antagonisms and access to rewards but also for how we understand human differences.[19]

My discussion has two related aspects that connect my understanding of race and social statistics. First, I account for the features that define the process of racialization and then show how social statistics developed and became what is at the moment under consideration. This allows me to dissect racial statistics, presenting its component parts as they have arisen over time and revealing the social circumstances from which each part has developed. For example, I am not seeking the instant when the Africans began to be a race; rather, I am interested in discerning the processes that give racial statistics meaning.

I have not attempted to be encyclopedic or panoramic in the empirical presentation of this book. The examples used are illustrative. My point is that to transform racial stratification and to develop theoretical analysis that might lead to such a transformation, we must endeavor to link race, social stratification, and statistical analysis. For the purposes of this book many of my examples will focus on the case of Africa and the African diaspora.[20] I do not want to suggest that only Africans have suffered from race, but that by focusing on their case we have much to learn about the dynamics of race and racial statistics.

A true human science will necessarily investigate population experience within the broader context of society. The creation of a truly African and African diaspora study—that is, a study of Africa and the African diaspora that begins by recognizing the commonality of experience but also includes an honest recognition of our differences—is imperative at this historic moment. As Du Bois notes:

> If we could have a scientific study of mankind in Africa without economic axes to grind, without the necessity of proving race superiority, without religious conversion or compulsions of any kind or exaggerated consciousness of color; if we could have the known facts of history set down without bias and the unknown studied without propaganda, we might come to know much better not only Africa but Europe and America and human nature in general.[21]

Such a perspective attempts to help us develop a true human science. The American and South African experiences play key analytical and explanatory roles in my formulation of the problem of the social statistics of race. It is precisely because these experiences are so different that they dramatically emphasize what is common in the racialization of social statistics.

# Part I
# Birth of a Problem

But the most weighty of all the arguments against treating the races of man as distinct species, is that they graduate into each other, independently in many cases, as far as we can judge, of their having intercrossed. Man has been studied more carefully than any other animal, and yet there is the greatest possible diversity amongst capable judges whether he should be classed as a single species or race, or as two (Virey), as three (Jacquinot), as four (Kant), five (Blumenbach), six (Buffon), seven (Hunter), eight (Agassiz), eleven (Pickering), fifteen (Bory St. Vincent), sixteen (Desmoulins), twenty-two (Morton), sixty (Crawfurd), or as sixty-three, according to Burke. This diversity of judgement does not prove that the races ought not to be ranked as species, but it shews that they graduate into each other, and that it is hardly possible to discover clear distinctive characters between them.

—Charles Darwin, *The Descent of Man* (1871)

# Birth of a Problem

While Africans were becoming the dominated subjects of the West, the European-origin population was experiencing a revolution in its own thoughts about freedom and equality. While Africans were enslaved, Europeans were arguing for democracy. The period of Enlightenment was distinguished by the establishment of European colonies in Africa and Asia and European settlement in America, Australia, and South Africa. When Africans were emancipated, colonization and Jim Crow dominated the day. These apparent contradictions needed justifications. Such justifications were developed. And these gave birth to the study of race in biology and social science.

The idea of biological differences was born in the late nineteenth century. In Europe, the biological sciences were growing rapidly, both in scope and in sophistication. Many intellectuals believed science explained why Europe was so dominant in its relations with the rest of the world. As African enslavement ended in the Americas, African colonization by European powers was born. Following the abolition of enslavement, the problem of racial stratification became the problem of the twentieth century.

Racially stratified societies had but one argument against yielding to the demand of humanity: they insisted on the importance of racial difference and on its essential role in producing the inequality between non-European-origin persons and the European-origin persons in Europe and in the areas of the European diaspora, especially in the Americas. In order to justify economic inequality, these societies fell back on a doctrine of racial classification, which they asserted made economic and intellectual equality impossible. Religious leaders reverted to the "Great Chain of Being"; scientists gathered and supplemented all available doctrines of white supremacy and racial inferiority; schools and periodicals repeated these myths, until for the average person it was impossible not to believe that civilization and science stopped with the African.

The espousal of the doctrine of racial classification was economically motivated by the need to support the slave industry and the settler colonial efforts; but to the watching world it sounded like the carefully thought-out result of experience and reason. And because of this, it was singularly disastrous for science and religion, for art and government, as well as for industry. These settler states could say that the African, even when brought into contact with "modern civilization," could not be "civilized," and that, therefore, she and the other non-European peoples in the world were so inferior to Europeans that the European world, the West, had a right to rule mankind for its own reasons. Racial classification was developed as part of the effort to justify racial stratification.

This book questions the nature of objectivity in the statistical analysis of racial differences. First, in part I, I describe the evolutions of racialized domination and racial classification. Next, in parts II and III, I show how current statistical methodologies were developed as part of the eugenics movement and continue to reflect the racist ideologies that gave rise to them.

# CHAPTER ONE

## Racial Domination

### Genesis of the Races

Beginning in the fifteenth century, Europeans experienced a flood of new contacts with peoples in faraway lands. European notions about the nature of the world were turned on their heads by "new knowledge" gleaned about plants, animals, and peoples in places such as Africa, Asia, and the Americas. European scientists attempted to fit this mass of new information into a logical framework that explained the world they lived in and the world they wanted. Race became a particularly important "scientific" notion. African colonialism and enslavement were two important moments in this process of racialization.

The concept of race is rooted in the fifteenth-century expansion of European nations.[1] The advent of racial slavery and colonialism marked a turning point in how physical differences were viewed. Orlando Patterson remarks that "there is nothing notably peculiar about the institution of slavery. It has existed from before the dawn of human history right down to the twentieth century, in the most primitive of human societies and in the most civilized."[2] However, the white supremacy that accompanied the racialization of slavery in the Americas has not existed since the dawn of human history, and it continues to exert a peculiar influence today.[3] The same can be said of colonialism. The racialization of colonization and slavery was historically unique, and its consequences have been lasting.

Most of the people enslaved throughout the Mediterranean before the seizure of Constantinople in 1453 were of European origin. There were African slaves as well, but slavery had not been racialized.[4] Between the fifteenth and sixteenth centuries, the European Christian rulers of Cyprus, Crete, and Sicily created the world's most profitable sugar plantations using a slave labor pool made up of Turks, Russians, Bulgarians, Greeks, and Africans.[5] These plantations were not governed by Roman slave codes, so they provided an opportunity for a new ethic of enslavement, and by the middle of the fifteenth century Cyprus had become the largest slave market in the Mediterranean.[6]

The victory of the Ottoman Turks over the Christians gradually pushed the Mediterranean sugar industry west to Spain and Portugal, and then to the Atlantic islands off the coast of West Africa, including the Azores, Madeira, the Canaries, Cape Verde, Fernando Po, São Tomé, and Príncipe. The supply of people for enslavement was plentiful and close at hand in sub-Saharan Africa, and the plantations were very profitable. The combination of African slaves and European capital became a model of success in Spain, Portugal, and Italy.

Gold- and slave-hungry explorers colonized the Atlantic islands with the blessing and backing of state and religious leaders.[7] The pope granted his approval of the practice between 1442 and 1456 with a series of papal bulls. And, in 1460, the Portuguese royal authorities licensed expeditions to contractors who, upon paying a fee, were given commercial rights to exploit areas of their "discovery." Portuguese adventurers such as Infante Henrique received state and church approval for colonization and enslavement of indigenous peoples.[8] Henrique visited North Africa briefly three times; however, he sponsored several expeditions that established trading posts and connections along the African coast and islands. "As a royal prince he was perfectly prepared to combine raids on the African coast with systematic work on island colonization" from his bases at Sagres in the Algarve.[9]

The soil and climate of the Atlantic islands were favorable to sugar cultivation.[10] This was especially true for São Tomé and Príncipe, which lay close to the equator. In the sixteenth century, São Tomé and Príncipe became major sugar plantations stocked with enslaved Africans. This early shift in the demography of the enslaved population was the historical precursor to the racialization of enslavement.

The colonial occupation of islands off the west coast of Africa is the historical precedent for the racialization of enslavement of African-origin populations. The colonization of these African islands coincided with

Dias's demonstration to Europe in 1488 that the Cape of Good Hope was the end of the African continent. While the creation of racialized plantation slavery first developed off the west coast of Africa, the state structures for racialized colonial rule in Africa developed in the Cape.

The European settlers came from developing states that experienced numerous wars in which plunder was a natural part. As the more powerful northwestern European states, like England and France, began to transform the weaker nations into economic satellites within Europe, they also initiated the process of transforming parts of Africa and Asia into economic satellites externally.[11] As Magubane observes in South Africa, the "Dutch settlers had come from developing capitalist states that had been forged after numberless wars, in which ferocious plunder was normal."[12] Between Africa and Europe, in the four centuries before colonial rule was dominant, the principal items of plunder were men and women. Europeans shipped enslaved Africans to European-dominated markets for profit. East Africa served as the point of departure for the other slave trade in Africans, the Arab slave trade. In the beginning, these colonial and slave experiences were typical expansions, with religion, fame, and economic gain as the sole driving forces. The same justification for dominating the weaker parts of Europe drove the expansion to Asia and Africa. The ideological justification was simple profit.

Two types of economic systems developed among European colonizers during the fifteenth and sixteenth centuries. The first was a diversified, self-sufficient economy of small farmers living off the land on which they toiled. The second was the export economy of large-scale plantations producing staple articles such as sugar.[13] It is the second type of colony that became the basis for the racialization of slave labor off the coast of Africa and in the Americas.[14]

By the end of the sixteenth century, settler colonialism had become institutionalized and spread in southern Africa. European colonization required the appropriation of land, a settling population as well as domination of a local majority, and the transformation of indigenous institutions into European constructs. As in all colonial situations, the settlers had to determine how a small and foreign minority could rule over an indigenous majority. Direct colonial rule was the initial response to the problem of administering non-European colonial subjects.[15] European law was to rule the land, and both the colonized and the colonizers could ignore indigenous institutions. All would be required to submit and conform to these laws, but only Europeanized (or "civilized") natives would have access to European rights.

Indirect colonial rule was the mode of domination over a semifree peasantry. In this context of restricted freedom, the community possessed land, and domination of the market was restricted to the products of labor; the indigenous population owned land and labor. The colonial authority dominated the market relationships in the political and civil life of the colonized. Indigenous customary law was used to regulate non-market relationships in the family and community of the dominated population.

The reality of indirect and direct colonial rule suggests that different colonial systems did not constitute radical breaks from what came before colonization; the social and economic practices of the epoch were themselves a complex product of things old and new. Although an ideological offspring of direct domination of the initial settlement of a colony, indirect rule was born of, and bore within it, a series of connections to direct colonial rule.

European settler colonies have different histories of racial and ethnic stratification. In South Africa racial tensions stem from European colonization, the enslavement of both Africans from other areas in Africa and Asians, and the spatial displacement of the native indigenous African population through colonization. The racial conflicts in the United States stem from racial tensions that began with a century and a half of race-specific policies such as enslavement and the colonization of Native Americans. In Brazil, the European settlers from Portugal initiated the racial tensions by colonization and enslavement first of the indigenous Native American populations and later the African-origin population.

Walter Rodney argued in his book *How Europe Underdeveloped Africa* that "the first significant thing about the internationalization of trade in the fifteenth century was that Europeans took the initiative and went to other parts of the world."[16] Europe exclusively established itself as the major power in the trade among Africa, Europe, and the Americas and became a formidable contender for control over the Pacific as well.[17] European interests owned the majority of the world's seagoing vessels that could travel the Atlantic from continent to continent, and they controlled the financing of the trade between these continents. The superiority of their ships and cannons gave Europeans control over trade across the Atlantic trade routes.

As part of the Spanish Empire since the rule of Hapsburg Charles V, the Dutch who occupied the seven northern provinces of the Low Countries fought for independence in the latter part of the sixteenth century.[18] The Dutch East India Company destroyed Portuguese domination in the Indian Ocean in the first decade of the seventeenth century. The Portuguese may have been the trailblazers, but the Dutch delivered Africa into the hands of the western European world-trading system. African incorporation into this trading system generated sufficient momentum to lead to European domination of the African continent and the Americas. The Americas illustrate how Europeans racialized colonialism and enslavement.

The European slave trade of Africans to the Americas began in 1502 with the Spanish. The end of the trade did not come until the 1850s in Brazil and Cuba. The racialization of America began with the dehumanization of the Native American population. In the New World, Native Americans became the first source of slave labor for the building up of plantations.[19] As in the Cape Colony, the European settlers and the indigenous Americans struggled for control of the land and the bodies of the colonized. In the sixteenth century, Portuguese settlements enslaved Native Americans ten to fifteen times as often as Africans. With the introduction of new diseases from Europe and Africa, the excessive demand for labor, and changes and limitations in their diet, Native Americans declined rapidly in number.[20] This demographic collapse was an additional stimulation to the European slave trade in Africans.

The Native American population decline stimulated by European contact affected Africa as well as America. It was not surprising that the Europeans turned to Africans as a replacement for Native American slaves. Africa's American diaspora was born. The need to justify the grand scale of African enslavement also came into play. Thus began the racialization of enslavement and the antiblack discourse on race.

Slavery was an accepted institution in Africa before the development of the European or Arab slave trades.[21] Consequently, commerce in slaves was not foreign to Africa. In Africa, slavery as an institution tended to be domestic and with few exceptions never developed into the large-scale plantation slavery that dominated the Atlantic islands under the Portuguese. This changed as the Portuguese explorers and traders established themselves on the sub-Saharan coast of Africa. The Portuguese slave trade stimulated an increase in the demand for African slaves. This demand transformed the market conditions in Africa and increased the African dependence on the slave trade. These changes occurred simultaneously with the Spanish conquest of the Caribbean islands and the Portuguese settlement of the Brazilian subcontinent, creating the American market for enslaved Africans.

In most cases Europeans did not invade Africa and enslave Africans; however, they did create the demand for slaves and promoted internal conflict through indirect military pressure by introducing military technology and political manipulation. At first, enslavement resulted primarily from the political-economic strategies of African kings and leaders. The African elite attempted to increase the size of their kingdoms by increasing the number of dependent subjects, entourages of clients, subjects, kin, serfs, and slaves. As these royal efforts became intertwined with international commerce with Europe, the search for dependents became a search for slaves, and eventually the slave trade dominated internal African markets.

The African diaspora in the Americas resulted primarily from the enslavement of Africans by Europeans. The literature on this enslavement is extensive, and I will not attempt to describe or summarize it. However, it is important to note that the arrival of Africans in the Americas in the sixteenth, seventeenth, eighteenth, and nineteenth centuries, became a central thread in the racialization of the Americas—at once a challenge to the idea of democracy and an important part of their economic histories and social developments.

Portugal took possession of the eastern coastline of South America in the early sixteenth century. The Portuguese Empire claimed the region during expeditions to the East Indies and, like the Dutch in the Cape Colony, had no plans for immediate development. However, it did not take long for the Portuguese to transport their experience in the islands off the coast of West Africa to their new American colonies.[22] They brought sugar experts from the Madeira and São Tomé plantations. This effort resulted in the first slave plantation system in the Americas and quickly outpaced the Atlantic islands in the production of sugar. By the seventeenth century, the northeast provinces of Pernambuco and Bahia had the most profitable sugar plantations in the world. Northeastern Brazil dominated the European sugar market. The trade in the enslaved and sugar gave the Portuguese a prize place in the New World market.

The Dutch had become deeply involved in the European slave trade as sugar producers and traders in enslaved Africans.[23] After establishing the Dutch West India Company, they took control of the Portuguese settlement of Pernambuco in 1630. By the 1640s, after they had captured the Portuguese El Mina fortress on the Gold Coast and the Angolan coastal region, the Dutch were a major colonial actor in the creation of Africa's American diaspora. Like the Dutch in South Africa when confronted by a superior European force, the Portuguese sought refuge in the domination of indigenous populations. To compensate for their defeats, the Portuguese increased Native American enslavement and their own settlement activities in the interior of the continent.

The Dutch exported the sugar plantation economy to the West Indies and expanded access to the sugar market within France and England. As Klein noted, "In the 1640s, Dutch planters with Pernambuco experience arrived in Barbados as well as Martinique and Guadeloupe to introduce modern milling and production techniques. Dutch slavers provided the credit to the local planters to buy African slaves, while Dutch West Indian freighters hauled the finished sugar to the refineries in Amsterdam."[24] However, Dutch settlers themselves proved decisive in the efforts to expand the sugar plantation system to the islands. The Portuguese had firmly implanted in Brazil their lessons of slave plantations from the Atlantic islands off the coast of West Africa. The extension of these methods to the Lesser Antillean islands and from the Amazonian estuary to Florida was carried forward by French and English settlers. After decimating the Carib population, European settlers were able to import first indentured servants and then slaves to establish profitable slave plantation economies.

These developments did not destroy the importance of the Brazilian sugar industry or its oppressive system of enslavement. By 1645, the Portuguese had recaptured their lost territory in Brazil and, by 1648, had recovered the colonial outpost in Angola and their islands in the Gulf of Guinea. They apparently never stopped resisting Dutch rule in the interior. The Portuguese were able to regain control of the European slave trade south of the equator; however, the Dutch continued to dominate north of the equator. Although Brazil never regained its sugar and slave monopoly, it was able to return to its exclusive dependence on African slave labor and continue to play a leading role in the production of sugar.

The Dutch West India Company successfully extended the slave plantation system in the Americas, and it benefited greatly from English and French dependence on supplies of slaves and technology. However, France and England did not allow their American settlers to become totally dependent on Dutch merchants. English and French companies competed with the Dutch in the European slave trade. This competition was in part responsible for the wars among the Netherlands, England, and France between 1652 and 1713.

The eighteenth century witnessed the opening of the slave trade to a host of individual merchants. African communities organized themselves to meet the growing demand for slaves resulting from the expansion of the slave plantation system in the Americas. Britain, France, Spain, Portugal, the Netherlands, and Denmark all thrived from their commercial activities with the settler colonies in the Americas. The expansion of new sugar plantations increased the ratio of enslaved Africans to the "free" Europeans and fostered a new industrial discipline using the gang system on rice, coffee, and cotton plantations.[25]

The United States was unique in that the sugar-plantation system arrived later than it did in other areas of the Americas, close to the end of the enslavement period. Thus, not as many enslaved Africans entered the United States as they did Brazil and the Caribbean. However, as in Brazil, enslavement in the United States became a racialized system. The settlers considered Africans to be natural slaves, indigenous Americans to be noble natives, and other Europeans as potential citizens. The problem of race was born.

## Race and the Problem of Freedom

The African diaspora, like the European diaspora, began during a time of great change and social transformation. The European Renaissance suggested a new freedom for the European spirit and body. However, it also suggested a newfound freedom to colonize and enslave Africans, Asians, and American Indians. The European world knew of these slaves, but they were slaves that came from various other regions and populations. The European Renaissance coincided with the rise of racialized enslavement and colonization.

The nineteenth century was the era of transformation in the status of the enslaved African-origin populations.[26] These transformations began in Haiti at the turn of the previous century and ended in Brazil on

May 13, 1888. A succession of revolts and wars swept away the systems of enslavement in the Americas and the Caribbean islands. Slavery was anathema to both the new industrial capitalism and the liberal democratic state. However, the result of emancipation—the transition from enslavement to free labor—exposed the contradiction of applying the idea of the liberal democratic state in a racially stratified society. The justification of racial stratification was an important means of evading the issue of persistent racial differences in societies that claimed to be democratic.

The transformation of enslaved Africans into wage laborers was not unique; it had a precedent in the transformation of European-origin agricultural workers into an industrial working class in the northern United States and Europe. Yet, the enslaved were by definition chattel, unlike the agricultural workers, and emancipation included the transition of the African-origin population to freedom.

The end of African enslavement accompanied the colonization of Asia and Africa, the expansion of colonization in the Americas, and state formation in nations such as the United States and Brazil. European settlers, dressed in their revolutionary clothing, sought to secure their freedom from the kings in Britain and Portugal and simultaneously the right to deny that freedom to the African and indigenous American populations.[27] The United States was the first of the racially stratified societies to gain independence from the mother country in Europe. And as Judge Higginbotham reminds us: "From the perspective of the black masses, the Revolution merely assured the plantation owners of their right to continue the legal tyranny of slavery."[28] In Brazil, Prince Regent Pedro and the merchants of Rio de Janeiro proclaimed independence in 1822. However, the slave trade continued well into the 1850s, and emancipation did not come until 1888. These developments required new justifications of racial stratification.

In 1794, France abolished slavery in her colonies and "apprenticed" the formerly enslaved people of Guadeloupe and Santo Domingo.[29] In 1802, Napoleon Bonaparte overthrew the abolition decree and forced the African-origin population into a battle for freedom and independence. The army of Toussaint l'Ouverture defeated Napoleon's troops, forcing the French to withdraw from Santo Domingo. Santo Domingo became independent Haiti, and the price of maintaining the enslavement of Africans in the Americas increased substantially.

Haiti was an exception in the transition to freedom among the formerly enslaved: it was a state formed by the enslaved as a result of war with the oppressors. The formerly enslaved were not emancipated; they were liberated. The Haitian revolution of 1792–1804 was the clearest manifestation of the rejection of African enslavement. After this the history of African emancipation was to be a different story entirely.

As Jay R. Mandle notes: "Everywhere in plantation America, with the exception of Haiti, the momentous transformation that the ending of slavery seemed to promise turned out to be far less than revolutionary. The slave-owning classes, by and large, were able to accomplish the transition from being what Gavin Wright calls labor lords to becoming landlords and, in the process, continue in their former role as the dominant class in society."[30] The ideas of freedom and equality were inconsistent with the economic and social system envisioned by the designers of emancipation and reconstruction. Several examples illustrate the illusion of freedom offered by emancipation. In 1838, the British emancipated all the enslaved under the British flag. As had been the case with the French, for the British Empire emancipation meant the replacement of enslavement with apprenticeship. Discussing the problems of the transition to freedom in Jamaica, Thomas C. Holt writes: "Apprenticeship was a halfway covenant in which the relationship between the planter and the worker was much the same as that between master and slave for forty and one-half hours of the work week, but during the balance of the week they were to assume the respective statuses of employer and employee freely negotiating conditions of work and wages."[31]

In the final year of the apprenticeship system, Holt notes, colonial administrations in the West Indies developed policies to restrict the freedom of the "freedmen." His citation of an administrator captures these inconsistencies:

> Given the demographic imbalances in the colonies, the "natural" effect of complete emancipation would be a general desertion of the estates to cultivate food crops. Eventually the growth of population might right this imbalance, but the plantations would be destroyed in the meantime. Thus the government must interdict the freedmen's natural—and, one might add, rational—proclivity to abandon the plantations.[32]

In 1865, the United States emancipated the enslaved African-origin population,[33] and racial enslavement was replaced with other forms of social and economic marginalization. As Du Bois notes:

It must be remembered and never forgotten that the civil war in the South which overthrew Reconstruction was a determined effort to reduce black labor as nearly as possible to a condition of unlimited exploitation and build a new class of capitalists on this foundation. The wage of the Negro worker, despite the war amendments, was to be reduced to the level of bare subsistence by taxation, peonage, caste, and every method of discrimination. This program had to be carried out in open defiance of the clear letter of the law.[34]

Brazil was the first country in the Americas to institute the slave plantation system, yet it was one of the last states to end its support of the European slave trade. Official Brazilian opposition to the slave trade coincided with a return to the rebellions of the enslaved in 1800, the 1820s, and the 1830s.[35] In 1831, Brazil signed an antislaving treaty with Great Britain, effectively ending the legal European slave trade to Brazil by 1852.[36]

In 1871, Viscount Rio Branco successfully proposed the "law of the free womb," which manumitted children born to enslaved women when they reached the age of majority. The bill was approved by the Brazilian parliament as the Rio Branco Law. On May 13, 1888, Princess Regent Isabel signed the Golden Law abolishing slavery throughout Brazil. With the Golden Law, legal enslavement in the Americas ended, and the last large African-origin population in the Americas was emancipated.

Following emancipation in São Paulo, as in the United States and Jamaica, the planter elite created a postemancipation system of racial stratification to secure their interests.[37] European-origin populations replicated this pattern throughout the Americas, and it continues to exert an influence on racial interactions. As in other postemancipation societies, because of their size and place in the economy the Brazilian freedmen (or *libertos*) were in a position to negotiate the terms of their labor and the political order of the day. In response the planters attempted to Europeanize Brazil. As George Reid Andrews observed:

> Far from doing away with "distinctions of class and race," as the black Republicans of Campinas had hoped, the Republic would cement landowner rule and then embark on a national campaign to "Europeanize" Brazil, a campaign in which the "whitening" of the national population, and the replacement of African racial heritage with European, would assume a prominent role.[38]

A similar policy was implemented in the United States.

In the West Indies, the United States, and Brazil, emancipation was part of a process that transformed labor conditions but did not end domination by the European settler elite. There were limits to the free-dom of the "freedmen" after emancipation. Being freed did not trans-late into equality or justice.

It is also interesting that as freedom was coming to those of the African diaspora, colonialism was arriving in Africa. As late as 1880, Africans ruled 80 percent of the continent of Africa. Between 1890 and 1910 vir-tually the whole continent was colonized by imperial powers. The resis-tance to colonial conquest was fierce and universal, as is illustrated by some of the more famous anticolonial struggles, such as the Hut Tax War in Sierra Leone, the Bailundu revolt in Angola, and the Maji Maji wars in German East Africa. This resistance mirrors the battles in South Africa, such as the "Kaffir wars" of the early nineteenth century. European pow-ers extended the model of racialized colonialism established in south-ern Africa to the rest of the continent. With the exception of Ethiopia and Liberia, European powers colonized the whole of Africa by 1914.

South Africa attracted settlers from Europe on a large scale and was the site of the establishment of growing colonial settlement. South Africa was uniquely suited to settlement from Europe, a fact to which it owes its environment, geographic location, and social history. However, South Africa did not follow the path of Canada, Australia, the United States of America, or New Zealand by almost exterminating the indigenous pop-ulation. Unlike South Africa, these new settler colonies became trans-planted images of Europe. In South Africa, the colonial settlers of Eu-rope "remained a small island in a black sea."[39] In this context South Africa has been a site in which the numerical majority has been mar-ginalized by a racialized minority. The arrival of European settlers in the sixteenth, seventeenth, eighteenth, and nineteenth centuries became a central thread in the racialization of Africa—a challenge to the notion of the civilizing mission of colonialism. Even though African colonial-ism did not become widespread until the end of the nineteenth century, the enslavement of Africans in the Americas played a key role in how Africans were to be viewed as a people in the twentieth century.

Rather than put an end to the racial hierarchy, emancipation became the next phase in racial stratification. The contradictions between free-dom and domination needed to be reconciled. The intellectual justifi-cation of racial stratification began with the idea of the Great Chain of Being but continued with the adaptation of the evolutionary ideas of Darwin.

# CHAPTER TWO

# The Evolution of Racial Classification

The racialization of social and economic stratification required the classification of human beings by their physical characteristics.[1] The physical classification of human populations took on added meaning during the process of racial colonization and slavery. Both racial slavery and colonialism required a dehumanizing discourse. One of the first intellectual articulations of this discourse was the Great Chain of Being. The classical idea of the Great Chain of Being ranked all creation, including the Creator, hierarchically. The Chain of Being classified creation from inanimate objects upward through lowly animals, women, and men, to God. In the European mind, the use of the Chain of Being to support and justify the enslavement of Africans was obvious.[2]

The Chain of Being maintained that humans shared a close affinity with beasts. It followed, therefore, that the lowest human beings were closely related to the highest animals. Given the belief in Europe that the ape was the highest animal, it followed that the lowest group of human beings would be apelike. The economic desire to justify the enslavement of Africans played an important role in shaping the eighteenth-century opinion among some European scholars that Africans were just above the ape on the Great Chain of Being.

The chain ranged from simple to very complex beings. Common descent was not critical to this idea. Stratification within a particular race and among different races was the work of the Creator. With European colonialism came knowledge of the "technologically primitive" populations of the Americas, Africa, Asia, and Oceania. Not only were there inferior races within Europe, but races inferior to those were found among peoples of color.

The idea of a racial hierarchy assumed a class hierarchy. Both colonialism and enslavement are class relationships, and the idea of a racial hierarchy justified the existence of these relationships in the past. The idea of the primitive African was key in discussions of the Great Chain. The Dutch settlers originally referred to the Khoikhoi as Hottentots.[3] The African "Hottentots" became a common reference to the bottom of the human population.[4] Eighteenth- and nineteenth-century intellectuals commonly referred to Hottentots as the lowest of the savage races.

Ideologies and social theories of racial hierarchy supported European colonization.[5] "Race" identified various forms of religious and social differences. That some people were less advanced technologically or militarily than others was seen as the will of God, the consequence of environment, or the outcome of differences in moral character. Within Europe the idea of the Great Chain of Being led British colonists in seventeenth-century Ulster to attempt to enslave the Irish. This attempt failed, but soon afterward Africans were successfully enslaved in Virginia, the Carolinas, and Georgia.

The racial theories of the seventeenth and eighteenth centuries were grounded in the notion of "divine providence" and justified the enslavement of Africans and the colonization of the Americas, Asia, and Africa. The theories held that God had ordained that Europe should rule the world, and various religious leaders were willing to give decrees to this effect.[6]

Justifying racial stratification was essential for the system of enslavement to exist in the Americas. Enslavement is a form of domination. Domination and its companions exploitation and marginalization refer to social relationships in which one population benefits as the other suffers. The degree of suffering can vary from society to society; however, the degree to which the dominant class depends on the exploited population does not determine the extent to which the exploited are marginalized. The dominant class's partial dependence may entail the destruction of the exploited class. This has been the case in the interaction of several indigenous Caribbean populations with European settler populations.[7] Or the dominant class's more general dependence may entail coexistence with the exploited population, as in the case of South Africa and Brazil, for example. This continuum of domination allows us to avoid extremist arguments without sacrificing the force of the idea of domination. The various degrees of dominant-exploited and dominant-marginalized relationships may be placed on a continuum ranging from a point prior to equality to one just the other side of extermination or genocide. Domination needs justification in an age of democracy. As racially stratified societies entered the twentieth century, they needed to justify this domination. Social Darwinism and eugenics provided the first scientific justification of continued racial stratification by "democratic" societies.

The nineteenth-century justifications of racial stratification are rooted in the eighteenth-century development of evolutionary theory in biology and social statistics. The shift from natural history to biology gave new life to old ideas of racial hierarchy. When the Great Chain of Being no longer carried the weight of legitimacy, science came to the rescue, beginning with the theories of evolution. The Swedish natural historian Carolus Linnaeus led the way, formulating the first scientific classification of human populations. His scheme was based on the outward appearance of specimens. In his *Systema Naturae* (1735) human beings made up one of several categories of animals but did not occupy a superior category. Human beings were divided into four subspecies (*americanus, europaeus, asiaticus,* and *afer*) on the basis of appearance and personality. He even suggested that the Hottentot and the European did not derive from the same origin and that the *afer* was black, impassive, and lazy compared with the white, serious, and strong *europaeus*.

Linnaeus's system was thought to be crude and inadequate, and refinements followed in Johann Friedrich Blumenbach's *On the Natural Variety of Mankind* (1795). Linnaeus's system was based on anatomical and cultural characteristics. Using only anatomical (morphological) characteristics, Blumenbach divided human beings into five categories: American, Caucasian, Ethiopian, Malay, and Mongolian. His five races became identified with the skin colors red, white, black, brown, and yellow. He maintained that all human beings belonged to one species and that his categories merely signaled breaks in a continuum. Blumenbach's work both clashed with and complemented the work of many naturalists of the time, but it was singularly important in challenging the legitimacy of the Great Chain of Being.

Linnaeus established the perspective, or more specifically the paradigm, within which scientific research on racial diversity was conducted. This perspective included the idea that the goal of data collection on human differences involved the determination of a small number of fundamental categories into which all human variation could be collapsed. Advances in statistics, craniometry, and genetics added information but did so within this paradigm developed by Linnaeus.

Many other individuals, particularly Jean-Baptiste de Monet de Lamarck, played key roles in the development of European theories of evolution and race.[8] As Charles Darwin himself noted, Lamarck was one of the first naturalists to formulate "the doctrine that all species, including man, are descended from other species."[9] Lamarck argued that evolution occurred through the inheritance of *acquired* characteristics, not natural ones. In his major work, *Zoological Philosophy* (1809), Lamarck also dismissed the possibility of taxonomic categories and random variation, arguing instead that individual organisms acquired new habits in new environments and that their anatomical structure responded to their habitat in order to survive. Through their responses, lower forms of creation were able to rise up the Great Chain of Being. Lamarck's views would play an important role in the development of social science nearly a century later, as we will see below.

The worldview of the seventeenth century, as envisioned by Thomas Hobbes, presented human existence as *bellum omnium contra omnes,* a war of all against all. In 1798 Thomas R. Malthus applied the Hobbesian worldview in his population perspective, linking the issue of survival to population growth and the competition for natural resources.[10] Malthus was the first to argue scientifically for population control, by showing that populations grew geometrically whereas resources grew only arithmetically. He argued that population growth had to be kept in check lest misery and poverty become the predominant conditions in society. Because the competition for resources was natural, he contended that the poor and the powerless constituted a natural social occurrence. Attempts by society to help the poor would simply add to the problem, by increasing their numbers, and so should be abandoned. Poverty was a fact of nature and a product of God's will.

At the same time Malthus emphasized personal responsibility as the operative factor in the competition for natural resources. The poor were poor because of their individual characteristics, not because of their social position or the society they lived in. Governmental intervention in the natural workings of the economy thus was bound to fail. The distribution of rewards within society reflected individual accomplishment rather than historical and social circumstances; to engineer a change within society by welfare or any type of "wealth transfer" would lead to more misery and would be an act against nature and God.

Malthus was concerned that Europe in general and Britain in particular maintain a naturally strong and healthy people.[11] For Malthus, the issue of civilization versus barbarism was the most important distinction among and within societies. In his view, the population problem was one of moral discipline and probity.

Malthus's ideas had a profound impact on the way people viewed population problems in society. It is too easy, however, to overstate his influence in the formation of the idea of race. The doctrine of colonialism did not wait upon Malthus's arrival, nor was the racism to come simply a result of Malthus's *Essay on the Principle of Population.* In fact, racism was not a result of conflict between the very dissimilar peoples of Europe (whites) and those of the rest of the world (people of color); rather, it was conceived in the class systems of Europe. Without relying on natural selection, post-Malthusian and pre-Darwinian thinkers such as Joseph-Arthur de Gobineau provided systematic explanations of why the uncivilized races could never achieve higher levels of civilization. In his landmark work, *Essay on the Inequality of Human Races* (1854–55), Gobineau explained that the principle of equality was misguided because of the superiority of the Aryan race. Gobineau, himself a count, argued that the nobility descended from superior progenitors and were therefore the only ones capable of ruling. The poor came from inferior progenitors and were thus politically incompetent.

Even before Malthus, states in the Americas were firmly grounded in the notions of European racial superiority.[12] The wars with the indigenous American population and the proslavery practices and arguments of politicians and propagandists made the idea of racial inferiority a living fact, one that was supported by the moral order of European people and "God." Europeans declared themselves owners and governors of the lands of nonwhite, "heathen" Others, and when they met with resistance, they were "forced into lawful war" in the name of preserving civilization and upholding righteousness. The colonial and slave practices of the era in which Gobineau lived required this new source of legitimacy.

However, Malthus's ideas were critical in the development of evolutionary thought. Charles Darwin himself observed:

> Fifteen months after I had begun my systematic enquiry, I happened to read for amusement Malthus on *Population,* and being well prepared to appreciate the struggle for existence which everywhere goes on from long-continued observation of the habits of animals and plants, it at once struck me that under these circumstances favorable variations would tend to be preserved and unfavorable ones be destroyed. The result of this would be a new species. Here, then I had at last got a theory by which to work.[13]

It is through Malthus's theoretical connection to Darwin that he had a critical impact on scholarly perspectives of ranking differences such as race. Malthus's perspective was both quantitative and tended toward ranking.

In 1859 Darwin fundamentally challenged Lamarck's argument with the publication of *On the Origin of Species by Means of Natural Selection, or the Preservation of Favored Races in the Struggle for Life.* Darwin's reading of Malthus's *Essay on the Principle of Population* alerted him to the struggle for existence that was, in his view, responsible for natural selection through competition. Darwin went a step further than Malthus did by applying the principle of natural selection to every living thing.

Darwin's work was another blow to the religious theories of race based on the Great Chain of Being. The morphological view of species—that they are fixed in form and structure—dovetails with the assumptions of the Great Chain of Being that the Creator designs each form of life. Darwin disagreed with this morphological view. He argued that species formed populations of diverse individuals who adapted to different environments in such a way that their successors' characteristics would change through natural selection. Species did not progress and become better; they became diverse. In addition, unlike earlier evolutionary theorists such as Lamarck, Darwin separated the idea of evolution from the idea of progress, shifting the focus from generational improvement to generational diversity.[14]

At first, social scientists saw Darwin's emphasis on heredity as a limitation to social reform. The idea that nature was continually selecting for fitness suggested that humanitarian attempts to promote equality were of little avail. Though Darwin would become the god of eugenics, European eugenicists persisted in ignoring the nonmorphological implications of Darwin's view regarding race. Some, such as Karl Pearson, would even advocate a morphological view of species. Despite these contradictions, social scientists called evolutionary theories of race Social Darwinism.

Darwin suggested that all animal and plant populations differ from one another; that the potential for natural increase in the population is greater than the resources available to support it, as Malthus argued before him; that as a result natural selection favors the survival of those individuals within the population best suited for the environment in which they live or exist; and that the characteristics of a population gradually evolve over time. A new, secular phase in the study of race began with the attempt to apply in sociology the principles Darwin set out in biology. For a considerable period social scientists took biological precepts as their guidelines, focusing on the definition of different races rather than on the relationships among them.

Darwin's theory of natural selection holds that one species evolves into another. With this revolutionary idea, debates about the human races were radically altered. Writers began to argue that if man evolved from apelike ancestors and there were no "white" apes, then the white race is the most evolved. Thus, the races of color, which Europeans considered culturally and spiritually more primitive, were closer to the nonhuman progenitor (the ape), and the white populations of Europe represented the latest and highest form of evolutionary progress.

Pioneered by the English sociologist Herbert Spencer in the late nineteenth century, Social Darwinism became the dominant theory of sociological thought and played an important role in the prevailing ideology of racism. Like Darwin, Spencer viewed Malthus's population perspective as the principal force in evolution. Unlike Darwin, however, Spencer based his view of evolution on Lamarck.

Social scientists tended to think that Darwin's theory of natural selection mirrored contemporary social processes.[15] The same competitive individualism lay at the root of laissez-faire capitalism and became the key to economic development and progress. According to economist John Maynard Keynes:

> Hume and Paley, Burke and Rousseau, Godwin and Malthus, Cobbett and Huskisson, Bentham and Coleridge, Darwin and Bishop of Oxford, were all, it was discovered, preaching practically the same thing—

individualism and *laissez-faire.* This was the Church of England and those her apostles, whilst the company of the economists were there to prove that the least deviation into impiety involved financial ruin.[16]

Darwin viewed species as a population of varying individuals with no fixed type, and contemporary political economists viewed society as individuals with different and divergent interests.

Darwin had maintained that certain biological differences conferred survival advantages on some organisms in the struggle for existence. Spencer interpreted Darwin's findings as demonstrating that the survival of the fittest resulted from the struggle for existence. Then, however, he applied Lamarck's theories, arguing that social evolution developed progressively. Spencer wrote:

> Whether it be in the development of the Earth, in the development of life under its surface, in the development of Society, of Government, of Manufactures, of Commerce, of Language, Literature, Science, Art, this same evolution of the simple into the complex, through successive differentiations, holds throughout. From the earliest traceable cosmical changes down to the latest results of civilization, we shall find that the transformation of homogenous into the heterogeneous, is that in which progress essentially consists.[17]

Spencer argued that the evolutionary laws applicable in the physical world paralleled those guiding human cultural developments. Civilization moved from the homogeneous to the heterogeneous, from the undifferentiated to the differentiated;[18] racial, social, and cultural differences represented various *stages* of evolution. At the turn of the twentieth century, Social Darwinism was extremely influential, and Spencer was one of the most popular academics in the world.[19]

American Social Darwinists argued that African enslavement gave Africans an unnatural advantage by *increasing* their life expectancy and health. Thus began the debate over the enslaved Africans' quality of life in the Americas. According to several prominent scholars, emancipation produced the conditions that would lead to the ultimate elimination of the African population in the United States, as the struggle for existence would find the free African wanting in the competition with a European-origin population. "Some southerners saw in emancipation nothing but extermination for the Negro Race. The Provisional Governor of Florida became almost tearful over the impending fate of the Negroes and the guilt of the North."[20]

The Social Darwinists' struggle-for-existence theory was supported by the "black disappearance hypothesis."[21] One of its first exponents, Francis Amasa Walker, a former Civil War general, was the census superintendent for the 1870, 1880, and 1890 censuses. Walker argued in 1891 that Africans were a distinct population with a limited ability to survive in a nation like the United States, thus leading to their disappearance.[22] Using census data, Walker suggested that the decline in the proportion of Africans in the United States indicated African inferiority; he connected this inferiority to the African physical appearance and inability to miscegenate with the European-origin population.

Five years later, Frederick L. Hoffman published his exhaustive study, "Race Traits and Tendencies of the American Negro."[23] Based on more than fifty years of data on population dynamics and race, Hoffman's article argued that emancipation was a positive process because of the anticipated devastation it would bring upon Africans in the United States. His study clearly attempted to bolster Walker's justification of racial stratification. Contrary to Hoffman's predictions, it became clear by the early twentieth century that Africans would not become "extinct" in the United States. However, social scientists continued to refer to this hypothesis in their justifications of racial stratification.[24]

Like Social Darwinists, black-disappearance advocates saw African-origin populations as inferior participants in the struggle for existence. But unlike Social Darwinists, black-disappearance advocates were influenced by the empiricism of the German School of History.[25] Walter Wilcox, a chief statistician for the 1890 census, a leading economist and a professor at Cornell University, and Hoffman believed that statistics lent legitimacy to their views on racial stratification, and both employed statistical and demographic analysis in their research. The list of racial statisticians reads like a Who's Who of early social statisticians.

These ideas of the struggle for existence and the black-disappearance hypothesis mark a transition in the theorizing of race and the elevation of racial statistics. The Social Darwinists' ideas assumed that racial differences were natural differences. Most scholars believed race was part of the *natural* world; they viewed racial differences as the natural order of the world. The black-disappearance hypothesis required a quantitative analysis of the racial struggle for existence and superiority.

Social Darwinism had a short life among American social scientists. By the turn of the century social scientists were turning their attentions away from Spencer's theories of evolution. Social Darwinism sought to defend the status quo on the basis of a laissez-faire attitude. Thus, it looked down on the intervention of the state in society. American sociologists tended to reject Social Darwinism and its evolutionary theories as the basis of social behavior and difference.[26] As Hofstadter notes, "The most important change in sociological method was its estrangement from biology, and the tendency to place social studies on a psychological foundation."[27] Lester Ward, the first president of the American Sociological Society in 1906, advocated the need for an evaluation of the psychic factor in civilization. The new social psychology portrayed the individual as being endowed with propensities, interests, and habits, and not simply bounded by pleasure-pain and stimulus-response processes.

Spencer, like Malthus, hoped that social science would provide the evidence that discouraged social reform. However, by the turn of the century the spirit of social reform had grown, and social science was increasingly supportive of this effort. As social theorists increasingly criticized Social Darwinism, the evolutionary perspective was revived in a new guise. The revolution in genetics research and a new statistical theory of evolution had serious consequences for social thought. Unlike Social Darwinism, the new evolutionary theory—eugenics—advocated social reform and suggested the most extreme forms of social engineering. This change was clearly articulated by Cooley:

> But why not make selection conscious and intelligent, and thus improve the stock of men somewhat as we do that of animals? There has, in fact, arisen a science of Eugenics, or Race-Improvement, seeking to stimulate the propagation of desirable types of human heredity and prevent that of undesirable types.... Scientific tests should be made of all children to ascertain those that are feeble-minded or otherwise hopelessly below a normal capacity, followed by a study of their families to find whether these defects are hereditary.[28]

Like many social scientists, Charles H. Cooley was a Darwinist but not a Social Darwinist. Cooley was clearly a believer in evolution and a follower of Darwin's evolutionary theory.[29] Also, his ideas show the significant influence of eugenics by the beginning of the twentieth century.

# Part II
# Racial Statistics

I began my study of the history too late, and after three years' work have only got to 1750 as yet. But I do feel how very wrongful it was to work for so many years at statistics and neglect its history, and that is why I want to interest you in this matter, that you may not be so ignorant as I have been.

—Karl Pearson, *The History of Statistics in the Seventeenth and Eighteenth Centuries against the Changing Background of Intellectual, Scientific and Religious Thought* (1920)

No more than there is equality between man and man of the same nation is there equality between race and race. This differentiation of men in physique and mentality has led to the slow but still imperfect development of occupational castes within all civilized communities.

—Sir Francis Galton, "Annals of Eugenics" (1925)

# Racial Statistics

The story of the numerical analysis of race is inextricably linked with the history of social statistics, touching on all the major themes of statistical methods. It provides insight into what has driven social statistics and perhaps what inspires social statisticians. Racial statistics are at the heart of an intriguing saga of tragedy, courage, brilliance, and cunning, involving all the greatest heroes of statistics.

In writing about this history, I have chosen a chronological structure that begins by describing the genesis of race. I have tried to illustrate this chronology by connecting the various characters involved in the process of racializing statistics within particular social contexts.

Historically, mainstream social scientists developed evolutionary notions of the biological superiority of European-origin populations. These scholars spoke against racial annihilation and racial degradation.[1] Consistent with the history of racialized enslavement and colonization, procreation between Europeans and non-Europeans was thought to produce non-European children and to threaten the survival of the European race; in the United States, such persons were referred to as mulattos, in South America as *pardos* and *mulatos*.[2] Additionally, many believed that the less intelligent seemed to outreproduce the intelligent within the European-origin population, leading to racial degradation.[3]

The history of social statistics reveals the ambiguities that underlie racial statistics and remind us how our racial concepts have influenced the logic of statistical methods. The population perspective in both demography and statistics corresponds to the tendencies of group objectification in social statistics. One tendency extends from Adolphe Quetelet's and Émile Durkheim's efforts to articulate a macrosociology. This perspective views groups as entities with collective traits that can be statistically described. The other tendency extends from the tradition of Galton, and while it recognizes different group statuses, such as race, it describes racial status as individual traits.

Raising questions about social difference and stratification called for more-developed statistical techniques than those employed in astronomy and other areas of science. The early success of Francis Galton, Karl Pearson, and Ronald A. Fisher in establishing statistics as a science must be credited as the foundation of modern social statistics and the first effort to legitimate statistical racism. Evolutionary eugenics provided a theoretical context for biological and social statisticians to employ enumerated data for understanding society.

Social statistics, biometrics, and genetics converged in the eugenics movement, where the phrase "survival of the fittest" had a fixed place despite the technical criticisms by other statisticians, biometricians, and geneticists. Eugenics views Africans and other non-European-origin populations as inferior because of their heredity, and this inferiority is thought to be of such a character that they are "distinct organisms."[4] From this perspective each race is viewed as an organic whole, bound together by heredity and social relationships. Eugenics racially ranks human groups on the basis of certain morphological characteristics; in this ranking the groups reify race on the basis of biological and social criteria. Social movements and scientific advances forced European eugenicists to reassert their arguments in new ways.

Evolutionary theory has historically had a dual potential and been capable of supporting opposite ideologies. The eugenic interpretations of evolutionary theory justified racial stratification as a result of the "all against all" version of natural selection. Eurocentric scholars were able to dramatize this vision of competition as a thing good in itself.[5]

Since 1950, there has been a renewed interest in the relationship between evolution and social science.[6] At first, this renewal tended to be presented without the overt racial implications of the politically incorrect eugenics, especially its Nazi manifestation. In the end social statistics had two faces: one reminiscent of the old classical eugenics, and the other based on an attempt to become more scientific.

Eugenics became genetically indefensible in principle and scientifically beyond practical consideration. Symbolically, these changes were reflected in the replacement of Ronald Fisher (who moved from Galton chair at the Galton Laboratories at University College London to Cambridge) by Lionel Sharples Penrose as the holder of the chair endowed by Galton. Penrose opposed eugenic determinism and openly advocated a need to understand the interrelationship between nature and nurture.[7] As recently as 1966, Lionel Penrose, with great confidence and support, declared at the Third International Congress of Human Genetics that, as of 1966, "our knowledge of human genes and their action is still so slight that it is presumptuous and foolish to lay down positive principles for human breeding."[8] Human genetics was by this time emancipated from the eugenics movement and could be seen as an "independent" scientific vocation. Yet, the emancipation of genetics from eugenics did not stop Arthur Jensen or Charles Murray from maintaining the classical eugenic tradition of Francis Galton. Nor has it hampered contemporary use of race as a biological indicator of social difference. Eugenic attempts to explain racial difference have left an indelible mark on social statistics.

# CHAPTER THREE
## Eugenics and the Birth of Racial Statistics

### Why the Social History of Racial Statistics

Understanding the history of social statistics is as important as understanding its logic. In fact, as Karl Pearson and Ronald A. Fisher note, context, especially historical context, is as important as the mathematics of applied statistical analysis. Social statistics begins at a point when mathematical statistics and evolutionary theory meet in the eugenic mind of Francis Galton, one of the most important statisticians of the twentieth century.

Francis Galton is the father of social statistics. His ability to translate evolutionary and social ideas into statistical logic set the stage for the major developments in social statistics. Prior to Galton most attempts to do social statistics were limited by the developments in statistical logic. Galton's focus on difference, especially human difference, played the key role in the development of statistical analysis of human society. More generally, his evolutionary ideas about racial quality had a fundamental impact on the logic of social statistics. Galton's methodologies were developed as part of his racial theory of eugenics.

I recognize the controversial nature of my interpretation of statistical history; however, we must return to the role of race in the development of statistical logic if we are to stop the misuse of racial statistics. Contemporary scholars have tended to sterilize the definition of eugenics. For example, in *The Dictionary of Demography* eugenics is defined as "*[t]he study of factors capable of improving the physiological and intellectual*

*status of populations by their effect on the conditions of human reproduc-
tion and on the physical environment.*"[1] My story is in part a historical
story; therefore, it is important that I place the definition of eugenics
within a historical and social context.

In a number of papers and books, Galton would advance the ideas of
heredity and the notion that human evolution could be accelerated by a
self-conscious policy of selective mating practices. Galton sought to
give a mathematical precision to his description of heredity and eugenics.

A critical component of Galton's ideas was his eugenic perspective.
Historically, eugenics has been characterized by three principles: the
unchangeable biological basis of class and race; the assumption that
"like begets like," or the hereditary basis of physical, mental, moral, and
behavioral human characteristics, qualities, and defects; and the biological evolution and the superiority of a particular race.[2] I use the term
*eugenics* to refer to its original intent and definition as biologically based
explanations and justification of racial stratification. In 1883 Francis
Galton (1822–1911), the movement's founder and intellectual champion,
coined the term *eugenics* from the Greek *eugenës,* meaning "well born"
or "noble in heredity."[3] Galton described the science of eugenics as giving "the more suitable races or strains of blood a better chance of prevailing speedily over the less suitable."[4]

In order to address biological explanations of racial stratification,
one must first understand the fallacies of the ranking and reification of
race.[5] *Racial ranking* refers to the tendency to order physical variation
on a gradual ascending scale. *Racial reification* refers to the tendency to
convert the abstract concepts of racial differences into a system of racial
classification. Race is a concept used to classify the groupings that make
up a species. The biological basis of human races is grounded in the morphological ranking of different populations.

The physical and social sciences have actively aided in the development
of race as a scientifically legitimate and socially acceptable concept. Some
of the most distinguished scientists apparently drew their inspiration
from racist notions, yet many were among the most politically progressive European intellectuals on issues of inequality. For example, the close
relationship between eugenics and developments in statistical theory is
found in the works of the most important innovators of social statistics,
including Francis Galton, Karl Pearson, and Ronald A. Fisher.

Both the experimental and inferential design in statistics guided the development of research on race in biometrics and genetics. Early in its development, social statistics was inextricably linked to the numerical analysis of human difference. Eugenic ideas were at the heart of the development of statistical logic. This statistical logic, as well as the regression-type models that the founders of social statistics employed, is the foundation on which modern statistical analysis is based. Before we outline the development of racial statistics, consider the birth of social statistics.

## Political Arithmetic

Social statistics used in social sciences took on new meaning with the availability of large-scale data at the beginning of the nineteenth century.[6] These data were made possible by the expansion of census enumeration activities undertaken by various government agencies in Europe and the Americas. A data revolution accompanied the social transformations that culminated in emancipation of the formerly enslaved Africans; the expanded colonial activities in Asia, Africa, and the Americas; and social unrest in Europe. These new data gave statistics a new area of study—society.

Statistics as a distinct field of inquiry came into being only in the twentieth century.[7] However, the discipline itself is much older than its institutionalized expression. The founder of the discipline is generally considered to be John Graunt, who wrote the *Natural and Political Observations Mentioned in a Following Index and Made upon the Bills of Mortality,* in 1662.[8] With their research, Graunt and other political arithmeticians demonstrated the efficacy of collecting social numbers.

Political arithmeticians convinced several European governments to expand the apparatuses for enumerating the population in the second half of the eighteenth century. In the spirit of the Enlightenment, political arithmeticians sought to improve governance. The movement sought to extend the use of statistical information by government bureaucracies and bypass the conservative interests of the church and nobility. In fact, political arithmetic helped consolidate state power, and the mass of private citizens were secondary beneficiaries if anything. Political arithmetic helped to centralize bureaucracies throughout western Europe. The new numbers helped to control the population by augmenting tax revenue, yet they also tended to individualize the population and to clarify citizenship.

The new uses of statistical information called for a new view of individual identity and a new conceptualization of accounting for the population. Until this point, populations were composed of estates, not autonomous persons. Individuals inherited privileges through birth; they were not born with individual rights. Yet, the spirit of the Enlightenment called for a new sense of individual value and worth.

Who are the people? This question is at the root of defining a "good" or complete enumeration. Answers to this question are based on notions of identity. The French Revolution led to new ideas of individuality and introduced the political need to account for all persons in the European population. The first statistical investigators were inspired by the social power revealed by the beginnings of the industrial revolution and the social dynamism typified by the French Revolution and unrest in the British, French, and Spanish Empires. These statistical investigators wanted to bring objective order to the confusion of self-interested political actors. As Porter explained: "They believed that the confusion of politics could be replaced by an orderly reign of facts."[9] Earlier, Malthus had maintained that population was a potentially unstable force requiring public education if social order was to be maintained.[10] This education required an understanding of political economy and the internal structure of human society that could be gleaned from social statistics.

The first social statisticians were driven by Victorian perceptions of reality. They defined social statistics as the empirical study of society. In the beginning there were two statistical perspectives: the inferential and the descriptive. The descriptive tradition grew naturally out of the work of the political arithmeticians and focused primarily on the recording of various data, leading to tables and figures that were adopted in the social debate around public policy. The inferential tradition grew out of mathematical statistics and focused on the analysis of social data that would yield laws of the sort attained in the statistical investigations of astronomy. As the French statistician Pierre-Simon Laplace (1728–1777) himself observed, "without any doubt, the regularity that astronomy shows us in the movement of the comets takes place in all phenomena."[11] Positivism was at the center of discussions of probability, on which statistics are based.

The positivistic model is based on the assumption that the laws of society and the natural history of humans can be modeled directly on what social scientists incorrectly conceived of as the objectivity of the laws governing the natural scientific world. Laplace advanced the use of the methods of the natural sciences in the social sciences. *Regularity, necessity,* and *determination* are part of a reductive language that was used by early European social scientists.

Demographic regularities in births, deaths, and marriages by age were viewed as examples of natural theology and the harmonies of nature. Even Immanuel Kant pointed to these results as supporting evidence of the divine and natural laws that guide the natural history of humans:

> Since the free will of man has obvious influence upon marriages, births, and deaths, they seem to be subject to no rule by which the number of them could be reckoned in advance. Yet the annual tables of them in the major countries prove that they occur according to laws as stable as the unstable weather, which we likewise cannot determine in advance, but which, in the large, maintain the growth of plants, the flow of rivers, and other natural events in an unbroken, uniform course.[12]

For our purposes, *probability* refers to the statistical presentation of partial certainty based on the vantage point from which we see the real world (both things and the universe). *Probability* describes our uncertain knowledge and ability to predict.[13] Probability is a statement of our limited ability to make predictions about causal processes. Statistical analysis provides an empirical methodology for the measurement of probability and for an examination and interpretation of our observations. Social statistics offers a quantitative technology to enhance our understanding of society. Laplace is credited with presenting "the first coherent theory of statistical inference."[14]

Causation is inferred from the observation of empirical objects. Empirical evidence is therefore the basis of inductive causal theories. Empirical induction is the process of reasoning from a part to a whole, from the particular to the general, from the individual to the universal, or from the sample to the population. Nevertheless, it is possible that a slight difference in the initial condition produces very great differences in the final phenomenon. A slight error in understanding the initial condition could result in an enormous error in the predicted outcome. Prediction thus becomes problematic, and we have what appears as a fortuitous phenomenon. Therefore, theoretically, induction requires a conceptualization of causal hypotheses, laws, theories, and causal effects—the cumulating of normal evidence suggesting their acceptance. The history of social statistics is the history of attempts to provide a basis for such conceptualization about society.

## Quetelet, the First Social Statistician

Lambert-Adolphe-Jacques Quetelet (known also as Adolphe Quetelet), who lived between 1796 and 1874, is credited with taking the first steps toward making the application of probability to the measurement of uncertainty in the social sciences a practical reality.[15] Quetelet was a Belgian astronomer and meteorologist; however, he was internationally known for his statistical and social science research. His social research focused on causes of phenomena like birth, death, marriage, crime, and suicide.

To establish the historical context of the development of social statistics requires some mention of the application of probability theory outside physical sciences before the time of Quetelet.[16] James Bernoulli clearly wanted to apply probability theory to "civil, moral and economic affairs" in part 4 of the *Ars Conjectanda* (The art of conjecturing, 1713) without much success. He defines probability as a measure of our certainty of the truth of a proposition. This revolutionary idea related probability to propositions and not events. His nephew and student Nicholas Bernoulli was more successful, as were Abraham de Moivre (1667–1754) and Nicolaas Struyck (1687–1769), in the application of probability theory to the stability of statistical ratios of the number of male and female births and rates of mortality. They applied life table methods to estimate the value of annuities. Marie-Jean-Antonine-Nicolas Caritat Condorcet broke new ground in his application of probability theory to the evaluation of the reliability of decisions made by an assembly or a tribunal. In the *Essai sur l'application de l'analyse à la probabilité des décisions rendues à la pluralité des voix* (Essay on the application of analysis to the probability of decisions rendered by a plurality of votes, 1785) Condorcet does not analyze any real data but applies probability to a sensitive and controversial social topic. He referred to his application of statistics to the political and moral sciences as "social mathematics."

Laplace presented social processes representing a statistical regularity that could not later plausibly be interpreted as indicative of divine wisdom and planning.[17] In his *Essai philosophique sur les probabilitiés* (published in translation as *Philosophical Essay on Probabilities*) he wrote an introductory section on the application of probability theory to moral sciences, followed by sections on the probability of testimonies, elections, decisions by assemblies, judicial decisions, vital statistics, and insurance.

The expansion in the scope of census enumeration accompanied the beginning of the nineteenth century. In addition to this expansion, censuses and other statistical data of the population were increasingly not seen as state secrets and became available to the scholarly community and the public in the form of official publications. It was in this environment that Adolphe Quetelet played a critical role in the transition of mathematical statistics from a focus on error theory to a theory of variation among individuals in social and biological sciences. Quetelet attempted to translate the application of probability theory using less mathematically advanced methods that were more familiar to social scientists and biologists who were ignorant of statistical theory.

In 1823, Quetelet visited Paris to study with the great masters of statistical analysis, Joseph Fourier and Pierre-Simon Laplace. As their student, he was given instruction in the instruments and methods of scientific observation. Moreover, he was introduced to the method of least squares in the Laplacian tradition, which associated the methods used to reduce astronomical observations with mathematical probability and formal demography.[18]

During this time, several statisticians sought numerical laws of society.[19] Quetelet agreed with Laplace's notion of a single method for every science and that the study of society could do no better than to imitate the celestial investigators.

Quetelet proposed a physicalist cosmology that presented regularity within a group as the natural outcome in both the moral and physical world. Society was therefore an independent entity not determined by the idiosyncrasies of its individual members.[20] Quetelet viewed statistical regularity as the key to understanding society.

During Quetelet's day, statisticians were concerned with subdividing and cross-classifying populations to avoid homogenizing different groups. They were also concerned with too fine a subdivision of homogenous groups that appeared different when analyzed using probability. (I might add that these are still concerns today.) Quetelet attempted unsuccessfully to solve the first problem. He maintained that all natural distributions followed a normal curve. Like his notion of the average man, his notions about the normal curve were flawed but influential because of the questions they provoked.[21] Quetelet mistakenly thought that if a group of measurements is normally distributed then the group is homogeneous.

Several problems are found in Quetelet's connections of homogeneity and the bell curve, or normal distribution. First, a heterogeneous group of measurements can be normally distributed. Second, Quetelet had problems fitting the normal curve to data. While this was not problematic in astronomical questions, the method was not directly convertible to social science data, which were often grouped and truncated. Third, Quetelet did not have a clear method of determining the adequacy of the fit of his data to the normal curve. As Stephen M. Stigler notes in *The History of Statistics*:

> Quetelet's method failed to solve the problem that was the main stumbling block to the advancement of statistics in the social sciences. It did not provide the key to evaluating and finding useful ways of classifying data for analysis, except in very specialized situations. It was, as I have argued, too successful in revealing patterns—in almost all cases where it was tried it revealed the same pattern. It was not sensitive to the more subtle types of inhomogeneities, such as age or diet, for which a method of analysis was needed. It could not even detect the presence of widely differing racial types. This is not to say Quetelet's work on this was without influence. To the contrary, it helped create a climate of awareness of distribution that was to lead to a truly major advance in statistical methods over the period 1869 to 1925, in works of Francis Galton, Francis Y. Edgeworth, Karl Pearson, and Ronald A. Fisher.[22]

Quetelet incorrectly assumed he could apply methods employed in the natural sciences to social phenomena. He assumed that there was a linear relationship between a social indicator and the probability of its observed manifestation. Technically, he maintained that a social indicator would have a deterministic relationship with its manifestation. In physics, for example, acceleration is deterministically related to the force of an object. The laws of physics dictate that we can take two billiard balls and set them up in such a way that if the first ball is hit it will knock the second into a pocket on the billiard table. In this context we can say that hitting the first ball caused the second ball to fall into the pocket. The laws of physics can address any doubt that the second ball will fall into the pocket. Social processes do not operate within such a deterministic context. In social science, hypothetical constructs like indicators and symptoms are probabilistically related to the manifestation of a social phenomenon.[23]

These new statisticians sought an accurate and exhaustive enumeration of "individuals" with an exclusion of the guesses and approximations of the past. Nevertheless, as in the Old Regime, the New Regime came with its own hierarchies. The New Regime saw individuals as being possessed with rights but hierarchically endowed in their abilities. This belief in the inequality in abilities was to become the driving force behind the development of racial statistics.

## Francis Galton, the Hereditarian Genius

European eugenics aimed at bettering the "more suitable races" by controlling reproduction and thereby influencing their genetic makeup.[24] Francis Galton believed that the human race could be improved in the manner of plant and animal selective breeding. He believed that humans could be bred for their abilities, especially their intelligence.

Understanding human variation required an understanding of the mechanisms of heredity. To understand the relationship between inheritance and human evolution, many European intellectuals turned to eugenics. Charles Darwin openly expressed his support for the work of his younger first cousin Francis Galton, the founder of eugenics. In his praise of Galton, Darwin suggested that the inheritance of intelligence was a key element in human evolution:

> The variability or diversity of the mental faculties in men of the same race, *not to mention the greater difference between men of distinct races, is so notorious that not a word need be said*.... [A]nd we now know, through the admirable labours of Mr. Galton, that genius which implies a wonderfully complex combination of high faculties, tends to be inherited; and, on the other hand, it is too certain that insanity and deteriorated mental powers likewise run in families.[25]

While Darwin demonstrated the possibility of evolution, he did not demonstrate exactly how this evolution occurred. The European study of eugenics aimed at filling this void by explaining the process and impact of heredity on society. Galton extended Darwin's evolutionary ideas to explain inheritance in human society.

Quetelet interpreted his statistical results as confirming that mean values were more important than understanding variation.[26] In fact, he felt that variation was governed by natural laws and could be neglected in the study of mean values. Francis Galton saw in Quetelet's work a tool for analyzing the nature and effects of variation. Social statisticians beginning with Galton extended Quetelet's application of probability-based statistics to the study of eugenics. Quetelet's research presented the first steps in establishing mathematics of variation, that would provide the statistical key to the study of heredity, leading eventually to eugenics and population genetics. However, where Quetelet's work used the bell curve, or probability theory, to get rid of variation, Galton's objective was to preserve and understand variation. Thus, in the process of understanding statistical variation, Galton sought to racialize inferential statistics.

Francis Galton was a key intellectual power behind the statistical revolution in the social sciences.[27] His imaginative ideas are the conceptual foundation of eugenic thought and inspired much of the early work in social statistics. Galton's research in *Hereditary Genius* (1869), *English Men of Science* (1874), and *Natural Inheritance* (1889) suggested that genius and success are inherited and that this process could be measured statistically. He was one of the first scholars to formalize the relationship among human potential, intelligence, and statistical analysis. This relationship continues to underlie much social analysis and public policy. Galton's rise to intellectual stardom in the British scientific community was initially based on his accounts of his travels in southwest Africa in the 1850s. *The Narrative of an Explorer in Tropical South Africa* documented his observations and opinions of southwest Africa.[28] Galton's African experience helped shape his ideas about race and was important in his formulation of eugenics.

Galton saw in Quetelet's formulation the ability to distinguish among populations. In *Hereditary Genius* he wrote:

> It clearly would not be proper to combine the heights of men belonging to two dissimilar races, in the expectation that the compound results would be governed by the same constants. A union of two dissimilar systems of dots would produce the same kind of confusion as if half the bullets fired at a target had been directed to one mark, and the other half to another mark. Nay, an examination of the dots would show to a person, ignorant of what had occurred, that such had been the case, and it would be possible, by aid of the law, to disentangle two or any moderate number of superimposed series of marks.[29]

Quetelet used the bell curve to demonstrate homogeneity; Galton, however, employed it to distinguish between populations and individuals. Galton used statistical analysis to make general statements regarding the superiority of different classes within England and of the European-origin race, statements that were consistent with his eugenic agenda.

In the first sentence of the first page of the original, 1869, edition of *Hereditary Genius,* Galton outlined why he wrote the book:

> I propose to show man's natural abilities are derived by inheritance, under exactly the same limitations as are the form and physical features of the whole organic world. Consequently, as it is easy, notwithstanding those limitations, to obtain by careful selection a permanent breed of dogs or horses gifted with peculiar powers of running or doing anything else, so it would be quite practicable to produce a highly-gifted race of men by judicious marriages during several consecutive generations.

Galton wanted to examine the inheritance of intelligence. He used data on the distribution of grades obtained by 73 Royal Military College candidates. Using methods developed by Quetelet, he found the distribution to be nearly normal. He assumed the distribution of intelligence was normal. He did not discuss the meaning of intelligence or how it was measured and how the measurement could influence the distribution. Some scholars continue to repeat this error today.

In 1889, in *Natural Inheritance,* Galton developed a solution that allowed the connection between the bivariate normal distribution and inheritance. His formulation of regression suggested that each generation moved toward the mean morphological features of the population. In fact, he argued that offspring returned partly to the mean. Galton's regression analysis showed that when midparental height (the average of the father's and mother's heights) was taller than mediocrity (the mean), children tended to be shorter than their parents; however, when midparental height was shorter than mediocrity, children tended to be taller than their parents. Thus, the stature of children was thought to regress toward the mean (or mediocrity).[30] Galton's regression analysis presented a statistical connection between two generations, and appeared to be free of bias and true for all but the most extreme cases. His analysis was both statistical and theoretical. His physiological theory of heredity was based upon Darwin's theory of pangenesis and integrated into his statistical ideas.

According to this hypothesis, every unit or cell of the body throws off
gemmules or undeveloped atoms, which are transmitted to the offspring
of both sexes, and are multiplied by self-division. They may remain
undeveloped during the early years of life or during successive
generations; and their development into units or cells, like those from
which they were derived, depends on their affinity for, and union with
other units or cells previously developed in the due order of growth.[31]

Galton embraced Darwin's theory of inheritance. Consequently, he
viewed his statistical analysis as a continuation of Darwin's evolutionary theory. Indeed, Galton's research attempted to extend Darwin's evolutionary theory to human inheritance, and from this he advanced the
political agenda of eugenics that helped transform social statistics. Scientifically, Galton's research surpassed Darwin's idea of pangenesis, and
he was to demonstrate the role of heredity in continuous variation.

In 1869, Galton did not understand how to connect the bell curve to
inheritance. Therefore, the statistical analysis in *Hereditary Genius* did
not play a critical role in his arguments.[32] However, his efforts to understand the variation among and within human populations led to the
development of the statistical measurement of correlation and to the
creation of modern social statistics.[33]

In 1875, Galton wrote an article, "Statistics by Intercomparison, with
Remarks on the Law of Frequency of Error," which suggested that measurement of two values—the median and the quartile—was sufficient
to characterize or compare populations.[34] In order to understand a
population or to compare two or more populations, one must arrange
the group in an ascending order. The middlemost person would represent the median. Individuals one-fourth and three-fourths along the
curve represented the probable error in the distribution. This method
was an outgrowth of Quetelet's ideas about probable error and proved
to be far more useful than the techniques used in *Hereditary Genius*. Like
Quetelet, Galton sought to bring statistical order to the chaotic patterns
of individuals within society.

Galton's method of inferential statistics by *intercomparison* also
demonstrated that bell curves exist within bell curves. Thus, if sets of bell
curves are superimposed onto each other, the result is a new bell curve.
Normal distributions exist within normal distributions. For Galton this
meant different populations could be represented in a bell curve of all
populations. Galton's original formulation of this point was illustrated

using the sizes of fruit from different parts of a garden in which he used the normal curve to examine heterogeneity.

According to Karl Pearson the "revolution" in statistics followed the publication of Galton's paper "Co-relations and Their Measurement, Chiefly from Anthropometric Data."[35] In this paper Galton drew on his earlier papers and research to advance statistical methods; he "formalized" his conception of correlation as a mathematical measurement of heredity and eugenic potentialities. "'Co-relation or correlation of structure' is a phrase much used in biology, and not least in that branch of it which refers to heredity. . . ."[36]

In the 1892 edition of *Hereditary Genius,* he noted that "the natural ability of which this book mainly treats, is such as a modern European possesses in a much greater average share than men of the lower races. There is nothing either in the history of domestic animals or in that of evolution to make us doubt that a race of sane men may be formed, who shall be as much superior mentally and morally to the modern European, as the modern European is to the lowest of the Negro races."[37] While this statement may be considered insignificant in the context of Galton's overall statistical contribution, it is fundamental in understanding the direction and purpose of his causal explanations.

## Bringing Galton's Message to the People

In 1885, Francis Ysidro Edgeworth (1845–1926) developed a test to ascertain whether different populations existed within the bell curve.[38] Edgeworth's test adapted the bell curve to assess the "significance" of differences among the subpopulations. He used Galton's 1875 formulation in "Statistics by Intercomparison" as a vehicle to employ classical statistical theory in understanding social statistics. Galton conceptually divided the bell curve into separate smaller bell curves on the basis of correlated measurements.

Edgeworth's economic research laid the foundation for the statistical analysis of time series and for the development of the modern systems of socioecomomic indicators. Edgeworth's extension of correlation was conceptually very important.[39] He was one of the first social statisticians to develop a cogent theorem for the multivariate normal distribution.[40] Edgeworth translated Galton's ideas into a generalizable statistical model.

Recognizing the power of Galton's ideas in Edgeworth's formulations, Pearson created a methodology and conducted the empirical research that popularized Galton's ideas in the scientific community. Pearson's first contribution to social statistics was an improvement in the estimates of Galton's and Edgeworth's work. As with earlier scholars Pearson's research consisted of fitting mathematical curves to frequency distributions of empirical data and of extensions in the measurement of correlation.

In the same year that Galton published "Co-relations and Their Measurement," Pearson met W. F. R. Weldon, the chair of zoology at University College, London. Weldon was attempting to adapt Galton's methods to the study of evolution in wild populations. Weldon turned to Pearson with a series of questions, to which Pearson responded in a series of papers known as Contributions to the Mathematical Theory of Evolution. Published between 1894 and 1916, the series was retitled Mathematical Contributions to the Theory of Evolution after the second in what became a series of about nineteen papers.[41] This series allowed Pearson and Weldon to develop their philosophy of the science of logical positivism into a new discipline of biometry or mathematical evolutionary biology. Around 1911 the Biometrics Laboratory and the Eugenics Laboratory at the University of London were combined and renamed the Department of Applied Statistics, with Pearson as the chair with the title of Galton Professor.

Edgeworth's contributions enhanced the meaning of Galton's earlier ideas; however, it was Pearson's elaboration of Edgeworth's theorems that advanced correlation theory into the main of social statistics.[42] In Pearson's third and fourth papers of the series Mathematical Contribution to the Theory of Evolution—"Regression, Heredity and Panmixa," and "On the Probable Errors of Frequency Constants and on the Influence of Random Selection on Variation and Correlation" (which he coauthored with L. N. G. Filon)—he provided a basic formula for estimating the correlation coefficient and a test of its accuracy.

Pearson, like Galton, identified good human stock with intellectuals, artists, musicians, and scientists. His statistical work was conducted "with special reference to what seems legitimate in the case of heredity."[43] The Pearson-led biometrical school of eugenics viewed evolution as an incremental process. However, it did not solve the problem of the transmission of characteristics from one generation to the next, which had stumped Darwin and Galton. However, it did establish a paradigm of introducing statistical methods from biometrics and genetics to the social sciences.

This paradigm introduced important statistical models such as regression and path models.[44]

In 1897, George Udny Yule provided the conceptual and statistical expression that completed Galton's project to apply statistics to the study of society.[45] Yule was one of the first social statisticians to demonstrate the relationship between regression and least-squares estimates. Yule was exceptional in that his application of statistics focused on causation in social sciences. For Pearson, causation was not the major issue. He was particularly concerned with correlation as a measure of the degree of association in biology.[46] And his primary interest was in making a contribution to eugenics and the theory of evolution. Pearson's main focus and contributions to statistical analysis were in the fitting of curves to observations and measurements. He did not develop a theory of estimation. He developed the chi-square measure as a measure of the goodness of fit.

Yule was attempting to investigate the "causal relations between economic phenomena."[47] For him, the regression line implied causation, not a eugenic law. In his view, regression was the process of fitting a straight line to a set of data. However, such statistical arguments "are almost necessarily circular."[48]

Yule extended the application of regression in one of the first regression analyses of poverty. Interestingly, Yule's analysis provided support for the conservative position advocated by Malthus at the beginning of the century.[49] Yule argued that providing income relief outside the poorhouse increased the number of people on relief. By 1920, Yule's approach to multiple correlation and regression predominated in social science research. As Stephen M. Stigler notes: "Galton, Edgeworth, and Pearson assembled the structure; Yule completed it by finding a variation on their advances that finally provided a formulation and analysis for questions in the social sciences."[50]

In the United States, social scientists began to embrace the statistical methods developed in the cause of eugenics. They embraced the methodological implications of the biometric model and followed Yule in giving it a causal interpretation. This commitment is reflected in the words of an important social statistician.[51] J. P. Norton noted in his manuscript *Statistical Studies in the New York Money Market*: "If the biologist can point to these correlations as satisfactory scientific laws, it is hardly more than fair to grant the same privilege to the economist. In short, it seems reasonable to conclude that economics may become almost as exact as biology."[52] Social statisticians could make categories. Not only did they claim to have scientifically codified and measured social reality, but also correlation and regression allowed them to understand the relationships among variables in this reality. Thus began the problem of positing causation when the most that has been demonstrated is an association of undetermined causes.[53] Ronald A. Fisher recognized this problem early on and suggested a strategy for using statistics in social science.

By 1922, Fisher had developed the tools necessary to present a theory of estimation for finite samples. He wrote his epochal papers "On the Mathematical Foundations of Theoretical Statistics" (1922) and "Theory of Statistical Estimation" (1925).[54] These two papers established the basis for Fisher's general statistical framework of a frequency-based general theory of parametric statistical inference. His work clarified the distinction between a sample statistic and population value (a parameter), and he emphasized the derivation of exact distributions for hypotheses testing. It is in these two papers that he formalized the distinction between probability and likelihood.[55]

Social statistics took another intellectual leap when Fisher published *Statistical Methods for Research Workers* in 1925 and *The Design of Experiments* in 1935.[56] Both books had a tremendous impact on the teaching and practice of statistics. In *The Design of Experiments* he discusses his notion of the null hypothesis. He points out that the null hypothesis can never be proved but can be disproved. These innovations remain critical to social statistics. He is credited with introducing the modern experimental design and consolidating statistical methods in the social sciences. In the introduction to *Statistical Methods for Research Workers*, he notes:

> Statistical methods are essential to social studies, and it is principally by the aid of such methods that these studies may be raised to the rank of sciences. This particular dependence of social studies upon statistical methods has led to the unfortunate misapprehension that statistics is to be regarded as a branch of economics, whereas in truth methods adequate to the treatment of economic data, in so far as these exist, have only been developed in the study of biology and the other sciences.[57]

During the first half of the twentieth century, eugenics continued to serve as an inspirational framework for developments in statistical analysis and the probabilistic language that accompanied its growth. During the second half of the twentieth century, probabilistic language offered a framework for thinking about many of the social issues that hitherto appeared beyond the empirical framework. I will return to the implications this has had for racial statistics in part III. First, we consider other historical developments in racial statistics.

## From Biometrics to Genetics

Gregor Mendel, the father of genetics, solved the "mode of inheritance" problem when he found the key to inheritance in genes. Mendel's research suggested genetic regularities in transmission of genes across generations.[58] He hypothesized that both the segregation of genes and their recombination are determined by chance. Therefore, the average or expected transmission of genes across generations may be predicted according to the rules of probability. Mendelian genetics suggests that the problems of heredity can be treated as statistical problems. The advent of Mendelian genetics opened up an opportunity to advance biometrics.

Advances in Mendelian genetics suggested that Galton's law of ancestral heredity was incorrect, even with Pearson's modifications. However, like Darwin, Mendel did not develop a statistical method for the analysis of his model. And Pearson's ideological objection to the Mendelian paradigm kept the field of genetics and biometrics apart for a period of time, especially in Britain.[59] Pearson unscientifically rejected the advances in genetics because Mendel's paradigm used theoretical concepts that contradicted Pearson's philosophical tenets. Pearson's effort to be "theory-free" led him to a "metaphysical trap" of interpreting his findings in ways consistent with his stated purpose but contradictory to his methods.

At the same time as Yule's article appeared, Gregor Mendel's famous paper was rediscovered. Mendel had published his results on plant hybridization in 1865.[60] Mendel presented his results in terms of the probability of inheritance of visible characteristics. As Yule's model of social statistics took root among social scientists in the United States (where human-genetic research was used against racially dominated populations) and elsewhere, plant and animal geneticists avoided human genetics because of its association with the eugenic doctrine.[61] Yet, this did not prevent prominent scientists from retaining the eugenic idea.

Fisher's efforts to merge genetics and eugenics occurred in the context of his political aspirations. In 1914 he wrote "Some Hopes of a Eugenist" for the *Eugenics Review*. In this paper he presents the pessimistic ideas of the eugenics movement. In his view the dysgenic problem resulted because "the socially lower classes have a birth-rate, or, to speak more exactly, a survival rate, greatly in excess of those who are on the whole distinctly their eugenic superiors. It is to investigate the cause and cure of this phenomenon that the eugenic society should devote its best efforts."[62] As a leading eugenicist, Fisher offered his own solution in 1917:

> To increase the birth-rate in the professional classes and among the highly skilled artisans would be to solve the great eugenic problem of the present generation and to lay a broad foundation for every kind of social advance. No object involves more profound social problems than this one or appears to offer more tremendous difficulties. The classes concerned are outside the scope of direct legislative interference, and owe their national value to the very fact that by their brains and skill they support society, and are not supported by it. To restore to these classes the conditions which they have previously enjoyed, to give to them more ample facilities for marriage and normal family life, and more promising prospects for their children of both sexes, is the social aim to which eugenists, however anxious they may be to avoid social controversy, inevitably become more and more committed.[63]

Galton's law of regression was developed in his work on heredity. He found that on average a child is halfway between the parent and the mean. At this point Galton had not made his conclusions on the basis of Mendel's ideas. Pearson also rejected Mendel's findings. It took Fisher's 1918 paper, "The Correlation between Relatives on the Supposition of Mendelian Inheritance," to introduce Mendelian genetics as an intrinsic feature of European eugenic thought.[64] Fisher demonstrated that the statistics of inheritance of quantitative traits was compatible with Mendelian theory. Fisher suggested a chance model based on Mendel's ideas that explained Galton's law of regression and the approximate normality of many physical characteristics, like stature. Fisher played the key role in developing the statistical techniques that helped reconcile the distinctions between biometrics and the Mendelian perspectives. He argued that the "great service which the modern development of statistics has rendered to eugenics is that it supplies a definite method of measuring and analyzing variability."[65]

Fisher's 1918 paper was followed by offers to teach at the Galton Laboratory under Pearson and at the Rothamsted Experimental Station. He chose the latter, the most pretigious agricultural institute in England.

While at Rothamsted, he wrote his famous genetics book *The Genetical Theory of Natural Selection.* In this book, he argued that a theoretical account of evolution by natural selection could be based on Mendelian genetics.[66] In this work Fisher also suggested the use of positive eugenics. He argued for family allowances proportional to wages, salaries, and professional fees. Such a strategy would favor the more prosperous and was thus consistent with the eugenic support for social class hierarchy in Britain.

American scientists embraced the Mendelian basis of eugenics early in the movement's development. In 1907, the Mendelian inheritance of human hair and skin color was demonstrated in the United States by the prominent biologist Charles B. Davenport, who became the leading European-origin eugenicist in the Americas.[67] As a consequence European eugenics in the United States took a strong Mendelian position regarding racial inferiority. From his laboratory at Cold Spring Harbor, on Long Island, Davenport studied heredity and evolution from a reductive Mendelian framework. Like other eugenicists, Davenport argued that each race had a fixed identity and that in racial hybrids—the result of race mixing—the inferior traits of individuals would be preserved.[68] He argued that biracial procreation produced inferior children.

Eugenic researchers collected information on human heredity by examining medical and genealogical records and with specialized surveys. In Germany and the United States, twin studies and family pedigree studies were examined within a Mendelian framework. Like most eugenic researchers, American and German eugenicists analyzed phenotypical and family records for the inheritance of medical affliction and social behaviors in genetic rather than biometric terms. Pearson, with his anti-Mendelian perspective, studied heredity by statistical analysis of relatives for the occurrence of medical affliction and social behaviors in biometric terms. Eugenic scholars exposed Mendelian patterns in the inheritance of well-specified traits such as color blindness, polydactyly, and albinism and for such diseases as hemophilia and otosclerosis.[69] Yet, race and class prejudice and domination clouded the social significance of the scientific value of the eugenic project. In Germany, for example, Eugen Fischer trained members of the SS and studied "material" from concentration camps.

A substantial and significant amount of genetic research occurred outside the context of the eugenic paradigm.[70] This line of research sought an "explanation of how organisms pass on traits of anatomy, physiology, and behavior to their descendants and of how each individual expresses those traits in its formation and throughout its life."[71] During the first fifty or sixty years, the most important developments in genetics were made in the study of nonhuman populations. Between Mendel's discovery and its rediscovery in 1900, biometrics and cell biology (cytology) developed enormously.

During this developmental period, genetic research increasingly provided evidence against eugenic arguments. Genetic research undermined eugenic notions of race and intelligence. In fact, the ability to locate the intelligence gene or genes appears possible yet far from our grasp as we begin the twenty-first century. Furthermore, the idea of what a gene is has been as dynamic as the idea of race.[72]

## From Genetics to Statistics

During the first half of the twentieth century, scientists sought to understand the subdivisions among populations dispersed geographically and in varying ecological niches. Race was a concept used to classify the groupings that make up a species. In the nineteenth century and the first half of the twentieth century, most "scientific" investigations of race focused on morphological traits of different groups (e.g., skin color and hair texture).[73] Eugenics used the morphological differences among humans to define race; indeed, from the sociological point of view, the biological basis of race is in fact morphological.

As genetic analysis came to be applied to the eugenic question, the morphological definition of a race was appreciably weakened, and the contributions of Ronald A. Fisher became increasingly important. In fact, prior to the major advances in blood-group serology, Fisher had seen such research as a potentially important aspect of eugenic research.[74] The inheritance of blood groups appeared to display patterns that conformed to Mendelian genetics. In 1935, with funding from the Rockefeller Foundation, Fisher set up a research unit to study serological genetics at the Galton Laboratory at University College. Serology offered an opportunity to separate eugenics from its racist and classist past.

Developments in serology advanced rapidly during and after World War II.[75] Morphologically populations vary; some of this variation is associated with environmental gradients. The distribution of these gradients along geographic dimensions may be referred to as a *cline*. In the beginning some of the new population geneticists associated the morphological races with different blood groups. However, the observation that the morphological variations among races were breached by the genetic distributions of different clines led to the undoing of a morphologically defined human race in genetics.[76] The fact that clines of genetic differentiation, like blood groups, transcend the supposed races weakened the scientific definition of race and, with it, most of the genetic support for eugenics.

Following World War II, the morphological bases of race that eugenics depended on for legitimacy were contradicted by genetic discoveries and challenged by several political events.[77] The success and failures of Nazism made the notion of scientific racism a caution for most scientists. The second edition of Arthur Ernest Mourant and his colleagues' book, *The Distribution of the Human Blood Groups and Other Polymorphisms,* rejected the scientific idea of race, so prominent in the first edition, and presented their discussion in terms of populations. Also, the liberation movements in Asia and Africa reinserted the unheard voice of the supposedly inferior races into the debate.

Despite the science of genetics, the European eugenics movement continued to reify the idea of race. Race was seen as not simply a social fact but also a genetic fact, a material reality that could be measured by the use of scientific observation. Conceptually, the use of statistics and morphological variation among human populations allowed the authoritative utterance of "facts" about racial distinctions. Racial elements could be reduced to morphological differences. Morphologically, racial difference was quantifiable and appeared with statistical frequency sufficient for analysis. Some eugenicists felt they had discovered the biological predictors of social and cultural quality.

Eugenics required an essential difference among humans in order to justify racial and class stratification. While mainstream genetic scientists were rejecting the idea of morphological races among human populations, psychologists were integrating the use of statistical methods into their analysis of human intelligence. As geneticists destroyed the biological basis of traditional European eugenics, psychologists developed the IQ (intelligence quotient) test, which became, with statistical support, the new source of support for eugenics. The IQ was originally defined as the ratio of "mental age" to chronological age by researchers like Lewis Terman, at Stanford University, but was later redefined in terms of standard scores for age levels. Testing was believed to be able to reveal the hidden reality of what was inside a person's head and predict their future performance on tests or in life generally. As the biological basis of race was undermined by genetics, the statistical basis of race was elevated to a new level of importance.

Recall that in his book *Hereditary Genius,* Francis Galton presented intelligence as the most important human trait and one around which society should be organized. He believed it was biologically inherited and that Africans and other people of color were inferior in intelligence to the lighter-skinned Europeans. Critical to his ideas of eugenics was the notion that the less intelligent populations were reproducing at a more rapid rate than the more intelligent ones and that this process would ultimately reduce the intelligence of all humanity.

Social Darwinism lost support among most American sociologists by the beginning of the twentieth century. It was psychologists who led the revival of the eugenic perspective in the social sciences in the United States. The developments in genetics did not necessarily support the racism implied by eugenics, but racial statistics continued to be the basis of eugenic legitimacy. Although genetics undermined the very notion of morphologically defined human races, eugenic researchers simply shifted their intellectual basis of support to psychology and maintained a belief in morphological human races.

The history of this shift overlaps with the development of biometrics and other forms of racial statistics. In as early as 1904, Charles Spearman published an article, "'General Intelligence,' Objectively Determined and Measured," which offered another avenue to justify racial stratification.[78] Published in the *American Journal of Psychology,* Spearman's paper offered a statistically based definition of intelligence. Spearman's method of *factor analysis* measured whether the common variance in a matrix of correlation coefficients could be reduced to a single general factor or to several independent factors.[79]

Consistent with the theory of correlation developed by Galton and Pearson, Spearman introduced the idea of correlational psychology. As a theoretical construct, Spearman's "rank-correlation coefficient" attempted to account for how those who scored high on one kind of test tended to score high on others, and it statistically defined the concept of intelligence.[80]

One year after the appearance of Spearman's paper in 1905, the French psychologist Alfred Binet devised the first test of intelligence. Several psychologists attempted to measure differences in mental ability; however, none was as successful as Alfred Binet and Theodore Simon, who developed an intelligence test for schoolchildren.[81] Binet and Simon meant for their test to be used to measure the "mental age" of slow learners. The original IQ test was not developed to measure intellectual superiority. Binet and Simon acknowledged that environmental and educational opportunity affected the test results. Their original research suggests that the test was only an approximate measure of intelligence of children from similar environments.

However, the original caution of Binet and Simon did nothing to stop the tide of misuse of these standardized examinations for the measurement of intellectual superiority of different racial groups and classes. Referring to this work, Spearman noted, "By this one great investigation the whole scene was transformed. The recently despised tests were now introduced into every country with enthusiasm."[82]

Spearman took the IQ test—a rather simple age-scale measurement—and applied the more mathematically complex method of factor analysis. His research led to the perspective that the mental test measured a *general* and a *specific* factor. He called the general factor $g$.[83] The acceptance of the $g$ factor theory legitimized the utilization of verbal and quantitative test items as measures of an underlying general intellectual capacity. Arithmetic and vocabulary problems demanding a firm knowledge of "Standard English" became the yardstick for measuring and evaluating the underlying intellectual ability of persons from various backgrounds, cultures, and lifestyles. IQ became the most respected of the measures of intelligence. The intelligence test became a measure of the innate capacity of the brain, a biological quality. Spearman shared a belief in the reification of intelligence. While others also shared their belief in intelligence, some questioned whether $g$ was an adequate measure of cognitive abilities.

Louis Thurston criticized $g$ as a misleading average of a set of tests with no "real" psychological significance. Thurston argued that intelligence consists of several *primary mental abilities* and that these abilities could be identified using a modified form of factor analysis.[84] Thurston called his modified form of factor analysis *simple structure*. In fact, Spearman's *principal component* method and Thurston's *simple structure* method are statistically equivalent. Thurston's major innovation was to redistribute the information used to calculate *g*. Spearman believed in a dominant innate intelligence, *g*, whereas Thurston believed in irreducible innate mental abilities and that *g* was a nonexistent oversimplification.

Many of the social scientists that rejected European eugenics embraced the new IQ test and the idea of standardized tests for the measurement of mental and intellectual ability. They embraced this idea despite the lack of evidence that there was a significant relationship among testing, ranking, and successful results.[85] Statistical examination of the test results *validated* the continued existence of "racial inferiority." The use of statistical methods was seen as a powerful tool in the observation and explanation of human biological differences. The circumstantial evidence of indirect statistical analysis replaced the biological basis of human difference. The trend against eugenics in genetics and biology had a big impact on those fields early on; psychologists were slower to respond. Following World War II, psychologists became the leading eugenicists, and IQ became the primary basis on which differences in human population quality could be explained.

By the end of World War II biologists had synthesized Darwinian evolution and its theory of natural selection with Mendelian genetics.[86] These changes coincided with the end of Nazi use of eugenic policies on a broad scale.[87] These two processes resulted in a transformation of eugenics. The new advocates of eugenics differed considerably from its founders. The new waves of eugenicists were convinced that genetics revealed the inherited inequality of humans. Biologically based differences in cognitive ability were manifest in the inequality of IQ scores of people within the same socioeconomic class and among different racial groups.

A classic example of these changes is the celebrated article of Cyril Burt and Margaret Howard, "The Multifactorial Theory of Inheritance and Its Application to Intelligence," published in 1956. As recently as 1975, one author characterized Burt and Howard's article as an "account, which is a generally accepted one."[88] Burt applied the technique of factor analysis to the study of mental testing. Like Spearman, his method depended on an assumption about the innate nature of intelligence with a statistical system to explain it.

To make matters worse, Burt was less than an honest scholar. He used fraudulent data in his analysis and fabricated the names of his collaborators.[89] He suppressed the results that he did not like and exaggerated the results that agreed with his preconceptions about human difference. The errors of eugenic psychometric analysis were well documented in 1974 by Leon Kamin, *The Science and Politics of IQ,* and in 1981 by Stephen Jay Gould, *The Mismeasure of Man.* However, the practice of psychometric eugenics continues, and its scientific credibility remains a problem.

Racial statistics of intelligence have a long history in the United States. Throughout this history, researchers have presented evidence of the influence of previously ignored factors on intelligence test scores. In 1935, Otto Klineberg's book *Negro Intelligence and Selective Migration* presented evidence that African American test scores went up among children who had migrated from the South to New York and that the rise increased with length of residence.[90] In 1948, Arnold Rose and Caroline Rose's book, *America Divided: Minority Group Relations in the United States,* presented evidence that African Americans from the North scored higher than those from the legally segregated South and that African Americans from some northern states had higher average scores than did European Americans from some southern states.[91] The racial statistics in this research provided evidence that opportunity was important and that the differences in test scores were not a result of selective migration. What was hitherto an innate ability was seen to be influenced by the social environment.

Studies like the two cited above did not destroy the eugenic orientation of much of the racial statistics on intelligence testing. However, these racial statistics redirected the discussion to the relative roles of environment and genetics. Such research was valuable in the recognition that environmental factors could generate large racial gaps in intelligence statistics; however, it was also important in helping perpetuate the problem of reifying race as a biological reality. While maintaining a biological conception of race, many researchers conducted racial statistical analyses that focused on environmental and social factors as causes of racial stratification. In the end this research only refocused racial statistics.

# CHAPTER FOUR

## Eugenics and Racial Demography

The central concept in demography is the idea of a population change. The forces of demography are both biological and environmental. Biologically, demography is the study of the processes of mortality and reproduction that determine the rate of population change. Environmentally, demography is the study of the forces that resist these biological processes and further regulate the rate of population change. Malthus, Graunt, Huygens, and Gompertz were all interested in population dynamics. The foundations of demography are both mathematical and theoretical. Demography shares its mathematical ancestors with inferential statistics.

Mathematically, the roots of demography began with John Graunt's *Observations upon the Bills of Mortality* in 1662.[1] Christiaan Huygens graphically presented Graunt's data on the age at death. Huygens also used Graunt's data to make the first estimation of life expectancy and the median age at death.[2] Demographic issues, especially mortality, were of increased interest to the major mathematicians and statisticians up to Laplace and Quetelet at the beginning of the nineteenth century. In 1825, Benjamin Gompertz proposed that the force of mortality increased exponentially with age for humans, over the range of adult ages for which he had data.[3] His observations were based on data from adults between the ages of twenty and sixty in England, France, and Sweden. Consistent with other social scientists during his time, Gompertz was concerned with understanding the laws of human populations. He saw in his analysis a "law of mortality." Likewise, Wilhelm Lexis's (1875) revolutionary diagram provides a convenient way of demonstrating the relationship between periods and cohorts. And, as we have seen, individuals like Pearson and Fisher maintained an active interest in demographic processes.

Theoretically, the roots of demography are connected with Malthus's theory of population. Malthus presented a perspective of population dynamics that has continued to influence demographic population perspectives. Malthus is also credited with giving evolutionary theory a new direction. Thus, it is appropriate that by the twentieth century the leading population perspective focused on the intersection between evolution and population dynamics. This perspective was eugenics.

Eugenics advocated the biological superiority of the European-origin elite even as it admitted their low reproduction rate. The notion of *dysgenesis,* in which certain population processes, such as births or migrations, promote the survival of biologically deficient individuals, suggested the contradictory idea that Europe was biologically superior yet socially and genetically vulnerable. The eugenics movement expressed the ambiguities confronted by societies influenced by Victorian morality in an age of European population dispersion around the world.

By the end of the nineteenth century, eugenics—and the biological justification of the racial "inferiority" of peoples from Africa, Asia, and the Americas—became a powerful force in Europe and the United States. In the United States, the Civil War was followed by the passage of antidiscrimination laws that restrained racist hostilities; within two decades, however, these statutes were repudiated and repealed.[4] In 1896 the Supreme Court's decision in *Plessy v. Ferguson* legalized racial exclusion, and racial stratification was reconfirmed in the era of liberal democracy.[5] Thus, the United States provided fertile ground for eugenics, which focused on identifying factors capable of improving the physiological and intellectual status of the European-origin population. Proponents of eugenics based their movement on biological explanations of racial superiority yet consistently ignored scientific facts that challenged their ideological beliefs. The most successful eugenics movement was Nazism in Germany. The political fallout that resulted from the Nazi defeat led to a change in eugenic rhetoric; however, the ideas remained fundamentally the same.

Eugenics played an important role in the development of the demographic perspective of racial differences. In the following sections I discuss the place of eugenics in the study of demography and its extension to the international justification of racial stratification.

## European Eugenics and the Population Perspective

Statistics, genetics, and demography all have eugenics in common. In its basic form, this commonality centered on the study of population quality or composition. Its major concern was preserving the quality of the European race. Consequently, the most popular population perspective in the first half of this century was eugenics. Eugenicists argued that racial differences in the population result from biological differences. The eugenics movement aimed at bettering the human population by controlling reproduction and migration and thereby influencing the racial composition of the population. Eugenicists defined the population in racial and classist terms and supported their arguments with whatever available science that would not undermine their determinism. Charles Spearman expressed an excellent summary of the demographic concerns of eugenicists:

> An accurate measurement of every one's intelligence would seem to herald the feasibility of selecting better endowed persons for admission into citizenship—and even for the right of having offspring. And whilst in this manner a suitable selection secures a continual rise in the intellectual status of the people taken in mass, the same power of measuring intelligence should also make possible a proper treatment of each individual; to each can be given an appropriate education, and therefore a fitting place in the state—just that which he or she demonstrably deserves. Class hatred, nourished upon preferences that are believed to be unmerited, would seem at last within reach of eradication; perfect justice is about to combine with maximum efficiency.[6]

In its *positive* form eugenics focused on increasing the breeding of the "most fit" individuals of the race. The *negative* form of eugenics focused on reducing the fertility and immigration of inferior races and individuals. Both the positive and negative forms of eugenics developed within a discourse about racial differences and racial inequality.

In the formative years of the institutionalization of population studies in Europe, the United States, and South Africa, eugenic research was an important and respectable population perspective. The eugenic population perspective was a fear of population decline leading to the decline of Western civilization. Between 1870 and 1950, many European-origin scholars (inside and outside Europe) expressed fears of population dysgenesis.[7] Population decline encompassed three interrelated fears of many scholars and politicians. The first fear was of decline in the quality of the population resulting from the reduction in the quantity of the upper-class population as a result of the prolific masses of poor and "less fit." The second worry was over the degeneration of the quality of the population as a result of racial differences in fertility and immigration. The third anxiety was over the problem of miscegenation. Miscegenation, or race mixing, was thought to be a degenerative act resulting in the undermining of "white" civilization. Feminists, social democrats, conservatives, and fascists all had in common these fears of the decline in the quantity and quality of the European-origin population.[8]

The defeat of German Nazism transformed the intellectual atmosphere in which population issues were discussed. Nazism compelled the world to reconsider the concept of race and the horrendous consequences of its misuse.[9] Recognition of how the Nazi regime used race led to the discrediting of the eugenics movement among population scientists. The "rejection" of the eugenics movement sent eugenic thought into hibernation. Eugenic researchers changed their language from a race-based rhetoric to a population-based rhetoric. The eugenic "concern with 'the race' was beginning to be replaced by attentiveness to 'the population.'"[10]

This change in perspective is reflected in various aspects of eugenic thought among leading demographers. The intellectual foundation of population studies in the United States was built upon the efforts of and in collaboration with eugenicists.[11] Historically, it is at times hard to distinguish between eugenicists and population scientists. For example, leading demographers like P. K. Whelpton, Louis I. Dublin, Warren S. Thompson, and Frederick Osborn were also supporters and advocates of eugenics. Each of these individuals was an important demographer, and each served as president of the Population Association of America.[12] P. K. Whelpton, the developer of the component method of population projections,[13] clearly exemplifies the crosscutting intellectual interest of early population scientists and eugenicists. In his *Needed Population Research*, published under the auspices of the Population Association of America in 1938, Whelpton argues:

> What may be the largest attempt to improve the biological makeup of a human population has recently been undertaken in Germany. By means of eugenic sterilization, it is planned to lower the incidence of certain undesirable qualities in the next generation. At the same time, an increase in the proportion of children from superior stock is being sought through the offering of larger economic inducements for additional children to families in certain so-called upper classes than to those in

lower classes. The steps taken to carry out the various phases of this plan should be watched carefully by populationists in all parts of the world and such tests of its effectiveness made as are possible.[14]

Whelpton's statement is in open sympathy with eugenics; it is by no means an isolated example of the association of population scientists with eugenic ideas.

Louis I. Dublin and Warren S. Thompson also expressed eugenic perspectives in their fertility research during this period. Dublin argued in 1918 that "[t]he best blood of America is being constantly thinned out by the exercise of a conscious limitation of births and is being replaced by a stock of a different order. Our national standards are being leveled to meet more and more the lower quality of our population."[15] Dublin's main concern was with the impact of immigrants on the racial quality of the American population. Unlike Whelpton, Dublin argued for positive eugenics. Like Dublin and Whelpton, Thompson also expressed concern for the racial quality of the population. Regarding the impact of European immigrants on the quality of the older Teutonic native-born American population, he noted:

> Thus *race suicide* becomes a problem in eugenics and anthropology. Is it desirable to have our natural population increase come chiefly from the rural districts and the poor class in the cities? Although the vast majority of people in these classes are biologically sound yet most of the biological degenerates in our population also belong to these two classes and at present they are propagating almost as rapidly as the sound stock. The upper classes—well-to-do and wealthy—probably do not propagate themselves, to say nothing of adding to the population. These classes contain much of the best ability in our population. To have them die without leaving fair-sized families is a serious matter. It means that much of the superior ability of the nation is used up in each generation. Able men and women rise into these classes and fail to propagate, thus eliminating their superior qualities from the population. If this process continues for any length of time it is bound to be harmful to the nation.[16]

Dublin, Whelpton, Thompson, and other population scientists may have come to regret their eugenics at a later point in time; however, their intellectual association with eugenics was important in the institutionalization of demography in the United States.

The ambivalence of some demographers toward the racist and classist views of earlier eugenicists is reflected by the work of Frederick Osborn. In 1940, Osborn published his book *Preface to Eugenics* in an effort to divorce eugenics from the race- and class-consciousness of the earlier eugenics movement. However, as late as 1968 his views continued to advance many of the old eugenic ideas. For example, in 1968 he published *The Future of Human Heredity: An Introduction to Eugenics in Modern Society*.[17] In this book he maintained the class- and race-consciousness of traditional eugenic thought.

Two central issues of eugenic research that have continued to spark interest among some demographers are the relationship between family size and intelligence and reproductive differentials by intelligence. Francis Galton was one of the first scholars to study the effects of birth order on cognitive achievement. Such studies have continued under the banner of the confluence theory, which maintains that as the number of siblings increases, the intellectual environment diminishes, because babies add little to the intellectual level of a household.[18] More recent research has suggested important refinements to the confluence theory.[19]

Another central concern of the early eugenics movement and its modern demographic counterpart is the contention that socially important physical, mental, moral, and behavioral characteristics are hereditary. The eugenicists believe that more-intelligent women have fewer children than less-intelligent women. This difference in fertility by quality of parent is thought to produce a downward shift in the ability of the population as a whole. This trend is referred to as dysgenic. Dysgenic fertility patterns are thought to promote the reproduction of weak and less well-adapted individuals at the expense of healthy well-adapted individuals. Because intelligence is thought to be different among racial subgroups, different racial groups are thought to make different contributions to the demographic development of the population.

In the early development of both demography and eugenics, there was much concern about the differential birth rate of different classes and races.[20] These early concerns focused on the impact of the relatively more prolific reproduction among the poor and racially "unfit." Additionally, many scholars were concerned with the possible population pollution that could result from immigration and miscegenation. For example, in October 1925, in the first volume of the *Annals of Eugenics,* Karl Pearson published a paper titled "The Problem of Alien Immigration into Great Britain, Illustrated by an Examination of Russian and Polish Jewish Children."[21] Pearson presented IQ and anthropometric evidence of Jewish racial inferiority. In this article he suggested that the English parliament follow the United States and enact a version of the Immigration Act of 1924 to keep inferior races out.

These early concerns have been reflected in the more modern concerns around "the population bomb." Though many have written on this topic none was as influential or popular as *The Population Bomb,* written by biology professor Paul Ehrlich of Stanford University, in 1968.[22] Though he depended on the rhetoric of eugenics, Ehrlich's book became a popular handbook for the population control movement that dominated the latter half of the twentieth century. Following the publication of his book, Ehrlich became a leading public authority on population issues.

The context of eugenic discourse has tended to reflect and support social inequalities. In societies where race was salient, such as the United States, the discourse of eugenicists focused on problems of racial differentials in fertility, miscegenation, and immigration of the racially "inferior." In societies where class was more salient than race, such as Britain, eugenicists focused on problems of class differentials in fertility and the immigration of poor uncultured persons from other areas of the world. The American anxiety over race finds its equivalent in the European fear of the lower classes.

Eugenic research and arguments are far from nonexistent in population studies. Some recent population research is clearly focused on issues critical to the eugenic tradition, even if the demographic findings are not strongly in favor of the eugenic argument.[23] Demography, like European eugenics, is concerned with social and biological aspects of human populations. This is a necessary concern if we are to understand population dynamics. There is nothing inherently wrong with studying the intersection of social and biological aspects of population differences. The problem has more to do with the history of eugenic research and the need to address this history as we move forward.

Eugenic research connects the "racial quality" of the population and demographic processes. The ideas of eugenics had an important influence on population growth research.[24] The connection between demography and eugenics is further confounded by the lack of discourse surrounding the meaning of race in most demographic research. This has led to the treatment of race by some demographers as an objective physical characteristic that serves as an identifier of racial genotype.

Not all of the connections between eugenics and population studies are conceptual. Many are organizational and programmatic. Many eugenic organizations have historically been connected to organizations within population studies. And, likewise, many of the most prominent eugenic scholars have been part of population studies. Several historical connections persist within the two perspectives. For example, the membership of both the Eugenics Education Society in Britain and the American Eugenics Society included distinguished scientists from the natural and social sciences, including many leading demographers.[25]

In 1973, the American Eugenics Society changed its name to the Society for the Study of Social Biology.[26] Four years earlier the society had changed the name of its journal from *Eugenics Quarterly* to *Social Biology*. The change in the journal name was purportedly because the word *eugenics* had a meaning too narrow to characterize the contents of the journal. However, the society maintained: "the change of name of the Society does not coincide with any change of its interests or policies. The founding of this journal twenty years ago marked such a change. The common interests that have long united the membership, and to which their scientific disciplines are relevant, are the trends of human evolution and the biological, medical, and social forces that determine these trends."[27] The Society for the Study of Social Biology is an affiliate of the American Association for the Advancement of Science. Its stated objectives "are to advance and disseminate knowledge about biological and sociocultural forces affecting the structure and composition of human populations."[28] And the membership of the renamed society continues to include distinguished scientists from the natural and social sciences.

Many of the concerns of European eugenics continue to be issues in demography (e.g., fertility limitation of the poor and selective immigration). The inverse relationship between fertility and economic development (that is, the increase in poverty that accompanies relatively higher fertility) at both the individual level (such as in the case of poor African

American women) and at the societal level (such as in the case of poor African nations) is generally assumed in demography.[29] Thus, the field of demography serves as an important link between the European eugenic conceptualization of race and modern society.

An important part of the eugenics movement has always been based on how the population is conceptualized. What sometimes appears as a small part of demographic research is in fact a large part of what justifies eugenic arguments. The basis of much of eugenic research is the concern of population quality. Thus, eugenicists have used demographic research to measure the level of population quality. Racial demography, which includes the examination of racial differences in demographic rates and processes, has played a key role in the eugenics movement.

## The European Eugenics Movement: 1900–1950

The basis of eugenic thought was developed in England; however, the movement had a powerful national and international presence, leading in some cases to state power and in other cases to restrictive and oppressive forms of legislation. For example, the research of leading eugenicists in the United States and Europe, like that of Charles B. Davenport, was used to support selective immigration laws and laws for selective sterilization of inferior people of color. Such policies helped the United States to avoid some dysgenic individuals (through restrictive immigration) and to reduce the numbers of dysgenic individuals already in the population (by use of sterilization). Such policies were a form of *negative* eugenics.

The Victorian middle-class fears of European-origin working-class militancy and the newly freed African-origin population, the social transformations accompanying industrialization and urbanization, and the need to provide a rationale for the colonial subjugation of non-European populations gave birth to an international eugenics movement by the early years of the twentieth century.[30] In 1907, Francis Galton created the Eugenics Laboratory at London University with Karl Pearson as its director. Charles Davenport created the Eugenics Research Station at Cold Spring Harbor Research Laboratory in 1904; in 1910 a eugenics records office was opened; and the Eugenics Committee of the United States (later renamed American Eugenics Society) was founded in 1921. The most prominent English-speaking eugenic institutions were the Galton Laboratory for National Eugenics, at University College, London; and the

Eugenics Records Office affiliated with Cold Spring Harbor Research Laboratory on Long Island, New York. In South Africa, the South African Association of Science in 1921 founded the Standing Committee on Eugenics and Genetics. A eugenics society was established in Paris, France, in 1912.

In Germany eugenics was represented institutionally by the International Society for Racial Hygiene, founded in 1907 and renamed the German Society for Racial Hygiene by 1924. In 1923, biologist Fritz Lenz assumed the chair for race hygiene at Munich. By 1927, the Kaiser Wilhelm Institute for Research in Psychiatry and the Kaiser Wilhelm Institute for Anthropology, Human Heredity, and Eugenics were institutionalized; the latter, in Berlin, was the most prominent institution in Germany.

Brazil led the way in the institutionalization of eugenics in Latin America.[31] Renato Kehl, a young doctor, called for the creation of a society devoted to the study of eugenics. In 1918, the São Paulo Eugenic Society (Sociedade Eugénica de São Paulo) was formed, only to die in 1919. However, in 1930, Kehl seized the moment during the Brazilian Revolution of 1930 and created the Central Brazilian Commission of Eugenics, a national organization. The Brazilian model was followed by the formation of the two most important eugenic societies in Latin America: in 1930, the Mexican Eugenic Society for the Improvement of Race (Sociedad Eugénica Mexicana para el Mejoramiento de la Raza) and, in 1932, the Argentine Association of Biotypology, Eugenics, and Social Medicine (Asociación Argentina de Biotipología, Eugenesia, y Medicina Social).

The formation of eugenic institutions in Latin America, Europe, South Africa, and the United States between 1900 and 1930 raises some interesting questions concerning the importance of eugenics and racism. International eugenic activities intensified after 1930. This intensification points to the importance of the movement for modern scientific understandings of race relations.

Thirty states in the United States passed sterilization laws between 1907 and 1931. In 1920, the House Committee on Immigration and Naturalization appointed a eugenic consultant, Harry Laughlin, who warned of the new wave of genetically inferior immigrants.[32] These laws resulted in sterilization of as many as twenty thousand individuals by 1935.[33] Symbolically, these laws codified the eugenic idea of restricting the breeding of the unfit population, and in the United States this meant Native Americans, African Americans, and the insane. By 1935, Switzerland, Denmark, Germany, Sweden, and Norway passed similar negative eugenic laws.

The International Union for the Scientific Study of Population Problems (IUSSPP) was the leading international professional association for individuals in population studies. In 1935, it initiated the International Congress for Population Science, which was held in Berlin and demonstrated the international support for Nazi eugenics by international population scientists.[34] "Scientists from Switzerland, Austria, Latvia, the United States, Germany, France, Hungary, Spain, Italy, and India reported about population movements in their respective countries."[35] The Nazi practices of negative eugenics found praise within the population community, both internationally and within the United States. Whelpton's written comments in 1938 were not an isolated event.

Francis Galton's original definition of eugenics outlined a system of *positive* race improvements. His eugenics was positive, because he concentrated on ways to increase the breeding of the "most fit" individuals of the race. He argued that eugenics would produce a true meritocracy rather than the old "class consciousness" based on custom, tradition, and the inheritance of family wealth.[36] However, the emphasis within the eugenics movement in the United States, and later in Germany, was *negative* and focused on ways to reduce the presence of inferior individuals within the population. Negative eugenics focused on reducing the fertility of inferior races and individuals and on reducing immigration from inferior nations by focusing on the dysgenic impact of free reproduction and immigration. Inferior races and individuals would reproduce their inferiority, and because of their high fertility, they posed a threat to the quality of life in society.

The majority of eugenicists combined their scientific and political agendas. Eugenicists generally agreed with the principle of distinguishing between inferior and superior elements of society. Some traced inferiority by emphasizing class; others emphasized race. European eugenics conceptualized race as a genetic trait. It is this aspect of eugenics that provided a common goal, whether the rhetoric was based on improvement of the race or the population.

The United States' version of eugenics advanced the cause by its early acceptance of Mendelian genetics and its success in influencing social policy. In the United States, European eugenics emphasized the combination of demography, statistics, and genetics. This emphasis gave the movement more scientific authority and legitimacy. The movement in the United States was a leader in its political influence on race-based immigration and sterilization laws. And, the United States movement was one of the strongest foreign supporters of Nazi eugenic policies in Germany. Eugenicists gave very important support to race-specific social policies and decisions.

Leading eugenicists, like Charles B. Davenport, published articles in German journals for racial hygiene and took a leadership role in the development of eugenic thought.[37] Furthermore, Davenport held positions on the editorial boards of two of the most influential German journals for racial hygiene.

Leadership within the eugenics movement began in England with Galton and Pearson, was taken over by the United States in the 1920s by Davenport and Harry H. Laughlin, and reached its zenith in Nazi Germany in the 1930s and 1940s. No example of these changes is as clear as the transition of leadership from the United States to Nazi Germany. The leadership of the Nazi race policy regarded the sterilization legislation as a lesson in eugenic policy.[38] In fact, a study of the impact of California's legislation served as the basis for the development of Nazi sterilization laws. Perhaps no foreign book did more to promote eugenic policies in Germany than Eugene S. Gosney and Paul Popenoe's book *Sterilization for Human Betterment: A Summary of Results of 6,000 Operations in California, 1909–1929.*[39] Gosney and Popenoe argued that negative and positive eugenics were complementary.

> Action is the more urgent because it is probable that a satisfactory positive program cannot be put into effect without a negative program to support it; and the longer the application of sterilization is postponed, the more difficult will it be to make a positive program of eugenics work. Even from this point of view, then, in which sterilization is regarded merely as a preliminary to direct measures for encouraging the reproduction of the eugenically superior, it cannot be avoided; and the time to begin it is now.[40]

Leading German Nazis and eugenicists, including Hitler, cited this volume. Nazi race policy is indicative of the international impact of the eugenics movement.

Eugenicists in the United States and the United Kingdom provided the intellectual basis for the international movement. However, each nation's unique history and culture of racial domination determined the

character and specific appeal of eugenics.[41] The eugenics movements in
Europe, the United States, Latin America, and South Africa were in essence
European eugenics. Support of European racial superiority and the politics of racial purification unified the international eugenics movement.
European eugenics in the United States differed from that in Latin America in its reduction of good human stock to the middle and upper classes
of native white Protestants.[42] The eugenics movement in Latin American
did not uniformly accept the superiority of Protestants. Among Latin
American eugenicists, race mixing with Native Americans was not seen
with the extreme repugnance expressed by the eugenicists in the United
States; however, as in Germany, South Africa, and the United States, eugenics in Latin America tended to be negative, especially toward African-
origin populations.[43] On the other hand, European eugenics in South
Africa was similar to that in the United States and Germany, because
South African eugenics advocated racial superiority and the politics of
racial segregation and antimiscegenation.[44] In South Africa, issues of dysgenesis (or racial degeneration) were also important, however, not as important as race.

The rise of Nazi Germany enhanced the racist character of the study
of human differences in genetics and biology in the United States and
Europe. With the rise and fall of Nazi Germany, European eugenics as an
international movement was in retreat by the 1940s. Many eugenicists
tried to save the movement from early Nazism. In 1939 at the Congress
for Genetics, several members prepared a resolution condemning racism
while still adhering to a eugenic ideology.[45]

Eugenicists applied the most advanced and sophisticated social statistics
to the study of the human population. On questions of society, however, as a rule they accepted simplistic distinctions between the civilized
and the primitive, heredity and environment, upper and lower classes. It
is important to note that the racial beliefs of these pioneers were not in
themselves based on science. To the contrary, their racial views were part
of a social ideology that employed science as a tool to legitimate their
ideological views and to justify racial stratification.

Eugenic ideals experienced a period of hibernation and transformation following the defeat of Nazism in Germany. The major transformation was rhetorical. Instead of improving the race, the new eugenics concerned itself with improving the population. Eugenics continued to attract

professors in the academy and members of leading research institutes, and they continued to receive support from major foundations.[46]

## European Eugenics after 1950

Earlier I indicated that racial statistics in the 1930s and 1940s redirected the eugenic discussion to the relative roles of environment and genetics. Such research was valuable in the recognition that environmental factors could generate large racial gaps in intelligence statistics. This research, along with the Civil Rights movement in the United States and the Human Rights and National Liberation movements in Africa, Asia, and Latin America, culminated in the 1950s and 1960s challenge of the notion that people of African origin were genetically disadvantaged. These movements demanded racial justice and equality. Social welfare programs for full employment, social security, medical care, educational improvement, equality in social access, and political power were justified, because politically dominated groups, like African-origin populations, were considered to be genetically equal to other human populations.

For example, the European eugenics movement argued that African cognitive abilities could not be improved. Thus, a key element of the African Liberation and Civil Rights movements was to provide resources to improve the skills of African-origin children to better enable them to make a contribution to society. In the United States, this meant attempts to end educational, political, and social segregation; in South Africa, this meant attempts to end Bantu education and social, economic, and political colonial domination.

These events also coincided with a rise in the use of test scores in the investigation of education opportunity, social mobility, and occupational and economic achievement. The importance given these test scores motivated Congress to mandate a large-scale examination of the policy implications of the social distribution of intellectual ability and achievement.[47] This research also focused attention on the environmental (school and family) factors relating to pupil achievement. The report resulted in the argument that African American achievement could result only from integrated education.[48]

European eugenicists like William Bradford Shockley and Arthur Jensen provided eugenic-based arguments in support of the segregationists' attack on the Civil Rights movement.[49] Shockley and other eugenicists were outraged about the government's intent to intervene on behalf of Africans and other genetic "inferiors." Shockely, a Nobel Prize–winning engineer, lacked formal training in psychology, and therefore credibility in most scholarly circles of psychologists, but he brought all the weight of his Nobel Prize to support his eugenic arguments.

Unlike Shockley, Arthur Jensen, a clinical psychologist, developed his European eugenic perspective after first arguing that the African-origin population had a "low-average IQ" because of "environmental rather than . . . genetic factors."[50] Jensen's sophisticated and scholarly argument added a fresh air of legitimacy to suggestions of African and Latino inferiority. Following the publication of Jensen's article "How Much Can We Boost IQ and Scholastic Achievement?" in the *Harvard Educational Review* in 1969, the eugenic argument resurfaced as a justification of racial differences and inequalities in society.[51] Jensen's work helped reinvigorate eugenics movements in the United States, South Africa, and Europe. Neo-Nazi supporters of apartheid in South Africa and segregationists in the United States often used Jensen's work to justify their negative eugenic plans for racial exclusion and domination.[52]

Many scholars criticized the assumptions and errors of the use of race and IQ as the basis for social policy.[53] Progressive and thoughtful scholars attempted to explain the erroneous assumptions of Jensen's research and to suggest why social policy should not be based on his findings. This line of research erroneously assumes that IQ-type tests measure intelligence; that racial groups are genetic populations and markers of group heritability; and that the intelligence measured by IQ-type tests is in part biologically based.

In part, the revival in eugenic research found support from eugenic writings that claimed to be able to locate the biological basis of inequality. Most of these claims can be traced back to Galton and Spearman. In 1979, Arthur Jensen published an eight-hundred-page defense of eugenic psychometric analysis. In 1994, Richard J. Herrnstein and Charles Murray published another eight-hundred-page defense of eugenic psychometric analysis justifying among other things racial stratification.[54] Perhaps no other authors in recent history have done more to promote the view that genetic differences are the cause of the respective intellectual measures of African-origin and European-origin populations in the United States and the rest of the world. The central theme of modern

eugenicists is that social stratification reflects the presumed mental limitations of a sizable number of citizens. Jensen, Herrnstein, and Murray
make arguments supporting the genetic stratification among human
populations.

The disciples of Shockley and Jensen have produced a new wave of
research that continued to receive public acclaim and attention in the
1990s.[55] Widely read eugenic books such as *The Bell Curve* present a range
of arguments on the benefits of using a biological model to explain social differences in society, especially the "deviant" behavior of the poor
and marginalized. Thus, the eugenicists have attempted to explain social
differences in crime, wealth, test scores, and social dislocation by reference to presumed intellectual aptitudes. Racial and class differences are
thought to be a reflection of more fundamental differences in intellectual and moral capacity. These works, especially *The Bell Curve,* make the
case for social policy that limits affirmative action, for seeking a less cen-
tralized administration of government, for halting governmental support (e.g., Aid for Dependent Children) for out-of-wedlock childbearing
and child rearing, and so on. In fact, *The Bell Curve* helped cultivate the
public policy environment that has greatly reduced governmental support for child rearing among the poor in the United States.

Echoing early eugenicists at the beginning of the twentieth century, current eugenicists argue that racial groups differ in their cognitive ability
and that these differences are genetic and underlie racial differences in
society.[56] These eugenicists, like the earlier ones, define race as a physical reality.[57] They proceed to discuss the demographic implications of the
dysgenic impacts of racial and class differences in fertility and immigration on the American population. First, they point to the importance of
differential fertility as a source of downward pressure on cognitive ability. They note that fertility among African Americans and Latinos is
more dysgenic than that among whites. Second, they note, "Latino and
black immigrants are, at least in the short run, putting some downward
pressure on the distribution of intelligence."[58]

Their dysgenic model suggests that the inequality of cognitive ability
and social achievement negatively impacts population quality. Thus, the
higher rates of fertility among poor and less intelligent races have resulted in increasing numbers of poor people and have increased the proportion of the population that is from the less intelligent races. A major

weakness in this perspective involves the question of racial intelligence and how it can be measured. As with Spearman and Burt, current eugenicists reify the meanings of intelligence and race.

Thus, their critique of liberal social policy is based on the negative effects of attempting to change biological processes by simple-minded social programs. The Great Society and other social welfare programs are seen as self-defeating, because their underlying assumption is that all groups and classes within society are equal. Consistent with other eugenic arguments, Herrnstein and Murray advance a set of social policies which would maintain the status quo while encouraging the "less intelligent" populations and individuals to accept their "place" in society. They employ the "authority" of statistics to legitimate their claims of European superiority and their fear of white genetic annihilation. European eugenicists support the notion of superiority of European-origin populations (some have added Asians and Jews to the list) with such things as the measure of their intelligence or their achievement on standardized tests.

We can surmise from eugenicists that differences in cognitive ability are mostly genetic and have consequences for understanding racial differences.[59] They advocate a social policy position similar to that of Malthus and Yule, however, unlike Malthus and Yule, eugenicists in the United States use racial statistics as a major component of their story. Racial statistics serve as a way to essentialize racial differences without biological support. Modern-day eugenicists need not justify race as biology when they have racial statistics to legitimate the "reality" of racial differences.

## African Eugenics? A New Twist

*Eugenics* refers to biological explanations of racial stratification. The Eurocentric explanation of eugenics assumes the superiority of European-origin populations. However, it is well within the logic of eugenics that the Eurocentric assumptions could be dropped. Several scholars within the African-centered tradition have challenged the Eurocentric assumption of eugenics.[60] The Afrocentric school challenges the conclusion that the African population is inferior to the European population while maintaining a biological explanation of racial stratification. As is true with European eugenics, African eugenics is a theory of biological superiority. Thus, African eugenicists tend to explain European domination as an indicator of Africans' social inferiority. However, as is the case with Eurocentric scholars, not all Afrocentric scholars are African eugenicists; nor are all African eugenicists Afrocentric. In fact, none of the "African eugenicists" that I know of has openly connected his or her research to the eugenic tradition.

Many African eugenicists attribute African biological superiority to melanin. From the African eugenic perspective, African depigmentation (albescentization) resulted in people less than equal to the original Africans. It is believed that European aggression is biologically caused and needs to be explained. This aggressive tendency on the part of European-origin populations is thought to be a genetic defect. For example, Frances Cress Welsing argues that white supremacy is a functional racism founded upon a pervading sense of inadequacy and inferiority among European-origin populations worldwide. This inferiority is based upon the lack of the genetic capacity to produce significant levels of melanin, which is responsible for skin coloration. Given the minority status of European-origin populations on earth, the fear of genetic extinction is thought to produce an "uncontrollable" tendency of hostility and aggression. Europeans the world over have manifested this tendency throughout the ancient and modern epochs as demonstrated by the consistent confrontations of whites with peoples of color. Welsing observes:

> The genocide of non-whites must be understood as a necessary tactic of a people (white) that is a minority of the world's population and that, because it lacks the genetic capacity to produce significant levels of melanin, is genetically recessive in terms of skin coloration, compared to the black, brown, red and yellow world majority. Thus, the global white minority must act genocidal against people of color for the purpose of white genetic survival.[61]

Furthermore, she argues, "Acutely aware of their inferior genetic ability to produce skin color, whites built the elaborate myth of white genetic superiority. Furthermore, whites set about the huge task of evolving a social, political and economic structure that would support the myth of the inferiority of Blacks and other non-whites."[62]

African eugenics consists of a continuous searching criticism of the assumptions and facts used by Eurocentric scholars.[63] Even though African and European eugenicists are alike in their view of race as a fundamental or primordial aspect of human differentiation, they differ in their view of interracial reproduction: European eugenicists view it as suicidal, whereas among the African eugenicists there is not as strong a repulsion to interracial reproduction. As Richard King writes in *African Origin of Biological Psychiatry:* "Humanity may differ in outer appearance, with variations of colors but internally they are all black, all African at the core."[64] The solution to racial stratification in the eyes of the African eugenicists is in recognizing the primordial importance of "blackness" and the significance of African depigmentation.[65]

By recognizing African superiority, nonwhite peoples will understand how they were manipulated into subordination as a result of European peoples' lack of melanin and numerical inadequacy. As Frances Cress Welsing notes: "This is analogous to the man with two eyes finding it difficult, if not impossible, to understand the behavioral patterns and motivations of the congenitally one-eyed man, who always looked upon the two-eyed state with jealous antagonism and perhaps, aggression."[66] It is thought that the European loss of melanin produced a sense of loss resulting in jealous aggression.

From the African eugenic perspective, Africans are not the biological out-group among human populations. They argue, and with much science to back them up, that Africans subsume the diversity within all other populations.[67] Thus, the African eugenic argument leads to a very un-eugenic conclusion. In fact, many who might be called African eugenicists use physical differences to explain the absurdity of racial differences. This observation is most likely a result of the position of African eugenic scholars in society. No African eugenicist has a tenured position at a major university, and many have been the victims of some form of racial marginalization and exclusion.

## The Limits of African Eugenics

Antiblack racism is the basis of both Eurocentric and Afrocentric eugenics. And the answer to both perspectives may be found in the origins of human beings. The African population is an old population; in fact, the African population is the original human population. Scientific evidence overwhelmingly supports the monogenetic origin of humanity in Africa.[68]

Paleontological research suggests that *Homo sapiens* originated in Africa. The African progenitors of humanity colonized much of the African continent's savannas and woodlands about a hundred thousand years ago. Apparently, Cro-Magnon migrated to the Eurasian continent from Africa about forty thousand years ago. As the place of origin of humanity, Africa has the most genetically diverse population.[69]

The monogenetic origin of humanity is a central idea in the African-centered population perspective. The African-centered argument is based in part on the thesis of African depigmentation.[70] African depigmentation is the process by which African skin color became lighter and lighter over a great number of years (about twenty thousand). The first *Homo sapiens* to inhabit Europe are believed to have been migrant African *Homo sapiens* who arrived over forty thousand years ago, twenty thousand years before the appearance of the "white" Cro-Magnon man in southern France. As Cheikh Anta Diop writes: "If one bases one's judgement on morphology, the first White appeared only around 20,000 years ago: the Cro-Magnon Man. He is probably the result of a mutation from the Grimaldi Negroid due to an existence of 20,000 years in the excessively cold climate of Europe at the end of the last glaciation."[71] African depigmentation produced the variety of races found on the planet.

Diop was not an eugenicist, but his population perspective serves as the basis of African eugenic thought. In a dramatic departure from Diop's caution that "there is no particular glory about the cradle of humanity being in Africa, because it is just an accident,"[72] African eugenic scholars have argued that nature made a value judgment in choosing Africa. Like their European counterparts, the African eugenicists believe in the essentialism of race. Diop's analysis guides the reader on an intellectual tour of human evolution in which we end up discussing physical differences and intelligence. The relationship between physical differences and intelligence is at the heart of European eugenics. And Diop's conclusion merits our attention.

> Molecular biology has taught us that, at the individual level, there are no two identical human brains; and it is this polymorphism which constitutes the "luck of the draw" in the human species, i.e., its power of adaptation. But these individual differences, like the lines of one's hand, do not in any way translate into racial hierarchism. As we have already seen, it would then be necessary to find a hierarchical difference among the races, particularly between Black and White, at the level of the brain in general and the interior part of the brain in particular.[73]

Diop, it seems, was not in support of the eugenic perspective. In fact, he argued that the relationship between the environment and the biological makeup of the human being was dynamic and had a big impact on human behavior but was, in turn, impacted by that behavior. Diop's more interactive perspective allows us to escape the trap of the racial reasoning explicitly endorsed by the eugenic perspective.

## Justifying Racial Stratification

Both African and European eugenics offer rationalizations for racial stratification. Both are ethnocentric perspectives. Both see race as an essentially biological aspect of human difference. Though the Eurocentric perspective continues to influence our research and social reality, it is rarely stated as blatantly as in Herrnstein and Murray's *The Bell Curve,* Dinesh D'Souza's *The End of Racism,* J. Philippe Rushton's *Race, Evolution, and Behavior,* and Michael Levin's *Why Race Matters.* The conventional European eugenic explanation is that racial groups differ in average cognitive ability and that these differences largely account for the racial differences in educational and economic success,[74] but this is not the only conceivable explanation. In *The Isis Papers,* Frances Cress Welsing argues that the fear of European genetic annihilation largely accounts for the racist behavior of European-origin populations.

A major difference is also found in the history of the two explanations. European eugenics was responsible for negative laws, deaths, and sterilizations of large numbers of "non-European peoples." African eugenics has not resulted in the mass sterilizations or deaths of any persons, nor has it been responsible for the passage of any laws limiting the participation of any persons in the United States or any other nation in the world.

The European eugenic argument maintains that inequality is natural and beyond human transformation, and people are destined by virtue of their native ability to fixed positions in society. The African eugenic argument maintains that racial inequality is unnatural and within the scope of human transformation.

The issue of the system of racial stratification has implications for the ability of eugenic arguments to influence social policy; however, the potential of eugenic arguments to influence social policy cannot be underestimated. Herrnstein and Murray build a case that critics have not dismissed out of hand for ideological reasons. Conservative scholars have tended to sympathize with the European eugenic explanation while not pursuing the implications of the African eugenic arguments.[75] As with earlier European eugenic arguments, the possibility of biological differences is seen as an important area of research. In *The End of Racism,* Dinesh D'Souza argues: "If biological differences do exist, they cannot be wished away. However unpopular the investigation, we have to take the possibility of natural differences seriously. What is at stake is nothing less than the foundation of contemporary liberalism."[76] This seems odd coming from a man who wishes away the possibility of African biological superiority. If biological differences do exist, they do not exist racially at the genetic level. For D'Souza and others, race is morphological. For ideological reasons, he, and others, insist that these morphological differences are the same as genetic differences and are reflected in human behavior.

In the same book that D'Souza praises European eugenics, he condemns African eugenics. "No doctrine of racism is complete without a theory of biological superiority. Predictably, black racists have concocted their own, and it attributes intrinsic black superiority to that colorizing agent in the human anatomy, melanin."[77] The inconsistency of the arguments of the D'Souzas and Herrnstiens and Murrays of the world points to the effectiveness of contemporary European eugenics. It is small wonder that the conservative discourse about the relevance of European eugenic-type arguments is divided along racial lines. Prominent African American scholars like Glenn C. Loury reject the European eugenic argument. In his review of the recent rise of eugenic thought, Loury argues: "They begin by seeking the causes of behavior and end by reducing the human subject to a mechanism whose horizon is fixed by some combination of genetic endowment and social law."[78]

# CHAPTER FIVE

## Noneugenic Racial Statistics

Racial statistics are not a fact of the past. Du Bois was of the opinion that the best minds should study racial statistics. He thought that statistical analysis could help in the development of a concrete understanding of the social status of the African American population. Unfortunately, this was not to be the case, because until the 1940s, social statistics remained closely identified with the racial reasoning of the eugenics movement. As the movement lost favor, most scientists, even the most dedicated eugenicists, moved away from any direct association with the movement's name. Nevertheless, genetics, statistics, and demography developed in the context of the eugenics movement, and the racial reasoning of eugenics continues to influence social statistics.

Social statisticians have long used race as a variable in their analysis. I am not talking here about the situation in which we are asked to give a detailed description that includes the color of a person's skin. In this situation skin color is being used like other biological traits such as eye color and hair texture. When used as part of a description to identify a given individual, the person's skin color is not a category that embraces a large number of people. Used in this way skin color is a distinguishing fact about the designated person. The history of this process is marred by patent ideological commitments to racial inferiority and superiority. In this chapter I would like to turn our attention to the use of racial statistics by scholars that do not profess such ideological commitments. My desire here is to show the continued influence of eugenics on racial statistics and to suggest that the time has come for us to reconsider how racial data are collected and used. I am concerned with the use of racial categories as a statistical device to demarcate groups of persons and how social statisticians view racial attributes as causes in the pursuit of racial justice.

## A Background to the Social Survey of Race

The background of descriptive racial statistics overlaps with the development in inferential racial statistics. Bureaus of official statistics and state statisticians were institutionalized by the mid-1800s. The statistical tradition most closely connected to these events is the descriptive framework. For the most part, state statisticians used rudimentary mathematical techniques and focused on the collection, codification, and tabulation of social data. By the end of the nineteenth century, social scientists began to make use of the results and methods of state statisticians. Especially important in this regard were their use of census data and the innovation of survey sample methods.

The social survey was preceded by the population census, of which social policy discussions were a by-product of government administrations. The social survey involves an effort to collect specific information to be used in transforming social relationships within society and can be designed by scholars and other interested individuals and organizations. It is much broader than the population census. The population census usually seeks a count of all persons and the basic structure and characteristics of the population for local areas within a given territory. Social surveys are confined to samples of the population, and because of their smaller size they can be designed to collect a wider variety of complete data for the examination of social changes and interrelationships among variables. Additionally, social surveys can be designed to fit specific research questions.

In 1802, Laplace convinced the French government to conduct a survey so that he could estimate the size of the French population. The survey was conducted in September 1802 and included selected communes with a total population of 2,037,615. His sample was not random but was a geographically representative, two-stage cluster sample. At any rate, Laplace was a pioneer in the theory of sample surveys. In 1891, Max Weber carried out a survey on the salaries of agricultural workers in East Prussia.[1] However, it was the work of Charles Booth that led to the formalization of survey techniques in social statistics.

Social surveyors also used social statistics to yield laws of society. In 1889, Charles Booth was motivated by the lack of population-bound accounts of urban poverty to undertake a vigorous analytical investigation. Three questions characterized the public debates about poverty in London: "how many were poor, why were they poor, and what should be done to alleviate poverty?"[2] A Victorian merchant, Booth responded in seventeen volumes of *The Life and Labour of the People in London*. Published between 1889 and 1903, these volumes introduced the social survey method. In *The Life and Labour of the People in London*, Booth developed an empirical basis for a discussion of social policy.

Booth sought to determine the distribution of the population among occupational categories and to construct a poverty baseline. The British census already categorized employment figures; Booth extended this categorization to an analysis of poverty.

At the inception of the social survey, research results were confronted with the developments in inferential statistics. In 1894, Booth wrote *The Aged Poor in England and Wales: Conditions*.[3] In this volume Booth claimed that there was no relationship between the ratio of welfare (out-of-doors relief) and workhouse relief (in-relief) and the incidence of poverty by parish (or poor law union). In 1895, George Yule challenged Booth's findings by constructing correlation tables of Booth's data. His results suggested a rise in the mean percentage of the paupers in the population as the proportion of welfare recipients increased. He proceeded to estimate the correlation coefficient and its probable error to support his argument.[4] In the 1895 article, Yule established an association between pauperism and out-of-doors relief. In his 1899 article, Yule used regression models to understand the *cause* of pauperism.[5] He argued that welfare that provided income to the poor outside the poorhouse caused an increase in the number of people on relief (pauperism).

Booth estimated the number of people below and above the poverty line. This effort was important and played an important role in the development of the use of social survey data for estimating population values. Booth's survey was local and comprehensive. He focused on gathering information for as large a proportion of the population as possible, and he worked with a research team that included fifteen assistants.

W. E. B. Du Bois conducted the first racial survey in 1899 and reported his results in *The Philadelphia Negro: A Social Study*. Unlike London's Charles Booth, who had fifteen assistants, Du Bois worked alone and was not wealthy, nor was he part of the European-dominated Settlement movement of his Hull House sponsors. A purposive social survey, Du Bois's study was also a community study. He focused his survey so as to define and capture the social dynamics of the African American community of Philadelphia. Unlike Booth's, Du Bois's study was focused on a community and what might be done to understand and change its social problems rather than the examination of a social problem like poverty. Du Bois did study poverty, but African American poverty was not the object of his study. The object of Du Bois's study was the African American community of Philadelphia.

According to Du Bois, "We must study, we must investigate, we must attempt to solve; and the utmost that the world can demand is, not lack of human interest and moral conviction, but rather the heart-quality of fairness, and an earnest desire for the truth despite its possible unpleasantness."[6] Like in most social science today, Du Bois created and defined the object of his study.

The very nature of his investigation presented the objects of his study—members of the African community of Philadelphia—as a "strange species" from which he would gain information for the College Settlement Association.[7] Yet the community did not fancy itself as an "Other" in need of a great intellectual savior; indeed, there was an obvious tension between Du Bois and the Philadelphia Negro elite. In the end, Du Bois interpreted the community's aloof reception of him as an indication that he "did not know so much" about his "own people." "First of all I became painfully aware that merely being born in a group, does not necessarily make one possessed of complete knowledge concerning it. I had learned far more from Philadelphia Negroes than I had taught them concerning the Negro Problem."[8] Yet, he maintained that his book did serve a positive purpose.

Du Bois's study provided a detailed empirical study of Philadelphia in general, using census data and a survey of the Seventh Ward. Booth in Europe and Du Bois in the United States established the tradition of presenting systematic and empirical statements on the study of communities and social problems based on a collection of individual-level data. They appealed for an objective scientific evaluation of issues that had been dominated by ideological partisanship.

During the same period as Du Bois's study, Durkheim made his considerable impact on the founding of social statistical analysis with his classic text *Suicide: A Study in Sociology.*[9] In *Suicide,* Durkheim presents a critique of Quetelet's notion of the average type while making use of descriptive statistics concerning causes of death. Durkheim distinguishes between the "average type" of Quetelet and his own notion of the "collective type."[10] Durkheim's notion of the collective type is the basis of his idea of "suicidal inclination," which is fundamental to his idea of the moral constitution of groups.

For Durkheim the collective moral sense can differ from the individual behavior of the majority of individuals. Therefore, according to Durkheim, Quetelet's notion of the average type leads to a view that the confused feelings of the average conscience represent the moral constitution of the society. For Durkheim it is not the mediocre morality of the average man but the collective tendencies that exist outside individuals. Durkheim distinguishes between the agglomeration of individual tendencies and the qualitatively different general will of the collective. The former produced the latter, but the product was qualitatively different. Moreover, this sociological reality, the general will, could be captured statistically. He wrote: "The regularity of statistical data, on the one hand, implies the existence of collective tendencies exterior to the individual, and on the other, we can directly establish this exterior character in a considerable number of important cases."[11]

Durkheim's critique of Quetelet's average type and Yule's critique of Booth's analysis of poverty demonstrate the early connections between descriptive and inferential statistics; however, it was not until the middle of the twentieth century that the two aspects of statistical analysis came together.

The early scholars like Du Bois applied the sampling method of purposive selection of groups of units. Du Bois selected a particular neighborhood within Philadelphia with complete enumeration of the African-origin population in the selected neighborhood.[12] Later, scholars like Adolph Jensen also applied purposive sampling by selecting a number of parishes within a county with complete enumeration of the units in the selected parishes.

It was not until A. L. Bowley's 1926 article, "Measurement of the Precision Attained in Sampling," that the foundation for the modern theory of the sample survey was formalized. And, it was not until J. Neyman's important paper in 1934, "On Two Different Aspects of the Representative Method: The Method of Stratified Sampling and the Method of Purposive Selection," that the foundation for replacing purposive selection with the stratified random sample of clusters of elementary units was established.[13] Following Neyman's methods, the U.S. Bureau of the Census began taking random sample surveys and led the way for the wide acceptance of this type of survey.

By 1930, about 3,000 surveys had been conducted in the United States and more than 156 in England and Wales.[14] The social survey had become a part of social science research. It was out of the social survey that the modern formal survey, in which members of a defined population have a known positive probability of selection, developed.[15] Although the method of collecting data became more scientific, where the issue of race was concerned, interpreting the results of these new data became more and more ideological. The logic of sampling methods improved at the same time as the analytical process was clouded by racial ideology.

## Some Nonrandom Examples from Descriptive Statistics

For Du Bois, empirical observation of human action was essential for understanding and changing society. Du Bois's sociological work shows clear signs of the influence of the positivist school in economic history, led by Germans Gustav von Schmoller and Adolph Wagner, Du Bois's professors, and the influence of the empirical work of Charles Booth.[16] Du Bois's empirical method consequently was based heavily on descriptive statistics, which he used to advocate social change. Du Bois's work is consistent with Quetelet's and Durkheim's macrosociological perspective. Like Quetelet and Durkheim, Du Bois viewed groups as entities with collective traits that could be statistically described. He added to these methods his desire to advance the status of the African American community.

The rise of eugenics represented the efforts to enhance racial domination. Du Bois connected this threat to the nature of racial research. African American survival depended upon scientific validation of their historical reality and humanity. Consequently, Du Boisian sociology provided a fundamental critique to both Social Darwinian and eugenic thought. For Du Bois, classes were not problems, races were not problems; on the contrary, the problems could be found in society.

In "The Study of the Negro Problems," published in 1898 in *The Annals of the American Academy of Political and Social Science*, Du Bois wrote: "... it is not *one* problem, but rather a plexus of social problems, some new, some old, some simple, some complex; and these problems have their one bond of unity in the fact that they group themselves about those Africans whom two centuries of slave-trading brought into the land."[17]

For Du Bois "a social problem is ever a relation between conditions and action, and as conditions and actions vary and change from group to group from time to time and from place to place, so social problems change, develop and grow."[18] Thus, he placed the study of the African American population into two categories: the study of African Americans as a social group, and the study of their peculiar social environment. As Du Bois himself recognized, these two categories are difficult to separate in practice.

Du Bois rejected the eugenic and Social Darwinian grand theorizing that dominated social research at the turn of the century. He advanced the need for empirical research grounded in statistical and historical analysis.[19] Du Bois entered this discussion by questioning social statistics. In discussing the credibility of the results of his study, he wrote: "The best available methods of sociological research are at present so liable to inaccuracies that the careful student discloses the results of individual research with diffidence; he knows that they are liable to error from seemingly ineradicable faults of the statistical method."[20] Indeed, Du Bois provides a rather astute description of social statistics at the turn of the twentieth century. *The Philadelphia Negro: A Social Study* is Du Bois's quintessential application of the ideas he outlined in "The Study of the Negro Problems." *The Philadelphia Negro* was the first social science study of race in urban America and the first social survey of any community in the United States done by a scholar.[21]

Du Bois's book "revealed the Negro group as a symptom, not a cause, as a striving, palpitating group, and not an inert, sick body of crime; as a long historic development and not a transient occurrence."[22] And in his effort to combat the justifications for racial stratification that dominated social research, he extended this research to other communities, in Virginia and Georgia, and to the United States as a nation.[23] Between 1898 and 1904, the U.S. Department of Labor financed and published four other studies by Du Bois and modeled after *The Philadelphia Negro*. Du Bois served as the chair of the sociology department at Atlanta University between 1897 and 1915, and during this period he and his students and colleagues produced more than nineteen studies and reports of African American life. In one way or another these studies were all modeled on *The Philadelphia Negro*.

Du Bois was not alone in his fight against Social Darwinian and eugenic thought. For example, Franz Boas developed a powerful critique of the eugenic doctrines.[24] In 1911, he published *The Mind of Primitive Man,* in which he argued that culture was the result of historical events, not racial ability, and the achievements of any particular race did not lead to the conclusion of racial superiority or unequal ability. Regarding racial differences in intelligence, Boas observed that Africans in America may not have the average intelligence of "the white race" and as a group may never reach the level of the average achievement of the white race, but there will be "countless numbers who will be able to outrun their white competitors."[25] For Boas, African-origin populations were fully capable of learning to participate in civilization, even if as a population they were *less than equal.*

Du Bois's analysis presented two pictures. In one view, the problems of African Americans resulted from enslavement and capitalism within the United States; in the other, they stemmed from African Americans' moral failings and included a lack of integration into the "greatest of the world's civilizations."[26] Du Bois's *The Philadelphia Negro* sought a balance between exploring the problems of a racially stratified society and unproductive behavior. Though he saw structural and behavioral problems as related, Du Bois was often apologetic regarding the cultural and historical distinctiveness of the African American population. He shrouded his discussion of African American oppression with admonitions and moralizing to African American people about their behavior.

These two problems would highlight descriptive racial research in the United States. It is true that the field of sociology did not appreciate Du Bois's model of investigation, particularly those University of Chicago scholars who, as the "Chicago School," came to dominate urban sociology. The prestigious *American Journal of Sociology* did not even bother to review *The Philadelphia Negro*. Furthermore, Du Bois was never offered a professorial appointment in a major "mainstream" university department, including the sociology department at the University of Pennsylvania, which had grudgingly extended him the title of "assistant in sociology" for the duration of his study of the Seventh Ward.[27] However,

*The Philadelphia Negro* received glowing reviews in the popular press and from liberal historians.

Many sociologists assumed European racial superiority.[28] It was this cultural perspective of European superiority that came to replace biological justifications of race. The move from eugenic to cultural arguments was a move from one type of essentialist perspective, the biological evolutionary, to another type of essentialist perspective, the cultural. This shift witnessed the birth of assimilation and a focus on unproductive behavior of the unassimilated as a dominant perspective—in a word, a return to viewing the "Negro as a problem."

Robert E. Park and Ernest W. Burgess are the fathers of classical assimilation. The assimilation school has tended to be Eurocentric and based on a process of assimilation into a single unit of several different races.[29] According to Park,

> Assimilation, as the word is here used, brings with it a certain borrowed significance which it carried over from physiology where it is employed to describe the process of nutrition. By a process of nutrition, somewhat similar to the physiological one, we may conceive alien peoples to be incorporated with, and made part of, the community or state. Ordinarily assimilation goes on silently and unconsciously, and only forces itself into popular conscience when there is some interruption or disturbance of the process.[30]

From this perspective racial solidarity is considered a natural state of affairs that leads to a state of racial conflict.[31] Robert Park argued: "For four hundred years and more Europe, and particularly Western Europe, has been preeminently the seat and center of greatest intellectual and political activity. During this period European commerce and European culture have penetrated to the most remote corners of the habitable world. As a result of this expansion, most of the world outside Europe has been reduced to a position of political and cultural subordination and dependency."[32] For Park, this domination is thought to have reduced the colonized and enslaved populations to a state of social and cultural dependence.

European American sociologists largely ignored Du Bois's insights.[33] They interpreted the urban plight of African Americans as comparable to the challenge immigrants faced in adjusting to American life. For European newcomers, the problem—and, in a sense, the solution—could be summed up in the word *assimilation*. But, Du Bois argued, assimilation was a solution to something quite different from the problems posed to a formerly enslaved population held in contempt and pity by Americans of European origin.

In fact, Du Bois argued that European immigration prevented the early advancement of the African American population in Philadelphia and other cities. Because of racial stratification, Du Bois observed, "[n]o differences of social condition allowed any Negro to escape from the group, although such escape was continually the rule among Irish, Germans, and other whites."[34] European immigrants could assimilate through economic advance, but the African American remained racially marginalized and segregated regardless of economic standing.

Some scholars have emulated Du Bois's descriptive model with important implications for understanding racial statistics and the need for a theoretically based analysis. One of the best examples is St. Clair Drake and Horace R. Cayton's use of descriptive statistics in *Black Metropolis: A Study of Negro Life in a Northern City*. Referring to the persistence of racial stratification, they observed: "[u]pper-class Negroes do experience discrimination and race prejudice in the form of inconveniences, annoyances, and psychic wounding. Exclusive shops and restaurants discourage or refuse their patronage. They cannot buy homes in most of the better residential neighborhoods, and in others they can do so only after protest, violence, and court fights."[35]

Drake and Cayton's *Black Metropolis* returned to the Du Boisian model of the race problem. Like Du Bois, Drake and Cayton emphasized the social relations of race and class positions within the society. Thus, class and culture included position in the racial hierarchy, family, clique, church, voluntary associations, school, and job, rather than the arbitrary approach of defining classes by looking at statistical distributions of income or rent. Like Du Bois in certain sections of *The Philadelphia Negro*, Drake and Cayton viewed the racial composition of Chicago as the product of racially prejudicial and calculated practices and decisions.

In the 1940s, The Yankee City series, edited by W. Lloyd Warner, presented descriptive evidence of how a large number of individuals from ethnic minorities had climbed up the class ladder away from others in their ethnic group. The social stigma of belonging to the ethnic group rapidly disappeared, freeing upper-class members of the group to try to move to higher levels; however, when this research was extended to issues of race in the South, it became apparent that alongside class stratification was racial stratification. In *The Deep South: A Social Anthropological Study of Caste and Class,* Allison Davis, Burleigh B. Gardner, and Mary R. Gardner argued that the social system supported the subordination of African Americans.[36]

Du Bois produced a mass of descriptive data, but his problems came in how he interpreted these data. Unlike inferential statistical analysis, descriptive racial analysis is often used to support arguments that posit causation to some larger social processes. This methodological process typified other descriptive studies that depended on the collection and analysis of large racial data sets. Drake and Cayton's *Black Metropolis* and Gunnar Myrdal's *An American Dilemma: The Negro Problem and Modern Democracy* (1944) are two of the most well-known examples of descriptive analysis that posit causation to larger social processes. These works are fundamentally important for understanding the structural dynamics of racial stratification, and they suggest that society must be changed in order to solve the race problem.

Du Bois confronted the paradox that the historical and social factors that racially oppressed his people were a "twice-told tale" that was growing old with his European American audience and patrons. Yet, he was intellectually committed to presenting this tale to them in a language they understood. Even in that language, the book must have startled these readers, given the extent to which it broke with the racial and intellectual orthodoxies of its day. *The Philadelphia Negro* showed Du Bois as one of the first scholars to pursue issues of racial justice in the analysis of racial data.

Du Bois's antiracist assumptions contrasted strongly with mainstream sociological research and the views of the general European American public.[37] In rejecting biological and other essentialist explanations of African American poverty and political powerlessness, the book described the importance of historical, structural, and cultural factors. In its conclusion, Du Bois argued that protesting the impact of racism was essential to the African American's future, "but he must never forget that he protests because those things hinder his own efforts, and that those efforts are the key to his future."[38] Du Bois's analysis provided a descriptive exposition of African American political exclusion and economic marginalization.

Several demographers at the University of Chicago's Population Research and Training Center picked up on the Du Boisian legacy and attempted to extend it beyond the case studies approach (i.e., the focus on single cities such as Philadelphia and Chicago) through a systematic delineation of intercity variations. On race, this effort, which grew out of the Chicago urban studies, began with Stanley Lieberson's book *Ethnic Patterns in American Cities* (1963). A tradition of research has followed the work of Karl and Alma Taeuber in their book *Negroes in Cities: Residential Segregation and Neighborhood Change* (1965), on residential segregation. The tradition has been maintained in the work of researchers such as Stanley Lieberson, *A Piece of the Pie: Blacks and White Immigrants since 1880* (1980); Douglas S. Massey and Nancy A. Denton, *American Apartheid: Segregation and the Making of the Underclass* (1993); and John Yinger, *Closed Doors, Opportunities Lost: The Continuing Costs of Housing Discrimination* (1995). The basic message of this research is that racial segregation in housing and private and public facilities (such as schools, hospitals, libraries, stores, and parks) is an essential part of racial stratification. This demographic tradition of examining segregation as an aspect of racial stratification is one of the uses of racial statistics for racial justice.

The most popular book using descriptive racial statistics in the twentieth century is William Julius Wilson's *The Declining Significance of Race: Blacks and Changing American Institutions* (1978), a structural perspective supported by descriptive racial statistics. Wilson clearly intended to provide a structural critique of racial stratification. He provided a structural analysis of descriptive racial statistics and does not attempt to justify the processes of racial stratification. In fact, Wilson made the leap to presenting one of the most powerful arguments for deracializing society and scholarly research.

A causal theory is a scientific theory describing aspects of the social processes by which the society changes. Du Bois and Wilson used racial statistics to support their causal theories. They based their arguments on numerical descriptions of various aspects of the social world. The authors provided much discussion about the underlying process at the observational level, stating how race is causally related to other social processes and examining the form of this relationship beyond that involved in the data under analysis. Such explanations are not the "true" underlying process but rather relate the phenomenon under study to other knowledge at a different level. For Du Bois and Wilson this different level of knowledge is found in the history of race relations.[39] Each author used racial statistics to pursue racial justice.

It is important to keep in mind that the power of the descriptive method is in the argument presented, not the data. Many of those objecting to the progressive orientation of Wilson and Du Bois embrace the validity of the data they present. That is, although they might question how to interpret the trends, they agree that the underlying data are the basis for understanding racial differences. So, for example, Charles Murray's *Losing Ground: American Social Policy, 1950–1980* could use the same sources of data as William J. Wilson's *The Declining Significance of Race* in coming to an opposite conclusion.[40] While Wilson argues in *The Declining Significance of Race* for more social programs, Murray uses the same types of data to argue in *Losing Ground* that social programs to help the poor are futile, foster increased poverty, and trap the poor in their situation.

## Modern Social Statistics

In chapter 4, I suggested that inferential social statistics are primarily concerned with *correlation* and *regression*. Since Yule published his paper on poverty in London in 1899, this concern has occurred in a context of establishing causality. Often investigators seem to view statistical modeling as being equivalent to a regression model. The reader is cautioned that my critique of regression analysis is not necessarily tantamount to denying the value of empirical research. However, I do think that a statistical model that predicts well or fits the data well is not necessarily connected with causation. From this critique the specification of a statistical model that includes all relevant "causal" variables is problematic.[41]

Modern social statistics involves the design of outcome variables and the analysis of their dependence on some explanatory or predictor variables. Most social statisticians confuse prediction with causation. This has led to the use of the language of cause and effect. In most of the social sciences, this has taken the form of "dependent" (outcome) and "independent" (predictor) variables. In experimental statistics, the two types of variables are "response" (outcome) and "factor" (predictor). In econometrics, the most common variable designations are "exogenous" and "endogenous."

Formally, the objectives of statistical design in the social sciences are description, experimentation, and inference. *Description* refers to statistical designs that attempt to understand the process by which the dependent variable is generated. Survey and demographic research characterizes descriptive designs. Demography is the study of the population, and social surveys are thought to represent the defined population. Demographic analysis is often based upon samples of census data. Formally, surveys consist of probability samples into which members of a defined population have a known positive probability of selection. Experimental designs employ a specific combination of values from the predictor variables within a statistical model to forecast the value of a dependent variable. In experiments all the extraneous variables have been either controlled or randomized.[42]

Statistical modeling of dependence in the social world differs significantly from statistical modeling in the natural world. First, statistical modeling in the natural sciences is generally *experimental*, and the explanatory variables can be manipulated and fixed by the researcher. In the social sciences, explanatory variables are usually random and lack the theoretical precision to attribute causation.[43] Second, in the natural sciences the use of experimental design usually affords researchers the luxury of selectively choosing a small number of treatment variables, unlike social scientists, who typically deal with a large number of possible explanatory variables. Finally, social scientists rarely specify a statistical model by making assumptions about the functional form of the error variance or about the distribution of the errors.

## Some Nonrandom Examples from Inferential Statistics

Examples of the confusion between attributes and causes fill the social science literature. For example, in several studies published in the journal *Demography,* authors examined racial differentials in mortality, fertility, and the labor market in the United States.[44] Each argues that because the "black/white" difference statistically disappears when other socioeconomic factors are "controlled," the racial disparity is due to these factors. While I agree with the spirit of these conclusions, they are perfect examples of how social scientists, particularly in more recent times, resort to racial statistics in an effort to refute racist arguments or vindicate past misdeeds. However, by employing racial statistics and interpreting race as a cause, they have actually legitimated the use of methodologies that perpetuate the problems they seek to overcome.

If the use of regression in racial research is a success, then it should be reflected in the routine paper in a "good" journal. I reviewed the leading sociology and demography journals in quantitative social science: *American Sociological Review, Demography, American Journal of Sociology,* and *Population Studies.* These peer-reviewed (refereed) journals accept very few of their submissions. For my examples, I selected papers that were published in the last ten years, included race as a variable that had a clear research question, and used regression to answer that question. The examples are too numerous for me to publish all of them; however, I have chosen for illustration three of many possible examples that I think have important findings but a problematic use of race as a variable. The authors' treatment of race as a causal variable leads to an essentializing of race as a variable, although the authors may not have intended this. They may themselves be thinking of race as a proxy for other social and biological causes that they have not specified. In general, my main problem with these articles concerns the language used to interpret their results, not their statistical results per se. I do not spend much time discussing the particulars of each article. My main purpose is illustrative.

Academic journals are full of this problem of interpretation and language in racial statistical articles. Examples of the language used in the interpretation of race as a variable in statistical papers point to the generality of the problem. Although the reader is invited to download the articles and read them, I will restrict my comments to examples of causal language in the discussion of race.

*Empirical example A.* In a study published in the journal *Population Studies* in 1993, the author examined whether differential mortality rates by social and economic status existed in the United States. He concluded that mortality differences among different racial groups are dramatically reduced when economic status is "controlled." The author gave the following example of a causal conclusion:

> Table 3 depicts the association between ethnic group and mortality.
> Blacks face greater mortality risks than whites, as is shown in Column 1;
> in fact, the *effect of being black* on mortality is equivalent to over five
> years of increased age. Controlling for background by using $p_i$ results in
> a small reduction of the "black" coefficient, but the effect of being black
> is still equivalent to over five years of increased initial age.[45]

*Empirical example B.* In a study published in the journal *American Journal of Sociology* in 1999, the authors examined whether the effect of alternative family structures on a child's education and occupational success has remained constant during the past three decades. The authors provided the following causal result:

> In fact, in the "raw" data the *effect of race* on occupational status actually increased from 1987 to 1993 (from –2.65 to –3.41). This empirical observation fits with wide speculation and other kinds of evidence that there has been a recent rise in race inequality.[46]

*Empirical example C.* In a study published in the *American Sociological Review* in 1998, two authors examined whether the subjective well-being of African Americans in the United States was significantly and consistently lower than that of whites over the twenty-four-year period 1972–1996. They conclude that quality of life continues to be worse for African Americans than it is for whites and that although racial inequality appears to be the primary cause of these differences, the exact processes producing them are unknown. The authors provided the following causal result:

> In Model 3, in which income, education, work status, marital status, and age are controlled, the *effect of race* declines significantly. Yet significant racial differences remain on all six indicators, and only marital satisfaction is a strict linear function of year. With these controls, blacks' disadvantage is most pronounced on mistrust and marital happiness.[47]

The authors clearly intended for the interpretations of their regression results to state that the "effect of race" could be measured statistically. However, an individual trait like race cannot determine another trait of the individual. The problem is determining when race is viewed as an unalterable characteristic of an individual and when it is seen as a cause that can act on individuals in the population under investigation. As an unalterable characteristic, race can be discussed only as an association. From my perspective, it is difficult to conceive how race could be a treatment in a social survey and, therefore, a "cause." The problem is not in the findings but in the authors' interpretations of their results. The authors' treatments of race lend themselves to inferring causality, although the authors may not have intended it.

The authors' models might be useful in predicting the results of interventions or in providing a better understanding of the racial stratification process. But this interpretation of their results must be based on a well-developed theory that connects their statistical calculations to the process of race.

Finally, the authors in two of the papers (involving empirical examples A and C) are concerned with determining which variables are important in their analysis. The authors in both papers have done what social statisticians refer to as controlling for the correlation of variables in their regression models. Researchers often estimate statistical models in which they believe a particular predictor variable is correlated with another variable, $X$, and thus has to be "controlled" in order to estimate the causal effect of $X$. Such considerations usually ignore the statistical implications of this concern, and the solutions presented are at best incorrect.[48] In fact, a causal effect that is the result of a controlled model must be seen as a mathematical result. It cannot exist in the real world, because the real world is what produced the process being controlled.

Social statisticians should avoid using race as a proxy for other social and biological causes. It is time that we collect the information on the social and the biological causes that race supposedly represents. As I indicated in the earlier chapters, race is particularly problematic as a proxy measurement of biological and individual behavioral processes. Furthermore, using race as a proxy for the causal effect of social processes introduces substantial bias depending on the researcher's preconceptions of racial difference.

By employing racial statistics and interpreting race as a cause, well-intentioned scholars often legitimate the use of methodologies that perpetuate the problems they seek to overcome. This is seen in the footnotes of two of the examples mentioned above. In one of the articles, the authors argue:

> We do not believe that the evidence strongly supports Herrnstein and Murray's (1994) hypothesis that the net effect of cognitive skills on socioeconomic outcomes has increased in recent decades. If their view is correct, however, then the t-ratios shown in Table 4 actually should be even more negative (at least for those minorities that show lower average levels of cognitive skills). Such a result would only strengthen our conclusion that we should reject the null hypothesis of no reduction in the net racial effect across this period.[49]

In another article, the author wrote, "The use of $p_l$ may be disputed, if there were, indeed, differences in longevity caused by ethnic genotype.

Being black means having black parents, and if genotype did matter, controlling for parents alive may be objectionable."[50] Race is not a reflection of genotype or cognitive skills. Reflections on causality where none has been demonstrated, or can be demonstrated using statistical methods, should be loudly challenged, not deferred to. Studies relying on assumptions that impose a decontextualized racial identity should not be the point of comparison.

By using the theory of probability, social statisticians engage in inductive reasoning, arguing from the particular to the general or from the sample to the population. Inferential statistics allows us to predict outcomes and discuss how variables are related. The practice of inferential statistics also commits social statisticians to a logical way of talking and thinking about causation. It is the confusion of prediction with causation that has caused many of the problems in interpreting statistical results. In part this confusion is the result of how social scientists think about causation, but the root of the problem is in how social scientists think about measuring the social world. The statistical analysis of race presents an important example of this confusion in the logic of analysis. This is the concluding issue that we turn to in part III.

# Part III
# Beyond Racial Statistics

It is an odd fact that subjective certainty is inversely proportional to objective certainty.

—Bertrand Russell, *Scientific Outlook* (1931)

When we speak of causes, we are not speaking of the world as God sees it. We are speaking of the world as God has arranged for us to see it.

—Glenn Shafer, *The Art of Causal Conjecture* (1996)

Mathematical definition is, however, often no more than a succinct statement of the axioms to be applied when the word occurs in deductive mathematical reasoning, and may pay less attention than is needed to the conditions of the correct applicability of the term in the real world. It is these conditions of applicability which are properly the concern of those responsible for Applied Mathematics.

—Ronald A. Fisher, *Statistical Methods and Scientific Inference* (1956)

# Beyond Racial Statistics

The purpose of statistical analysis is the reduction of data. Census or survey microdata are of such a quantity that analysis is impossible without some process of summarizing the data. The human mind cannot look at 250 million individual records of information and make any conclusions. The mere bulk of the data is incapable of entering the human mind. The object of statistical methods is to replace this bulk of data with a relatively few numbers that will adequately represent the entire population in the original data. The object of racial statistics should be to help us understand the process of racial stratification, not to justify its existence.

Often race is seen as a proxy for genotype or culture. This tendency has led many researchers to view race as a cause of some social process. I argue that race as a variable cannot be a cause. And to depend on causality where none has been demonstrated is a mistake. Race as a variable must be placed within a social context.

Studies should not rely on a decontextualized racial identity. It is, in fact, this decontextualization that leads to a form of racial reasoning. Statistical research can go beyond racial reasoning. It is not a question of fancier statistics. What is needed is a better understanding of our theories and how they relate to our research methods. We need a better understanding of how racial data are related to our research methods and how causal effects relate to our causal theories.

The United States censuses contain the longest-running consecutive compilations of data on racial classification in the Americas. The 1777 racial classification that allocated three-fifths apportionment for each nonvoting enslaved African and the nineteenth-century classification of mulattoes, quadroons, and octoroons all point to the ideological and biased nature of racial classification in the United States.

Likewise, the South African censuses contain the longest-running consecutive compilations of data on racial classification in Africa. The official classifications of different racial groups have been dynamic. Not only has the terminology changed, but also the groups represented by the terms have changed. Racial classification in the South African censuses is related to the social and political context by its definition and measurement.

The current practice of classifying individuals with partial African heritage as black or mixed continues the tradition of racist practices. And the dominate position given to the questions regarding race on the 2000 round of census questionnaires in both the United States and the Republic of South Africa only proves that racial classification is an obsession in racially stratified societies, one that is difficult to move beyond. Both nations had heated public debates regarding which categories must be used. And both expended great resources to attempt to make the racial classification process more scientific. The problem does not end with the collection of racial data; it only begins. The problem accelerates when we attempt to analyze these data statistically. This problem is especially acute in our efforts to understand race as a causal process or variable.

Using racialized census, survey, or other social data is not in and of itself problematic. The racialization of data is an artifact of both the struggles to preserve and to destroy racial stratification. Before the data can be deracialized, we must deracialize the social circumstances that have created racial stratification. Some scholars have suggested an end to the collection of racial data.[1] While I agree with the deracialization of data as an objective, the elimination of the collection of racial data should occur as a process leading to the end of racial stratification. Racial blindness should follow the process of a racially conscious effort to end racial stratification.

Racial data do not represent a genetic or biological population. Recent studies have questioned and criticized the social concept of race.[2] Statisticians are in the process of an important discussion on the issue of using attributes like race in social statistics.[3] The statistical discussion has not focused on the issue of the conceptualization of race. It nevertheless places a considerable theoretical burden on social statisticians who use race as a variable in their statistical analysis to predict social outcomes.

Several scholars have reintroduced critical evaluations of the use of race as a variable in health research. This volume has attempted to focus on the methodological implications of the use of race.[4] I suggested a new logic for understanding racial statistics. This new perspective is developed on the basis of my readings among Quetelet, Galton, and the reflexive discourse among statisticians. Causal effects from data sets are different from causal theories partly derived from the conclusions of empirical research. It is important that we revise our interpretations of the causal effects determined from racial data and that we place these findings within a context that is theoretically based.

Apparently conflicting interpretations of racial statistics result from the different ways in which race is interpreted. The conceptualization of race is fundamental to all subsequent use of racial data. This use of racial data influences our understanding of the logic of statistical analysis and how this analysis has developed in the study of human beings.

Before Galton, attempts to do social statistics were flawed. Galton's focus on difference, especially human difference, played the key role in the development of statistical analysis of human beings. Galton's methodologies were developed as part of his racial theory of eugenics, and his ideas about racial quality had a fundamental impact on the logic of social statistics. Fisher challenged these ideas by separating statistical logic from evolutionary theory. Fisher's challenge has a direct implication for the examination of racial data: it involves the issues of method and theory. In statistical research we must pay closer attention to the method being used and its connection with theories of society. The logic of racial statistics is connected to theories of race in society. Seeing race as a cause in racial statistics helps justify racial stratification.

The statistical logic of racial justification is based on how individuals and population are defined. In statistical analysis a population consists of an observational record of a particular characteristic. Thus, the number of Asians in South Africa or the United States could be determined by either asking who in the population is Asian or by sending out "trained" enumerators to count the number of Asians on the basis of some preconceived notion of who is an Asian. These are, in fact, the ways that census bureaus have generally handled the counting of race and in doing so have contributed to the reification of race. The census is primarily concerned with classifying rather than measuring. Thus, genetics and demography have tended to use statistical notions of race in their justifications of racial stratification.

Empirical social science is both descriptive and inferential. Most empirical social science involves numerical descriptions of various aspects of the social world. Inferential statistics summarize data using mathematical tools. Statistical reasoning is part of the discourse that motivated the creation of the variables. Statistical analysis makes sense only in a context of a common language, marked by some level of agreement about the technical and social purpose. The variables and conventions that serve as the basis of statistics follow political, social, and mathematical developments. Public debate that uses statistical reasoning is limited by the logic of statistics and our ideas about how society should operate. Du Bois's legacy is important, because he does challenge us to look at social stratification.

Some will argue that causal models are the best way for social scientists to make public policy statements. They will say that statistical models used in this way allow us to elaborate on how and what produces particular effects. This may all be true, but human knowledge is uncertain and imperfect, and it is not clear how statistical models contribute to this uncertainty.[5] Interpreting the results of a statistical analysis should be connected to an underlying causal theory. The results themselves do not prove anything beyond the statistical relationship between two or more variables. The connection of these variables in the real world requires a causal theory. It is possible that the causal language used by many social scientists is not reflective of an unarticulated causal theory but is simply the careless use of language. Such research should be considered within the context of causal effects. Causal effects research provides basic materials for the elaboration of a causal theory; however, it is not essential that these basic materials all be of the causal-effects type. Ethnographic, historical, and other domains of research are also essential for the development of a powerful causal theory.

Our theories of society, not our statistical methods, will continue to guide how we interpret racial data, (or any other social data, for that matter). It is important to remember that what social scientists see as the strengths of statistical analysis in other sciences has more to do with the strength of their theory than with their statistical methods.

# CHAPTER SIX

## Challenging Race as a Variable

Race continues to be seen as a biological and demographic variable by many scholars, even though it has been argued for years that race is, biologically and demographically speaking, an exceedingly complex matter and that subjective predispositions and biases, more than biology or demography, govern the way people think about it. Racial statistics are not biologically or demographically based, because both demography and biology developed ideas about race under the sway of the eugenics movement. This continued bias results from the acceptance of the statistical definition of race as real rather than as a simple reflection of the classification process itself.

Changes in the natural and social sciences transformed how we understand race. Evolutionary thought offered an opportunity to synthesize research in both the natural and social sciences; however, this effort was polluted by the dominance of the eugenic perspective. The extent to which evolution accounts for our social world nevertheless remains a legitimate question. Indeed, this question has brought a renewed interest in the relationship between the evolutionary and social worlds, as echoed in Lucius Outlaw's noteworthy text *On Race and Philosophy*:

> Though evolutionary—as opposed to typological—thinking, in some form, is at present the dominant intellectual framework for systematic reconstructions and explanations of human natural and social history, it, too, has been enlisted in the service of those who would have "science" pass absolution on their political agendas: i.e, to legitimate the empowerment of certain groups, certain races, over others.[1]

The evolutionary aspects of race have been incorporated into cultural, political, and social justifications for racial stratification.

Social statistics have been used to justify racial stratification. Among social statisticians an implicit tendency to accept the underlying logic of racial reasoning has developed. And as Patricia Hill Collins notes in *Fighting Words: Black Women and the Search for Justice:* "Although the 'master' may have meant for scientific words to be used one way, reclaiming scientific tools and recasting them for different purposes can benefit both science and subordinate groups."[2] It is rare to find social scientists that criticize the methodological foundations of racial statistics. Instead, the most advanced-thinking social scientists usually appropriate the legitimating function of statistics to refute racist or sexist arguments. This project of appropriation may be logically flawed and could contribute to the process of legitimating and perpetuating the methodologies that justify racial stratification in modern social statistics. As Lewis Gordon notes: "How can there be a science of human beings, the challenge goes, if there were no ontological dimension of human beings? Similarly, how can one study antiblack racism and black people when there are already problems involved in studying people? A clue rests in what is at bottom required of the interpreter of human phenomena."[3]

Along these lines we could attempt to engage in social statistics in a way that keeps the human being and human effort evident. This effort requires that we avoid studying society while rejecting the humanity of the population under consideration. In order for modern social statistics to make efforts to pursue this direction of research, we must change some of our ideas about the study of racial statistics.

Racial data continue to play the contradictory roles of being essential in the profane fight against racial stratification and in reifying race in the study of society. Deracializing data must be a process that coincides with the deracialization of society. The deracialization of data is a process. Let's begin with the anthropological or biological measurement of difference and its deracializing implications.

## Anthropological Measurement and the Death of Racial Reasoning

Human biological variation is real.[4] But race as a way of organizing that variation is false. This view is important because it should dispel any remaining doubts concerning the essential and physical reality of race. Racial stratification is real, but biology is not its root cause. Race is often referred to as either a biological (anthropological) or a demographic characteristic. In reality it is neither.

The basis of racial classification has been skin color. Variation in skin color among groups is larger than variation within some groups, making it amenable for the study of human quantitative traits.[5] Theoretically, we can group human populations on the basis of skin color. However, such a grouping is based on our arbitrary distinctions. The difference in skin color between people of African and European origin is believed to be the result of three to six polygenes. Yet, as we enter the twenty-first century, the mode of inheritance of skin color remains unknown.

From a scientific point of view, advances in biological anthropology and human genetics signaled the death of biologically based notions of race. Population geneticists have tended to define a population as a community of randomly mating individuals.[6] They study the frequency and distribution of genes and other hereditary units within entire populations. Given that human beings are one species with a tendency toward amalgamation—whenever and wherever they come into continuous contact—racial classifications are culturally determined. As James King observes:

> Whether two individuals regard themselves as of the same or of different races depends not on the degree of similarity of their genetic material but on whether history, tradition, and personal training and experiences have brought them to regard themselves as belonging to the same group or to different groups. Since all human beings are of one species and since all populations tend to merge when they exist in contact, group differentiation will be based on cultural behavior and not on genetic difference. True, there is great geographical variation within the species but even at its most extreme there is no biological barrier to interbreeding and population fusion. In these circumstances, whatever classification of human beings is to be made will be determined by the cultural practices of the classifiers.[7]

In the most comprehensive analysis of genetic data on human difference, population geneticists L. Luca Cavalli-Sforza and his colleagues make the following observation:

> By means of painstaking multivariate analysis, we can identify "clusters" of populations and order them in a hierarchy that we believe represents the history of fissions in the expansion to the whole world of

anatomically modern humans. At no level can clusters be identified with races, since every level of clustering would determine a different partition and there is no biological reason to prefer a particular one.[8]

It is important that Cavalli-Sforza and his colleagues use a factor analysis to genetically classify populations. Factor analysis was developed within the context of eugenic research on race and intelligence. However, it is equally important that they distinguish their populations from traditional notions of race. For Cavalli-Sforza and his colleagues, population differences are not directly observed; their populations are "latent variables" and, like intelligence, must depend on a theoretical justification.

Biological research has helped us dismiss the biological reality of race itself, and therefore it has contributed to understanding racial stratification. James E. Bowman and Robert F. Murray's book, *Genetic Variation and Disorders in Peoples of African Origin,* uses biological research to describe disease among African-origin populations. For population geneticists like Bowman and Murray, African Americans, blacks in Europe and Latin America, and Africans south and north of the Sahara are all peoples of African origin. In reference to African Americans they note:

> Within recent memory, blacks in the United States were referred to as colored, and later, as Negro, African-American, and an assortment of unmentionable pejorative names. No matter what African-Americans may be called in the future, they will remain peoples of African origin— at least in terms of some of their ancestors. Many African-Americans are also equally peoples of European, Asian or Amerindian origin, or of multiple origins; to say otherwise would lend credence to an anachronistic social definition of race and ignores biological reality.[9]

Unlike eugenics, this research does not embrace a biological understanding of racial differences, but it does enhance our knowledge of population differences. The human species is a potentially interbreeding natural population that reproduces exclusively within the human group regardless of racial classification and stratification.[10] Populations vary in accordance with the geographical origin of the members of the population. Thus, we can speak of the African-, Asian-, and European-origin populations. African Americans are an African-origin population; however, Europeans of Zimbabwe and South Africa can be considered European-origin populations, and Asian Indians, Chinese, and other post-fifteenth-century immigrants from Asia can be considered Asian-origin populations.[11]

Although more genetic variation exists within defined human populations, some variation also exists among such populations. These variations are the result of differences in the historical and environmental conditions and have resulted in diverse genotypes and morphologies.[12] The relationship between the genotype and the "racial morphologies" continues to be a major question in the social sciences. It is often assumed that skin color (a morphology) is a good predictor of genotype.

Research in genetics that was inspired by eugenics nevertheless undermined the eugenic arguments about racial differences by pointing to the racial unity of the human population. However, genetics does recognize the differences among populations on the basis of the frequency that different alleles occur within each of them. Allele similarities allow the grouping of populations on the basis of genetic similarity. These differences have developed over a long period of time, and since 1492 there has been extensive interpopulation reproduction. The differences in morphologies used to racially classify the population do exist.

Various physical traits occur with definite frequencies among different populations, so that any individual from a particular population picked at random is very likely to possess a combination of the most frequently occurring physical traits observed in that population.[13] For example, if we were to compare a population of Scots from England with a population of Zulus from South Africa, it would be obvious that for various characteristics such as height, weight, hair texture, and skin color each population would have an average and a distribution around the average. The distribution of differences around the given traits that distinguish each population is determined by the cultural practices of the classifiers.

Population differences do not always translate into racial differences. A classic example of this is found in South Africa. Afrikaners and Coloureds are two of the racial groups within modern South Africa. Apparently, in 1688 when Dutch orphans were brought to serve as wives for Dutch settlers, they introduced an allele that explains a founder effect in the Afrikaner population.[14] By studying porphyria geneticists were able to trace the allele back through several generations of the Afrikaner population from living sufferers from porphyria. Thus, this allele could be used to describe the Dutch-origin population. Yet it fails in allowing us to make distinctions between the current Afrikaner and Coloured races, because the trait is present among both Afrikaners and Coloureds.

Race is defined within a society by the importance attached to certain morphological characteristics and is more a measure of a relationship than of an individual characteristic; that is, race is theoretically a classification of a social relationship, not an unalterable individual trait. Yet many social scientists continue to conceptualize race as an unalterable trait, and indeed race may be an unalterable trait within certain social contexts, such as in the United States or South Africa. Whether two individuals are regarded as members of the same race depends on their history, traditions, and personal experiences, not their genetic material.

*With the exception of Nazi Germany, there is not in existence, nor has there ever been, a society or scientific community that attempted to make its racial classifications on the basis of genetic examinations of the population.* Such a scheme is doomed to failure given that genetic variability is greater within populations than among them. Nazi Germany was forced to rely on genealogical records. Such a scheme may be technically practical as a result of recent developments in genetics; however, these same developments suggest that the skin color that serves as the biological basis of current racial classification may not apply to populations defined by genetic examinations.

## Biology in the Study of Racial Stratification

Genetic identification of each individual is theoretically possible. In principal, DNA segments can be used to distinguish among individuals and populations.[15] But this differentiation of the population is not consistent with any known system of racial classification.

Biology may be a necessary starting point for understanding population differences; however, it is not sufficient to explain racial stratification. Population differences are geographically patterned and are far more permeable than racial classifications imply.[16] For example, the three major regimes of immigrants to the United States are from West Africa, western Europe, and eastern Asia. Among West Africans there is a great degree of diversity; in fact, Africa may be home to the most genetically diverse human population. The construct "western European" masks the great diversity among the populations in the western portion of the Eurasian continent. And "eastern Asia" does not begin to describe the diversity of the Asian-origin populations. However, in the context of the system of race, being of Asian, European, or African origin has a social and political meaning independent of biology.

A population's health status results from interacting pathways. His-torical, genetic, social, and environmental interactions have a profound impact on population health and mortality.[17] HIV, the sickle-cell allele, and hypertension all illustrate the interrelationships among society, en-vironment, history, and biology and their impact on population dy-namics, indicating that the social reality of race has biological as well as social implications.

Some epidemiological researchers have adopted a perspective that looks at the African population and the African diaspora as a solution to race-based analysis. Richard S. Cooper and his colleagues, in a series of epi-demiological studies, have suggested that hypertension among African Americans arises through complex interacting pathways. This interac-tive perspective involves external factors (such as stress, racism, and diet) and internal physiology (such as the biological systems and the genes that regulate blood pressure).[18] This research does not deny the impor-tance of genetic research in the understanding of racial differences with regard to hypertension. However, it suggests that "not a single shred of direct (i.e., molecular) evidence exists to support the contention that higher rates of hypertension among Blacks have a genetic basis."[19]

Social epidemiologists have been able to successfully examine the health impacts of racial stratification. For example, Sherman A. James and his colleagues have conducted a series of studies on the psycho-social and behavioral determinants of cardiovascular disease in African Americans.[20] Dr. James has advanced the concept of "John Henryism," which hypothesizes that repetitive, high-effort coping with social and economic adversity is a major cause of the high rates of hypertension typically seen in poor and working-class African Americans. This research suggests that the structural impediments or racial stratification takes a health toll on poor and working-class African Americans who exhibit high levels of John Henryism. Thus, low-income African Americans who emphasize the "American values" of the strong work ethic and self-control are also more likely to be hypertensive.

Some anthropologists have used Africa and African human variation to understand the measured and quantifiable aspects of human differ-ence. These scholars have focused on the anatomical, physiochemical, and molecular aspects of human difference. In fact, from this perspective it would be a liability not to recognize the importance of African biodi-versity. Fatimah Jackson and her colleagues have developed a perspective based on Africa and African human variations to "illuminate world patterns of human biodiversity."[21] This perspective seems to follow logically from the work of Luca Cavalli-Sforza and his colleagues, who "start with the continent where the genus and probably also the subspecies to which we belong have first developed, Africa, and then proceed with the other continents successively occupied, though not in the strict order of occupation: Asia, Europe, America, and Oceania."[22] Professor Jackson and her colleagues have challenged the Human Genome Diversity Project to pursue a more scientifically based agenda. They argue that the key to understanding human biological variation can be found among African-origin populations. And they argue for a reconstruction of human variation on the basis of "ethnogenetic layering," which is dynamic, interactive, and highly flexible. From this perspective there is one human race, and it is basically out of Africa.

Our ability to understand the role of biology in the study of racial stratification has suffered from conceptual limitations. Genes exist and have a function within the context of a specific environment. An argument that views genes or environment in isolation as the reason for a racial difference is incomplete and maybe even unreasonable. Indeed, some racial differences are simply the result of social circumstances, while others require that we understand human adaptation to social evolution.

## The Demography of Racial Stratification

Demography is an observational science. Demographic analysis focuses on the size, composition, and growth rates of human populations. The traditional approach within demographic analysis focuses on understanding variation among and within populations. This variation is seen as a direct result of changes in births, deaths, and migration—demographic rates.

While for statisticians *population* refers to the measurement of some characteristic, demography defines *population* as living persons residing in a specified space at a given moment in time. Typically, demographers define *population* on the basis of some specifying criteria. For example, they refer to the "European American population on July 1, 1999," or to the "population of African American elderly in Philadelphia on December 30, 1999." In both examples, the specifying criterion refers to a set of operational choices designed to clarify the specific collection of persons in the population.

Demographic accounts of the processes of births and deaths in a population require an understanding of both biological and social factors. A failure to account for the biological component of demographic processes can lead to misinterpretation. For example, the fertility of human populations has both biological and social aspects.[23] The reproductive physiology of human fertility focuses on the processes of ovulation, spermatogenesis, and fertilization and the regulation of these reproductive processes with contraceptive technology. Most researchers recognize the logical need to integrate the biological with the social approach for a complete understanding of human fertility. However, when we consider the issue of race, the connection between the biological and social aspects of fertility takes on new importance. This importance is complicated by the historical connection of fertility research to eugenics.

Like most social statisticians, demographers use race as a category that distinguishes the population socially and biologically. In one recent article published in *Demography*, the authors define races as "genetic entities because generations of 'reproductive isolation' have led to differences in gene frequency across racial groups. During prehistoric times, the physical barrier of the Sahara Desert reduced gene flow between Europeans and sub-Saharan Africans. For many traits, including those physical traits that visibly differentiate the groups (e.g., skin color and physical features), gene frequencies are sharply different." They also argued that "race is a social category."[24] This was all said in a context where genetic research has discredited such arguments. However, this article was successful in the review process and published in what is arguably the flagship journal of American demography.

The estimation of most demographic measures assumes the ability to exclusively define racial populations. In the comparison of two populations, population A cannot overlap with population B. The African American population cannot overlap with the European American population. If children from European American men and African American women are classified as African American children, the internal integrity of both populations is compromised. And any comparisons of the two populations are erroneous to the extent of interracial reproduction and racial "misclassification."[25] It would be like comparing individuals of ages ten to fifteen with individuals ages twelve to sixteen. These age groups, like race, do not distinguish two separate populations. The estimation of demographic rates is prone to errors as a result of the current conception of race. However, this statement may be too strong, because the known methods are not the problem. The problem resides in the application and development of these methods to the understanding of multi-group populations.[26]

Another problem results from demographers treating statistical populations, such as races, as if they were demographic populations. Thus, demographic analysis focuses on the demography of people classified as races but interprets the results as if they are analyzing the demography of races. It is not unusual for demographers to estimate an aggregate-level process, such as life expectancy, and to translate it into statements about the demographic circumstances faced by an average or randomly chosen individual of a particular race.

One way to enhance the discourse about race is to distinguish between racial stratification and population differences. The demography of race is a question of the impact of racial classification. This simple shift in perspective begins the deracialization of demography while we examine the processes of racial stratification.

Population membership depends on the context of the discussion. With the exception of the statistical definition, a population is not the same as a race. In most social science research the statistical definition of a population predominates. The problem lies not in the use of the statistical definition of race but in its employment as if it has the same meaning as the demographic or genetic definition of a population. Eugenicists used the statistical definition of population as an erroneous justification for racial stratification, and many demographers today replicate this error. A solution to this problem may lie in reconceptualizing race as a variable in the statistical analysis of demographic processes.

In recognition of the biological and social connections in demographic processes, demographers have begun to reintegrate biological and social factors into their models of population variation.[27] This new effort also attempts to understand biological processes outside the political framework of eugenics and has been most successful in the analysis of births and mortality. One potential benefit of this research is as a scientific alternative to using race as a proxy for genetic variation. Using race as a proxy subverts even the most positive attempts to understand the impact of genetic variation.

Future research in this area has significant potential. In the future more biological data will be collected in demographic surveys. These new data will open new opportunities for the examination of the relationship between biology and social and economic processes. However, researchers must be vigilant about not committing the errors of the past.

## The Politics of Racial Classification

Racial classification depends on the social and historical context. In the system of race in South Africa, Brazil, and the United States, being of Asian, European, or African origin has a social and political meaning that differs among these places. *Origin* takes on a unique meaning depending on the social and historical context.

The United States provides an excellent example of how historical origins and race are interrelated in racially stratified societies. In the United States, Africans did not come to America as blacks or Africans; they came as Akan, Yoruba, Ibo, and Wolof. Immigrants from Europe did not come as white or Europeans; they came as English, Scottish, French, and Irish. Likewise, immigrants from Asia are not coming to the United States as Asians; they arrive as Chinese, Japanese, and Koreans. And the migrants from Latin America do not come to the United States as Hispanics or Latinos; they come as Mexicans, Cubans, and Dominicans. Typically, historical origins are thought to confer ethnic identity. And ethnic relations are thought to be temporal. Ethnicity refers to differences of culture and historical genealogy; however, unlike with race, with ethnicity the importance of physical differences is not insurmountable. Both ethnic and racial differences can and do exist in the same society.

Origin and race are confounded by the legacy of physical distinctions that are necessary to justify racial slavery and colonialism. Thus, whiteness, or Europeanness, identifies European-origin populations in the United States despite the fact that they have come from a variety of nations and cultures. In fact, each individual's origin could in itself be the result of multiple national and cultural origins.[28] The nature of racial classifications is bound by historical struggles that reflect the tendency to identify Europeanness as a positive attribute. An example of this tendency is found among the Mexican American community in Texas. In the 1940s, the League of United Latin American Citizens (LULAC) fought against Mexicans in Texas being classified as "colored."[29] LULAC pressured politicians and government enumerators to classify Mexicans as white.

Racial classification is a perfect example of what Paul Starr refers to as *legitimate classifications* and *legitimate use* of classifications.[30] According to Starr, governments must determine which classifications will be used in political discourse and administration of the states. "Legitimate classifications" reflect the government's decisions as to which classifications will be used and which classifications will not be allowed. More than simply a personal choice, classification of social difference by the state is part of how societies socially differentiate. As such, legitimate classifications can fight or aid social stratification. The government must also determine when and how legitimate classifications can be used. For example, how will statistical information be organized around them? Legitimate use poses a problem in the political choice of legitimate classifications.

The Republic of South Africa provides an example of how race is used as a legitimate classification in the political process. From 1921 to 1996 the South African government used four broad racial categories in its censuses: Africans, Asians, Coloureds, and Europeans. These four classifications were determined at a Statistical Council meeting in November 1921.[31] Ethnic groups within these classifications have been shifted from time to time. For example, Syrians were included under "Asians" in 1921, but were switched to "Europeans" thereafter. The most dynamic classification was that which was ascribed to the African population. It changed from Bantu to Natives to Bantu to Blacks and finally to African/Black over almost a century of enumeration. The other dynamic aspect of this era in South Africa's history is that of the increased usage by the state of these socially defined racial classifications; they controlled every aspect of life of the subordinate groups within the country. The legislation that had the greatest effect in this capacity was the Population Registration Act of 1950. Under this act, there were only three racial classifications: White, Coloured, and Native. The last two were classified additionally according to ethnic group.

In the 1950s, influx control became a compulsory policy throughout South Africa. The Population Registration law assigned every person an identity number. For Africans, the population registration system was particularly onerous, because they had to carry reference books, also known as passes, to travel in the country and to prove that they had a right to live or work in certain areas. These passes had to be shown whenever and wherever requested by the authorities, and failure to do so often resulted in imprisonment, a fine, or both.

In the case of South Africa, state-ascribed racial classification systems manifested as a public policy of racial stratification. In part, the South African racial data represent the racial distribution of the population at different times. On another level, they reflect a history of governmental policies of racial stratification in southern Africa.

The history of the development of the South African state and Afrikaner identity played an important role in the development and the composition of the country that is today known as the Republic of South Africa. As one Afrikaner leader noted, "The Afrikaans Language Movement is nothing less than an awakening of our nation to self-awareness and to the vocation of adopting a more worthy position in world civilization."[32] In fact, the Afrikaans Language movement was to become a major site of the struggle against apartheid by the Black Consciousness movement. Unlike the English-speaking white identity with its international identification with European imperialism, Afrikaans and Afrikaner racial identity were based on a specific notion of bringing civilization to and developing it in South Africa. European origin was equated with civilization, and the new Afrikaner culture was seen as the most recent manifestation of this cultural transformation. Thus, if Afrikaans became the language of the nation, it would also result in a modernization of the population's "self-awareness." This ethnocentric concern with language served as a model for partisan demographic research as well. No single demographer expressed this fact as clearly as J. L. Sadie. In 1949 he wrote:

> In South Africa the outstanding problem, dominating all others, is the relative numbers of the different races constituting the Union's population, and their differential rates of growth. For in the long run numbers must count. In this connection it is the numerical relation between Europeans and non-Europeans, and in particular between Europeans and Natives, which commands our attention. A complacent attitude towards this problem on the part of the Europeans, who as a minority still rule the country, is, to say the least, irresponsible.[33]

Historically, the census has provided social contexts for political discussions about racial categories. In the South African state, racial classification was incorporated into the administration of the state. The colonial governments of the past found it necessary to classify the population racially in order to levy taxes and allocate benefits. This classification of the African population facilitated the process of exploiting the colony and transforming indigenous identities to support the colonial process. Administrators and scholars viewed the census as demonstrating South Africa's civilization to the world.[34] Thus, the act of enumeration was an act of defining the colony for the civilized European world. The pre-modern censuses were a key element in the colonial process of transforming the identity of the African subject.

Official classifications influence personal identities as well as social science research. Given the influence of the government on a society, these classifications leave an important imprint on that society. Official classifications change as a result of changes in the social structure. Therefore, there is a symbiotic relationship between the state's efforts to develop and use racial classifications and the society's use of, adherence to, and development of these classifications.

Racial classification of the South African population has been used for political purposes. In particular, apartheid used racial classification to signify African marginalization. On a broad level, apartheid laws sought to ensure that elite whites maintained social, economic, and political control over the country and over Africans. This was deemed necessary, since the African population greatly outnumbered the white citizenry. As in the United States, in South Africa the practice of racial classification is a political and cultural process tempered by specific historical circumstances.

The United States serves as an ideal example of the political legacy of the collection of racial data. The United States Constitution directed enumerators to count three racial groups in the census: whites, enslaved Africans as three-fifths of a person, and "civilized" Native Americans. Since then, the census has facilitated the development and public awareness of social statistics and demography, and now the public is served a steady diet of racial statistics. Almost a third of the 2000 census short-form questionnaire asked about race.

The general public acts and thinks politically within the confines of racial categories, and the government makes policies that determine "who gets what" on the basis of these differences. Racial data are used for legislative redistricting; monitoring civil rights legislation, such as enforcement of Title VII of the Civil Rights Act of 1964, which prohibits discrimination in employment based upon race, color, sex, religion, and national origin, enforcement of the U.S. Civil Rights Act of 1991, which prohibits discriminatory employment practices having a "disparate impact" on women or minority populations unless the practice is a business necessity, and enforcement of the Voting Rights Act of 1965, which prohibits discrimination in the electoral process; and for estimating race-specific population size and change. The definition and classification of race are essential for the enforcement of civil rights laws.

Since 1977, the Office of Management and Budget (OMB) has had the responsibility to establish the official classifications of race and ethnicity in the United States. The original OMB Statistical Directive 15 recognized four racial categories, namely, American Indians or Alaskan Natives, Asian or Pacific Islanders, Blacks, and Whites, and two ethnic groups (Hispanic Origin and Not of Hispanic Origin). These OMB classifications fit each person in the population into one racial and one ethnic category.

Following the 1990 census enumeration, the OMB racial classifications came under criticism. Critics argued that the directive did not reflect the increasing diversity of the population that resulted primarily from growth in immigration and in interracial marriages. These criticisms resulted in congressional hearings held in 1993 with Representative Thomas Sawyer as the chair of the subcommittee to conduct a review of the current categories for data on race and ethnicity.

In 1997, the OMB extended the number of racial categories by breaking apart the "Asian or Pacific Islander" category into two categories— "Asian" and "Native Hawaiian or Other Pacific Islander." They also changed the ethnic category from the single term "Hispanic" to "Hispanic or Latino." This change reflects regional usage, with "Hispanic" being common in the eastern portion of the United States and "Latino" being common in the western United States. OMB rejected the call for a "multiracial" category; however, it allowed individuals to report more than one race by allowing multiple responses to a single question in the 2000 census questionnaire.

## To Classify or Not to Classify?

Racial data are necessary for viewing the effects of racial prejudice on socioeconomic status and individual well-being. The current debate over the use of racial data is polarized around whether public policy should be race-blind or if racial data should be used aggressively to reverse the history of racial bias and neglect.

Racial data are essential if we are to achieve racial equality; however, this does not mean that every statistic should be presented racially. In fact, much that is presented as racial statistics has only helped aggravate the problem of racial conflict by making it appear that race causes people to behave or respond in particular ways.

Racial classification of data based on "benign prejudice" or racial justice is just as political as classification inspired by malicious racial prejudice. In each instance it is political. However, there is no equivalence between a policy that is designed to perpetuate racial stratification and one that seeks racial justice by seeking to eradicate domination.

Contrasting perspectives have influenced decisions to collect racial data. One view, the major topic of the preceding chapters, is marked by an insistence on the essential biological reality of race. The second perspective, less influential historically than the first, rejects the legitimacy of racial stratification and white supremacy. It insists that race is a social construct for the purpose of the social stratification that legitimates white supremacy.

The question whether, or under what circumstances, racial data should be collected and analyzed frames a context in which these competing perspectives converge. The matter is more complex than the polemical battle suggests. For debate over the proper response to racial data rages not only between white supremacists and nonracist scholars; it rages as well within the ranks of the scholars who pursue racial justice.[35] Two key concerns characterize this debate: (1) to engage in "race-blind" analysis (viewing race as an irrelevant trait); and (2) to pursue racial justice by "race-conscious" statistics. Both concerns are essential elements in deracializing society, but essential in different ways. The first focuses on the rights of individuals and the social processes of the status quo and does not pay attention to history. The second concern considers the social disparity caused by racial stratification and focuses on opportunities and outcomes within a historical context. The tension revolves around the pursuit of racial justice by violating the desired race-blindness.

I am not suggesting that we ignore differences in population composition or how the environment impacts these differences. Why not eliminate race as a proxy for social economic and biological processes? Typically researchers use race as a proxy for biological or other traits. By proxy, I mean scholars believe that race is related (statistically correlated) with some other trait (like intelligence or crime). We may all react to people on the basis of traits that we believe they possess and that we think are related with those traits in which we are primarily interested.

Racial classification came of age as part of the racial legacy that partitioned the population into upper- and lower-status persons, beginning with colonialism and slavery, thriving through Reconstruction, Jim Crow, and other forms of apartheid. Applying the concept of race uncritically continues to reflect the biases that gave rise to the classification itself.

Supporters of both race-blind public policy and a race-conscious program have resorted to racial statistics to refute each other. Nonracist and racist alike have regularly resorted to racial data in an effort to advance racist arguments and to refute racist arguments without acknowledging the biases already infused in the notion of race. By employing racial data in their arguments, without challenging the basis of the construction of race, public policy advocates of both camps may have legitimated inequalities based on race. Statistical scholarship has always been part of the profane world of public policy and thus cannot be judged by ahistorical or decontextual appeals to race-blind policies. In the future we may be better off if we phase out the use of racial data. However, to stop collecting racial data prematurely in a racially stratified society would be like *putting the cart before the horse*. A first step could be to change how we interpret racial statistics. Although racial statistics have been used to justify racial stratification, recasting them for racial justice can benefit and has benefited both science and subordinated racial groups.

Researchers employ observational records to define abstract concepts like race. The researchers or the subject (as in self-administered surveys or censuses) can make the observation; however, the researchers and the purpose of their study determine the meaning of the record. This is how empirical research reifies race. If we have records of racial classification, the population of races rather than the population of persons is open to statistical investigation; yet in social statistics it is always a mistake to think of a population of races as a genetic population. A population of races in this sense is a statistical concept based on a crude system of measurement that has been politically constructed.[36]

Whether we ought to authorize the collection of racial data and how we should analyze these data are important questions. To avoid trivializing the issue to a simple question of language, consider the practical issue of how racial statistics are analyzed. This is the subject of the last chapter.

# CHAPTER SEVEN

## Deracializing the Logic of Social Statistics

### Causation

Much of the field of statistics developed as the study of population variation, and most social statisticians are primarily concerned with the cause of this variation.[1] Discussions of causation in social statistics accelerated after Otis Duncan's introduction of path analysis in 1966.[2] Within these discussions, explanation, prediction, and causation are often mistakenly seen as synonymous. In the following, I will address myself specifically to the use of race as a cause in social statistics. For the most part, the analysis extends with no difficulty to gender.

In statistical analysis the issue of causation is not a simple matter. In theory, causal relations between social processes like race and economic phenomena always run the risk of being circular.[3] Thus, as a rule, social statisticians ignore the discussions about the meaning of race and the implications this meaning has for their statistical models.

Researchers typically use selected variables in a statistical model that purports to correspond to a poorly explained substantive theory. They then use some data to estimate the parameters of the model, and these parameter estimates and their functions give the effects of interest. However, this strategy makes too many unsubstantiated assumptions.

Deriving a statistical model of social relationships requires an elaborate theory that states explicitly and in detail the variables in the system, how these variables are causally interrelated, the functional form of their relationships, and the statistical quality and traits of the error terms. Once we have this theoretical model we could estimate a regression model.[4] Rarely, however, does social science research provide the level of theoretical detail necessary to derive a statistical model in this manner.

The alternative is a data-driven process. To derive a statistical model from data we assume the model is a black box and "test" it against our empirical results. From this perspective, data analysis is synonymous with social research.[5] The statistical model is raised to the substantive level, and the statistical equations provide the causal model and the causal theory of society. Data-driven statistical modeling perverts the substantive basis of theory and seeks to reformulate social reality as a mathematical equation.

Both the theory- and data-driven statistical models attempt to provide a parsimonious and generalizable account for the phenomenon under investigation. Statistical models attempt to provide a rigorous basis, rooted in abstract statistical theory, for determining when a causal relationship exists between two or more variables in a model. However, unless we start with prior knowledge about the causal relationship, the calculation of the regression equation refers to a regression model and its system of equations, not to the "real" world that the model cannot purport to define empirically.

There is a tendency for social statisticians to gloss over the causal and racial concepts in their research. They usually conceptualize race as an individual attribute. Racial classification typically occurs at birth but in some societies can change during a person's lifetime. When an individual's race can change, race is not an attribute but a dynamic characteristic dependent on other social circumstances. In the United States and South Africa, an individual's race is assumed not to change and thus is considered an attribute reflecting racial stratification. As such, social statisticians may have measured racial classification "correctly." The major error is in how race has been interpreted. I am suggesting a new language to express things that our current language handles inadequately. This new language attempts to increase the efficiency of communication about the statistical analysis of race.

The statistical definition of causation is limited by the lack of an explicit notion of an underlying process at the observational level stating how the variables in the system are causally related and the form of this relationship beyond that involved in the data under analysis. Such explanations are not the "true" underlying process but rather relate the phenomenon under study to knowledge at a different level (for example, relating a demographic finding to some biological process or, as David Cox notes, relating "an epidemiological finding to some biochemical or immunological process").[6]

Historically, Fisher demonstrated that Galton's statistical law of regression on heredity was in fact driven by knowledge (or processes) at a different level—at the Mendelian genetic level.[7] Galton was not aware of the genetic processes that defined the causal relationship he observed in his regression of heredity. Without Mendelian genetics, Galton's statistical results refer to a regression model and its system of equations, not to the "real" world that Galton thought it empirically defined.

## Causal Effects versus Causal Theories

One way to avoid Galton's error is to distinguish clearly between causal effects and causal theories. Causal effects can be observed in a random experiment, and in principle they can be estimated in observational studies.[8] A causal effect is a comparison of two or more potential responses that are observed from each individual in the population. A causal theory "is a scientific theory describing aspects of the various biological, chemical, physical, or social processes by which the treatment produces its effects."[9] Causal theories present principles that explain existing evidence and the processes that produce this evidence. A causal effect is the effect of a factor on a given response variable, whereas causal theories consider how and why the effect operates. Causal effects are more important in experimental studies. In experimental studies causal theories can be called into question if they contradict the results of the study.

The causal theory serves a more fundamental purpose in social statistics. If the causal theory is contradicted by the results of a well-designed study, and the causal theory is supported by evidence from other studies and by well-developed arguments or perspectives, questions can arise regarding the assumption of the method.[10] Yet, many social statisticians give little if any attention to the causal theory of their research. And rarely have the implications of this issue for racial statistics been systematically considered.

Causal theories are not the opposite of causal effects. Rather, causal effects are an essential part of causal theories, since causal theories should be based on all known information about the subject being studied.[11] Causal theories attempt to predict events beyond those observed; however, they also deal with known empirical information about the subject that includes what is known about causal effects. In this I am suggesting a probabilistic view toward understanding causation. And, as Lieberson states, "specifying that a given set of conditions will alter the likelihood of a given outcome, not only will the reality of social life be correctly described, but we will also be freed from assuming that negative evidence automatically means a theory is wrong."[12]

Statistical methods and the technology for their application have increased our ability to evaluate the accuracy of our research results. However, evaluating the accuracy of causal effects is not equivalent to determining the relevance of these results for our causal theory. The developments in statistical methods and technology have improved our understanding of how to perform statistical analysis. Yet, most research continues to lack a clear sense of when a causal theory is supported or undermined by the results of research. Usually researchers can decide if the data are consistent with causal effects, but we are less able to determine how much the results strengthen or weaken our confidence in the causal theory.

Causal effect research is important for advancing our understanding of society. The problem occurs when we treat such research as the examination of a causal theory or when the methods are not sufficiently critical.

I would like to suggest a reconsideration of racial statistics in light of these distinctions between causal theory and causal effects and developments in statistical analysis. In so doing, I would like to suggest that we incorporate the theory of manipulative causation into racial statistics. I must be explicit in this suggestion of manipulative causation so that I can present the foundational elements of the causal process in statistical modeling and exemplify the problem with race as a cause in such models.

## Manipulation as Causation

The cause of a given effect must necessarily be revised as our understanding about the phenomenon being analyzed increases. For example, at one point Western scientists thought that bacteria caused disease. With further investigation it was observed that the toxins that the bacteria produced, not the bacteria themselves, caused the disease. After some time it was observed that in fact certain chemical reactions are the "real causes" of diseases. And, as we dig deeper and deeper and our knowledge about disease increases, our view of the *cause* of this given effect is subject to revision. Thus, any formal theory of causation is stronger if it begins with the effects of given causes. Therefore, the appropriate question is not Do bacteria cause disease? but rather, What is the effect of bacteria on disease? or What happens to disease as different bacteria are introduced?

Researchers revise their interpretation of race as a cause of a given effect on the basis of different causal assumptions or theoretical arguments. For example, different scholars have argued that genetics, or culture, or discrimination cause racial stratification.

Because most social science researchers study causal effects for the purpose of making inferences about the effects of manipulations to which groups of individuals in a population have been or might be exposed, causes are only things that can, in theory, be manipulated or altered. This recognition forces us to consider the ability to vary of the individuals or units we study. This type of clarity is essential yet absent in most policy-oriented social research, in which decisions to manipulate the real world often depend on social researchers' causal inferences. A lack of clarity in the statistical analysis of racial processes has contributed in great measure to the confusion about how to resolve issues of racial stratification.

The language of causation originates in the experimental framework of modeling causal inference.[13] Probability is the mathematical language of causal modeling in statistics. Statistically, causation has a particular meaning. Investigators are concerned with the presence of causal connections, with the relative strengths of those connections, and with ways of inferring those connections from social data. Probability theory provides the logical context for statistical analysis. For example, if $A$ stands for the statement "Jesse L. Jackson will seek the nomination for president in year 2004," then $P(A|K)$ stands for my belief in the event described by $A$ given a body of knowledge or information described by $K$, which could include my assumptions about racial politics discussed in the preceding chapters.

Measuring the effects of causes is done in the context of another cause, hence $X$ causes $Z$ relative to some other cause that includes everything but $X$. In the context of causal inference, each individual in the population must be potentially exposable to any of the causes. And, as the statistician Paul Holland notes, "the schooling a student receives can be a cause, in our sense, of the student's performance on a test, whereas the student's race or gender cannot."[14] For example, being an African American should not be understood as the cause of a student's performance on a test, despite the fact that being African American can be a very reliable basis for predicting test performance. The logic of causal inference itself should give every nonpartisan scholar reason to avoid flamboyant rhetoric about the genetic-based cognitive causes for racial and gender stratification.

To see this point of view in a social context, consider the following nonexperimental study, in which causation assumes only two causes, denoted by $t$ (private school) and $c$ (public school). Now let $P$ be a variable that indicates the cause to which each individual in the population, $U$, is exposed. In this case $P = t$ indicates that the individual is exposed to $t$ (private school). In social statistics $P$ is generally determined by factors beyond the researchers' control. The point here is that the value of $P_u$ could have been different for each individual in the population. That is, in this example, the researcher does not determine who attends private school; yet each individual theoretically could have attended private school.

The response variable $Y$ (test scores) measures the effect of the cause and has values that are theoretically determined after exposure to the cause. Causes have effects for the reason that the particular cause, $t$ or $c$, to which each individual has been exposed, potentially affects the values of $Y$. The potential responses are denoted as $Y_t$ and $Y_c$. For any given individual in the population denoted as $u$, we interpret the response variable $Y_t u$ as the value of the response that would be observed if the student attends private school and $Y_c u$ as the value of the response that would be observed for the same individual if she attends public school.

Finally, the effect of the cause "public versus private school" on each individual as measured by $Y$ (test scores) and related to the cause of not attending private school is the difference between $Y_t u$ and $Y_c u$, and is expressed by the algebraic difference $Y_t u - Y_c u$. This represents the causal effect of private school relative to public school on each individual in the population as measured by the test scores.

In social statistics, inferences about causal effects are statistical inferences about effects on collections of individuals in the population. For our example, the average causal effect of private school relative to public school is denoted as $T$ over the population $U$ and is the expected value of the difference $Y_t u - Y_c u$ over the individual $u$ in the population $U$.[15]

This experimental model contains three variables $P$, $Y_t u$, and $Y_c u$; however, only $P$ and $Y_p$ are observed. Remember, it is $P$ that determines which value— $Y_t u$ or $Y_c u$—is observed for a given individual. If $P_u = t$, then $Y_t u$ is observed, or if $P_u = c$, then $Y_c u$ is observed, and the observed response on individual $u$ is $Y_{pu} u$.

Inferences in social statistics employ (usually implicitly) a model that corresponds to the statistical model outlined above. To further illustrate these points, I offer an example. To estimate the effect, we can compute the mean difference in subsequent test scores between private school and public school students. This is "true" when $T$ is independent of subsequent test scores (under either treatment).[16] If $T$ is not independent of subsequent test scores, the researcher would have a good estimate of $E(Y_t u \mid T = t)$ but not $E(Y_t u)$. In this case the mean difference in test scores between public and private school students estimates the actual average difference between the two groups and not the average effect. We would have what economists call selection bias.

Increasingly, statisticians agree that in social statistical analysis (observational studies, quasi experiments, social surveys, etc.) only those variables that can be manipulated conceptually are eligible to represent causal processes. It must make sense in the context under examination that for any individual the causal variable might have been different from the value actually taken. Thus, race is not a causal variable but rather an intrinsic property of the individual. If we accept the perspective of manipulation as causation, racial change (i.e., passing from black to white in the United States or from *preto* [black] to *pardo* [brown] in Brazil), racial prejudice, and possible racial discriminatory employment or payment practices are exceptions.

Race and gender as unalterable characteristics of individuals are not causal variables in inferential statistical analysis. Statisticians have questioned and criticized the use of such attributes—unalterable properties of individuals—in inferential statistical models.[17] Most social statisticians, however, continue to treat race and sex as an individual attribute in their inferential models. *Statistical models that present race as a cause are really statements of association between the racial classification and a predictor or explanatory variable across individuals in a population. To treat these models as causal or inferential is a form of racial reasoning.* The study of association is important for the advancement of social science research. The study of association helps to establish the basis for empirical prediction and helps in the isolation of conditional independence structures, which may provide the basis for developing causal explanations.

## From Causation to Association: One Step Back

According to the causal theory of manipulative causation, an unalterable characteristic cannot be a cause in inferential statistical models. Causal statements involving unalterable characteristics are really statements of association between the values of an attribute and a response variable across individuals in the population.

I begin with a population-based model of associational inference involving race.[18] This statistical model relates the distribution of two variables over a population. Again, I am explicit in this section so that I can present the foundational elements of the suggested clarification of race in statistical modeling.

A population-based statistical model starts with a population of units. You will recall that an individual in a population is denoted by $u$. Individuals are the basic objects of investigation. In this discussion human subjects are the basic units. A variable is a characteristic or function defined on every individual $u$ in population $U$. The basic elements of social statistical models are a population of units and variables defined on these units.

For example, suppose for each unit $u$ in population $U$ there is an associated value of $Y_u$ of a variable $Y$. Also suppose that $Y$ is a variable of interest, and we want to understand why the values of $Y$ vary over the units in the population. $Y$ is the variable to be explained. In associational inference we discover how the values of $Y$ are associated with the values of other variables defined on the units in the population. Now let race be $R$, another variable defined on the population. I distinguish $R$ from $Y$ by referring to it as an attribute of the units in $U$. In a more general sense $R$ could be any unalterable characteristic of units in the population, like gender. In this context the meaning of race takes on added importance. Both race and $Y$ are on an equal footing, since they are both variables defined on the population. $R$ is analogous to variable $P$, mentioned above, but with the essential difference that $R_u$ indicates a property or characteristic of $u$, whereas $P_u$ refers to exposure to a specific cause. In my example the value of race could not have been different, whereas the value of $P_u$ for each individual could have been different.

Probabilities, distributions, and expected values of the variables race and $Y$ are computed over the population. A probability in this case is equal to a proportion of units in the population. The expected value of a variable is the average value over all of the population. And the conditional expected values are averages over subsets of units, where each subset is defined by conditioning in the values of variables. In this sense social statistical models are population-based.

If we let $Y$ equal some variable of interest (such as intelligence or income) and $R$ equal race, then the most detailed level of measurement we can have in this model is the values of $Y$ and $R$ for each of the individuals in the population. The joint distribution of $Y$ and $R$ over the population, $U$, is specified by the probability of $Y$ being equal to $y$ and of $R$ being equal to $r$, which equals the proportion of individuals, $u$, in the population for which $Y_u = y$ and $R_u = r$. In more formal notation, we can write this probability statement as $\mathbf{Pr}(Y = y, R = r)$. $\mathbf{Pr}$ is short for *probability*.

The conditional distribution of $Y$ given $R$ is specified by the conditional probability for $Y$ being equal to $y$ given that $R$ is equal to $r$. In more formal terms this means that the $\mathbf{Pr}(Y = y \mid R = r) = \mathbf{Pr}(Y = y, R = r)/\mathbf{Pr}(R = r)$. This describes how the distribution of $Y$ values changes over the population as race varies. In the social sciences a typical associational parameter is the regression of $Y$ on $R$, that is, the conditional expectation: $E(Y \mid R = r)$.

Associational inference involves descriptive statistics and consists of making statistical inferences (estimates, tests, posterior distributions, etc.) about associational parameters relating $Y$ and $R$ on the basis of data gathered about $Y$ and $R$ from individuals in the population. For example, it is usually a mistake to use the association between race and intelligence as evidence of a "causal link" between them. The data involved in this debate are purely associational. Most of these studies ascertain only racial status and test results on sets of subjects.

I am suggesting that in this case race be considered an individual attribute rather than something that can be manipulated. In the context of research on intelligence, one cannot be more or less of one race; such a notion is impossible to measure, because race is thought to be an unalterable characteristic. Thus, one cannot use race as a cause in statistical analysis.

## A Hypothetical Example

The problem with race as a variable in social statistics might be clearer in a hypothetical example.[19] Consider two examples that involve causal statements:

(A)  *European-origin populations do well on tests because of their race.*

(B)  *African Americans do well in college because of the affirmative action taken by universities.*

The meaning of *because* is different for each of these statements. The effect, doing well, is the same in each statement. In *A* the cause is assigned to an *attribute* that European-origin individuals possess. This is the underlying thesis of *The Bell Curve,* by Herrnstein and Murray. In *B,* the cause is assigned to an *activity* performed by others. The causal statement in *B* is the subject of *The Shape of the River: Long-Term Consequences of Considering Race in College and University Admissions,* by William G. Bowen and Derek Bok. The causal statement in *A* suggests that, in some sense, whites do better on tests than nonwhites. This statement presents race as a determining factor in test taking. The causal statement in *B* means that, without the advantage of affirmative action, African Americans would not do as well as they do. Statement *B* presents a comparison of the responses to two causes. In *A,* all that can be discussed is association; it is difficult to make a connection between the data being analyzed and human agency. Race is an attribute. This use of race is consistent with the eugenic heritage of racial statistics, but the underlying logic is problematic. According to the theory of manipulative causation, we can measure the causal effects in example *B.* Example *B* allows us to see human and social agency at work on a particular outcome. In this context, racial statistics that allow human and social agency (example *B*) differ both methodologically and theoretically from those that view race as an intrinsic attribute (example *A*).

Hypothetical example *B* mentioned above is easily interpreted in terms of measuring causal effects from the perspective of manipulative causation. The interpretation is that, without the advantage of affirmative action taken by the university, African Americans would not do as well as they do. It implies a comparison between the responses to two causes and is appropriate for causal inference. In example *B,* a biologized view of race is not an issue. Yet, as seen in our substantive examples in part II, it is not unusual for individuals to look at hypotheses like that in *A* and treat them like that in *B*.

Association may not prove causation; however, it may provide the basis for support of a causal theory. Association is evidence of causation when it is buttressed with other knowledge and supporting evidence. When we discuss the effect of race, we are less mindful of the larger world in which the path to success or failure is routinely influenced by other contingencies or circumstances.

Usually, social statisticians argue that race causes a person to be in a certain condition or state. To argue that race causes an individual to make less money on average or to have less intelligence on average is arguing either that race causes income or intelligence like smoking causes cancer or that race is a proxy for some genetic relationship. I am suggesting an alternative perspective. I am suggesting that we place our statistical analysis of race within a historical and social context. It is not a question of how race causes disadvantage and discrimination. The real issue is the way the society responds to an individual's race. The question has to do with society itself, not the innate makeup of individuals. Racial statistics have been used primarily for the justification of racial stratification. To alter this misuse we must recast our perception of how we think about what race and causation are in society.

## Probable Causation

Some statisticians reject the theory of manipulative causation and thus the possibility of our establishing causation with social statistics. Statistical models are assumed to generate results that show a significant discrepancy or difference from a certain hypothesized state or process (namely, in this case, the hypothesis that social status is in no way influenced by race) or, and on the other hand, results that show no significant discrepancy from this hypothesis. Even if we accept race as a causal factor, it cannot be proven to have caused social status by the use of statistical analysis alone. In order to establish causation we must go beyond the data and results at hand. As Fisher noted:

> In relation to any experiment we may speak of this hypothesis as the "null hypothesis," and it should be noted that the null hypothesis is never proved or established, but is possibly disproved, in the course of experimentation. Every experiment may be said to exist only in order to give the facts a chance of disproving the null hypothesis.[20]

One study cannot prove anything. It can contribute to our understanding of causal theories, but it can never give us an understanding of the "real world." Support or lack of support for any particular hypothesis "does not authorize us to make any statement about the hypothesis in question in terms of mathematical probability, while, none the less, it does afford direct guidance as to what elements we may reasonably incorporate in any theories we may be attempting to form in explanation of objectively observable phenomena."[21] Fisher was concerned primarily with experimental analysis. And, with the exception of social psychology, rarely is social science research based on experiments. Yet, the experimental notion of causal inference is the implicit guide in the selection of observations in quasi-experimental research and in the model selection, design, and statistical analysis of nonexperimental data from sample surveys.[22] Most social scientists use experimental language when interpreting empirical results, thereby entailing a commitment to the experimental mode of analysis.[23] My point is that social statisticians must appreciate the consequences of adopting the experimental model as a guide in the design, collection, analysis, and interpretation of social science data. If this is done, we might be more careful about what we call a cause, and then no single finding will be considered proof of causation. As Lieberson notes, each study "consistent or inconsistent with a theory is incomplete information; what is needed is the frequency distribution for a set of observations."[24]

## Racial Statistics for Racial Justice

Even if we insist that race is a social construct for the purpose of racial stratification, we can use statistical analysis in the pursuit of racial justice. I agree with the race-conscious use of statistics. Statistical analysis can help focus our attention on opportunities and outcomes within a historical and social context. Rather than use race as a proxy, we can analyze racial stratification directly by focusing on discrimination. For example, consider the statistical analysis of racial discrimination.

Race, or more specifically the process of racialization, may be the stimulus for how racially classified individuals respond to or interact with one another. The examination of discrimination and prejudice provides a solution to the trap of racial reasoning. Probability enters this discussion in three ways. First, did an employer racially discriminate? Second, how do individuals use probability to shape their opinions about other persons? Third, what is the meaning of racial statistics that help individuals form these opinions?

Following the passage of civil rights legislation, the U.S. courts have embraced statistical evidence of racial discrimination.[25] The courts have looked to statistical analysis to decide on the substantiality of evidence of illegal discrimination. Consequently, some effort has been expended to understand the place of racial statistics in the legal process. As within other institutions legal statistics depend on a foundation of understanding statistical science in general and racial statistics in particular. Social statisticians have participated in the process as expert witnesses in adversary proceedings, and they have written about statistical discrimination as part of the statistical reasoning of employers.

The current use of statistical evidence in employment discrimination cases can be traced from *Giggs v. Duke Power Company,* where the Supreme Court established the idea of "disparate impact" as the basis for challenging employment selection procedures under Title VII of the Civil Rights Act.[26] As a consequence of the ruling in *Giggs,* the use of a qualifications test for employment that has a pass rate of African American applicants that is "substantially" less than that of whites is illegal unless the employer can demonstrate that the practice constitutes a "business necessity." Under this ruling the prima facie showing of disparate impact is sufficient for the plaintiff to prevail. Disparate impact cases depend on the interpretation of the term *substantial* and on how much disparity should be judged substantial. Disparate impact cases are by definition statistical.

In *International Brotherhood of Teamsters v. United States* (1977), the Supreme Court established the use of statistical evidence in cases alleging "disparate treatment." Disparate treatment cases require a showing of discriminatory intent, with the burden on the plaintiff. As with disparate impact cases, disparate treatment cases raise the question of deciding how large a disparity must be to demonstrate an inference of discrimination.

The introduction of statistical inference in the demonstration of employment discrimination first occured in *Castaneda v. Partida* in 1977. In *Castaneda,* a jury discrimination case involving the Texas "key man" system, the Supreme Court ruled that "if the difference between the expected value and the observed number is greater than two or three standard deviations, then the hypothesis that the jury drawing was random would be suspect to a social scientist."[27] This adoption of formal statistical language was important in this case, because the Mexican American jurors were almost 29 standard deviations.

These cases culminated in the *Hazelwood School District v. United States* case. In *Hazelwood*, 405 school teachers were hired by the defendant school district and only 15 were African American. The plaintiff, the United States, claimed that the population of St. Louis County was 15.4 percent African American. The defendant claimed that the relevant population of possible teachers did not include the city of St. Louis, reducing the population of teachers to 5.7 percent African American. In *Hazelwood,* the Supreme Court refers to "gross statistical disparities." The court remanded for a determination of whether the United States' position on the labor pool was correct. In this case, the Court ruled that "in a proper case" statistical evidence can suffice for a prima facie showing of employment discrimination. In *Hazelwood,* the court discussed the use of statistical tests of significance in employment discrimination cases.

Statistics alone cannot ascertain whether social reality is one thing or another. Thus, statistics alone cannot ascertain whether racial discrimination exists. For example, by definition, hiring does not proceed by random selection from a pool. Neither a standard significance test nor regression analysis alone can establish the presence of illegal racial discrimination. However, both a significance test and regression could serve as useful tools to establish benchmarks for the presence of discrimination.

For example, if the difference in black and white hire rates is small enough to have arisen by random sampling from the appropriate population, then we might conclude that there is not statistical evidence of racial discrimination. Such a conclusion would not, however, rule out the possibility that discriminatory hiring took place. The courts have tended to use statistical measures of discrimination with a practical understanding of their significance. Finding a statistically significant difference does not prove that the difference is the result of illegal racial discrimination. In order to establish illegal racial discrimination, one must show legally cognizable discrimination as well.

The use of racial statistics in legal cases can lead to substantial misunderstanding. The employment process and workplace require multiple variables for a basis of understanding. Understanding racial discrimination through regression analysis has increased following the Civil Rights movement. A feature of the use of regression analysis of employment discrimination is a condensed presentation or summary of complex information or numerical tables.[28]

Since no complete model of the economic process exists, the social statistician cannot completely predict the effects of discrimination on the system. The social statistician formulates models representing her uncertain knowledge about the relevant aspects of the reality of the economic system and computes posterior (subsequent) probabilities given the data at hand. For example, a model is constructed to examine the posterior distribution of the effects of discrimination in the context under study. The models should be constructed as an objective presentation of the evidence in favor of the proposed representations.

## Statistical Racism: Old Practice with a New Name

In statistical models of employment discrimination, the employer is also an actor in the formal system under consideration. The employer is the individual decision maker or person responsible for rewarding each employee. The employer's decision is the basic unit of analysis. The employer's decision to reward a particular employee with $Y_i$ produces a sample of $n$ such decisions and rewards: $Y_1, Y_2, \ldots Y_n$.[29] Social statisticians assume that nondiscriminatory employers determine employee productivity by processing the information available on each employee.[30]

The economic study of statistical racism exemplifies the problems inherent in racial statistics.[31] The causal factors in statistical racism are discriminatory practices by employers, not the races of the people involved.

It is important to distinguish between the "statistical" reasoning by an employer and the statistical reasoning discussed in this book, which focuses on social scientists engaged in a very different sort of statistical reasoning from that of an employer. All individuals discriminate when they make decisions; however, racial discrimination is not a benign form of discrimination. The econometric "theory" of statistical racism maintains that racial preference of an employer for a "white" job candidate over a "black" job candidate who is not known to differ in other respects might stem from the employer's previous statistical experience with the two groups. That is, the employer may have accumulated his or her own personal racial statistics about the productivity of different racial groups from past experience or socialization.

In my opinion, individual racial discrimination is best viewed as a form of domination. In some cases it is simply commensalism, and the impact of it on the victims is not beyond a minor nuisance. But at the society wide level, individual racial discrimination is a direct source of exploitation that prevents full participation in society. Whether such decisions are probabilistically or statistically based makes no difference. The only difference is the logical basis of how the individual made the race-based decision.

According to my argument, statistical racism is a difficult process to examine. An employer's assessment of the expected productivity of employees in less-favored groups may be wrong in a way that a longitudinal study could effectively demonstrate; however, such a study is still prohibitively expensive. Also, an employer's perspective may be invalid because it does not incorporate certain systemic mechanisms of other types of prejudice, such as the effect of higher rewards themselves on the productivity of employees in a less-favored race.

The issue of statistical discrimination could facilitate a better understanding of the practice of racial prejudice. Employers argue that they are not prejudiced against Africans (blacks). It's just that, for whatever reason, they are statistically (probabilistically) less qualified and/or less productive than those of European origin (whites). This might be interpreted as an honest attempt to assess productivity. Such employers are not only judgmental beyond the statistical evidence available to them but also capricious in regard to equality.

The sociological study of environmental racism also exemplifies the problems inherent in racial statistics. The analysis of environmental racism examines whether facilities for the treatment, storage, and disposal of hazardous wastes are located disproportionately in communities of the less favored race.[32] Although the study of statistical racism focuses on intentional prejudice and the study of environmental racism has focused on dumping prejudice, both depend on inequitable distributions as evidence of intentional prejudice. The causal factors in environmental racism are discriminatory practices by institutions in the location of hazardous waste sites, not the racial composition of the communities.

Is the behavior of judgmental employers economic? Is the dumping behavior of corporations economically driven? That is, are they simply making good business decisions? The answer to all of the above is yes.

In sum, an employer's racial judgment is simply a form of discrimination. In this case, equal opportunity is inhibited by racial prejudgment and is justified as being a scientific decision because the individual considered probability in coming to his or her decision. Profitability from racial discrimination is old news dating back to the days of slavery. The practice of environmental racism may also follow this pattern. Determining discrimination as a form of domination requires information beyond the statistical data but should remain at the core of how we interpret racial statistics.

Racial discrimination can result in racial inequality. Racial prejudice can cause racial inequality. Indeed, the purpose of racial discrimination is to justify racial stratification.[33] Lawrence Bobo has outlined areas in which racial attitudes play a role in the production and reproduction of racial inequality. He argues that prejudicial racial attitudes contribute to high unemployment faced by African Americans and to the perpetuation of residential segregation by race, in political elections, and in attitudes about public policy.[34] Statistical analyses must link the measurement of prejudice with the structural processes of discrimination in order to contribute to our understanding of racial stratification. These analyses must be placed in a context that helps us move beyond simple explanations, because such explanations become forms of justification.

# EPILOGUE

## Toward a New Analysis of Difference

The parents of social statistics are political arithmetic, mathematical statistics, and efforts to describe trends and patterns in social data. In the past this legacy has placed social statistics at the center of some of the most controversial issues of our time. These issues have ranged from Malthus's "Second Essay," in which he dealt with the Poor Laws in England, to our more recent discussions about the role of biology and inequality in population dynamics. Demographic structures and processes have become increasingly important for social science theory. Social statisticians are concentrating more on models that incorporate the entire causal process of population and social changes. Methodological and technological advances have allowed social statisticians to focus our research more on the time dimension of social processes, changes, and structures, and the micro- and macrolevel factors associated with human behavior. It is important that we return to the question of what difference means in this context of improved statistical techniques and technology.

A number of scholars are engaging in discussions that help us understand that race need not determine the structures that organize the distribution of life chances and well-being.[1] These scholars suggest a change in our perception of race and how we use it in our research. They suggest a view of racial difference that does not assume a monolithic and homogeneous objective. This new view embraces diversity, multiplicity, and heterogeneity.

Research on difference is not new in the history of social statistics, yet what makes it novel is how and what constitutes difference. How differ-

ence is viewed in statistical analysis and the ways that highlighting issues of difference (like age, race, gender, nation, biology, and region) are
increasingly new suggest a discontinuity from previous forms of statistical analysis.

A deracialized perspective has great potential for helping us to understand variations in population composition. In fact, if we deracialize our
analysis we could examine the cultural, biological, and social factors that
affect population differences without the mystery of race. If race is not
biological, then it is not a good proxy for understanding biological processes. If race is, as I have argued, a signifier for the impact of racial stratification, then we may well learn much by developing better measures of
social and economic processes. Cultural differences among different populations do exist; however, race is not a satisfactory measure of these differences. It is time for us to focus on the development of better measures
of cultural, social, biological, and economical processes.

We must demystify aspects of currently accepted notions of racial statistics by showing the extent that this research has been shaped by ex-
trinsic factors such as the interests and social position of particular writers and debated issues long since forgotten. Most research on race has
not yet come to terms with the full range of problems to which the idea
was originally addressed, and, in this way, we may be led to new ideas or
to new applications by returning to the source of the idea.

To this end, I have argued that race is a social construct. Within this
construct, the person of color does not exist outside his or her other-
ness.[2] It is the international belief in race as real that makes race real in
its social consequences. Nevertheless, a belief is not a fact, and we should
question how and why we believe something to be real. My desire is not
to diminish the social significance of race but to bring into view the reality of racial stratification, the reality of the experience of race, and the
rationality of those who study racial dynamics and processes. If race were
to exist only on its condition of being believed, its life would have ceased
long ago.

It is in the collective belief that humans are divided into races, built
into the experience of everyday life, that the idea of race to which we are
subordinate gains its place in the "real world." In order to understand
and to evaluate who humans are, we must look beyond our own personal
or historical experience. And in order to change the place of race in the

world, we must change not merely our own thinking but also the social conditions of everyday life that facilitate beliefs in race.

## A Final Word

In the preceding pages I have attempted to clarify the meaning of racial formation with a sharper focus on the concepts of racial statistics by directing our attention to our own acts in the use of these concepts, to our powers in carrying out our research, and so forth. This is not a book on race in the same sense as other racial research is. Rather, it proposes a technique to produce in us a new state of consciousness in which we describe in detail the basic concepts we use in racial research or grasp other basic concepts yet to be uncovered. Empirically oriented persons have no reason to reject such reflections, for that would imply that their empiricism is, in reality, an apriority with its sign reversed.

Not only is there no unbiased reason for rejecting reflection, but also, on the contrary, we can conclude with reasons in its favor. If one considers the development of racial statistics, one notices that it has proceeded in two directions: it consists, on the one hand, of classifying humanity according to race and, on the other hand, of the development of a language of probability to explain the racial differences observed in a racialized population. With respect to the development in this second direction, one can justifiably say that racial statistics has passed through various states of understanding; for example, one can say that a higher state of understanding was attained when social statisticians applied probability to the analysis of social processes and, similarly, at the moment when Fisher formalized a logic of statistical inference.

Now one may view the whole development of racial statistics as a systematic and conscious extension of what social statisticians did when they developed in the first direction. The success of the procedure is indeed astonishing and greater than expected a priori: after all, it has led to the racial basis of our identity in recent times.

We are not born as members of racial groups. The conflicts among racial groups cannot be explained in terms of fixed invariables like biological identity. Otherwise, the problems of racial conflict would always be the same at all times and places; and further, there would never be any solution to racial conflict except through a change in that which is permanently fixed. The solution to racial conflict must be sought through a change in how we view and practice race and a change in how race is used in the social world.

Most racial statistics lack a critical evaluation of racist structures that encourage pathological interpretations. These pathological interpretations have had a profound impact on our causal theories and statistical methods. Our theories of society, not our empirical evidence, guide how we interpret racial data. Fancy statistics come and go. We need a better understanding of how our statistical methods relate to society. I am not suggesting that we discredit research findings because they lead to unwanted political conclusions. I am suggesting that we have a better understanding of the political and theoretical ideas that motivate different interpretations of social science results. We must recognize that the researcher is part of what he or she observes. We do not passively or objectively observe the statistical universe as scientific outsiders.

# Notes

## Introduction

1. Michael Omi and Howard Winant "define *racial formation* as the sociohistorical process by which racial categories are created, inhabited, transformed, and destroyed" (*Racial Formation in the United States: From the 1960s to the 1990s* [New York: Routledge, 1994], 55). According to political scientist Melissa Nobles, "race is not something that language simply describes, it is something that is created through language and institutional practices. As discourse, race creates and organizes human differences in politically consequential ways" (*Shades of Citizenship: Race and the Census in Modern Politics* [Stanford: Stanford University Press, 2000], 12).

2. See Alfred Tarski, *Introduction to Logic and to the Methodology of Deductive Sciences* (1941; 2d ed.: Oxford University Press, 1946; reprint of 2d ed., New York: Dover, 1995), chapter 1.

3. My view is similar to that of Lewis R. Gordon when he argues that racial classification "is a form of value built upon racism. We therefore assert that one of the attitudes of an antiblack would be that white people and black people are essentially white and black. People in between are sometimes regarded as either more black or less white, though such subtlety of difference seems to be present only in 'black' societies. For the most part, whiteness is pure, and all others are colored down the line to blackest. The initial encounter with this attitude does not automatically entail one's being in bad faith. But the preservation of this attitude is a form of bad faith. A child may be shown that one person is white and another is black. But for the child to live with this distinction requires an uncritical attitude toward these distinctions that can transform his attitude, as he goes on in years, into bad faith. This is because the distinctions themselves cannot sustain the force of existential criticism. The adult who introduces racist notions may be a figure in bad faith" (*Bad Faith and Antiblack Racism* [Atlantic Highlands, N.J.: Humanities Press, 1995], 94).

4. Below I address the role of psychology in the development of racial perspectives among social statisticians; however, the psychological definition of race has tended to depend on either statistical or genetic perspectives. Also, although they

are mentioned here, I will delay a more detailed discussion of the statistical and de-mographic perspectives until part II.

5. Eugenics is the study of factors capable of improving the physiological and intellectual status of a race by their effect on the conditions of human reproduction and on the physical environment. I discuss eugenics in detail in parts II and III.

6. "In its simplest sense the Enlightenment was the creation of a new framework of ideas about man, society, and nature, which challenged existing conceptions rooted in a traditional world-view, dominated by Christianity. The key domain in which Enlightenment intellectuals challenged the clergy, who were the main group involved in supporting existing conceptions of the world, concerned the traditional view of nature, man, and society which was sustained by the Church's authority and its mo-nopoly over the information media of the time" (Peter Hamilton, "The Enlighten-ment and the Birth of Social Science," in *Modernity: An Introduction to Modern Societies,* ed. Stuart Hall, David Held, Don Hubert, and Kenneth Thompson (Cam-bridge: Blackwell Publishers, 1996), 24.

To grasp the significance of modernization to the founders of European social science, the reader is invited to read three classical texts: Karl Marx, *Capital: A Cri-tique of Political Economy,* trans. Samuel Moore and Edward Aveling (1887; reprint, New York: International Publishers, 1976); Max Weber, *The Protestant Ethic and the Spirit of Capitalism,* trans. Talcott Parsons (1920–1921; reprint, New York: Charles Scribner's Sons, 1976); Émile Durkheim, *The Division of Labor in Society,* trans. George Simpson (1926; reprint, New York: Free Press, 1964).

7. Ibid. Also see Stanley B. Greenberg, *Race and State in Capitalist Development: Comparative Perspectives* (New Haven: Yale University Press, 1980), chapters 1 and 2, esp. pp. 9–11; and Harry Liebersohn, "Weber's Historical Concept of National Iden-tity," in *Weber's Protestant Ethic: Origins, Evidence, Contexts,* ed. Hartmut Lehmann and Guenther Roth (New York: Cambridge University Press, 1987), 123–31.

8. In *Economy and Society,* Weber asserted: "We shall call 'ethnic groups' those human groups that entertain a subjective belief in their common descent because of similarities of physical type or of customs or both, or because of memories of colo-nization and migration; this belief must be important for the propagation of group formation; conversely, it does not matter whether or not an objective blood relation-ship exists. Ethnic membership (*Gemeinsamkeit*) differs from the kinship group pre-cisely by being a presumed identity, not a group with concrete social action, like the latter. In our sense, ethnic membership does not constitute a group; it only facili-tates group formation of any kind, particularly in the political sphere. On the other hand, it is primarily the political community, no matter how artificially organized, that inspires the belief in common ethnicity. This belief tends to persist even after the disintegration of the political community, unless drastic differences in the cus-tom, physical type, or, above all, language exist among its members" (Max Weber, *Economy and Society* [1956; reprint, Berkeley: University of California Press, 1978], 389). Weber expressed some of the most advanced thinking on the issue of race among nineteenth-century social scientists of European origin. For Weber racial identity was a particular form of ethnic identity, and both "dissolved" in the context of the nation. Also, Weber's article suggests a heavy debt to Du Bois. In fact, Weber was himself influence by and predisposed to Du Bois's work (see his letter to Du Bois in 1905 in W. E. B. Du Bois, *The Correspondence of W. E. B. Du Bois,* vol. 1 (Amherst: University of Massachusetts Press, 1973), 106. Yet, his notion of ethnic

group identity differed significantly from Du Bois's idea of racial identity. Du Bois was careful to distinguish between ethnic and racial identity and social processes.

9. Racial stratification means "the differentiation of a given population into hierarchically superposed racial groups." Its basis and very essence consist in an unequal distribution of rights and privileges among the members of a society. For a thoughtful and provocative review of this perspective see Eduardo Bonilla-Silva, "Rethinking Racism: Toward a Structural Interpretation," *American Sociological Review* 62 (1997): 465–80.

10. W. E. B. Du Bois, *Black Reconstruction in America, 1860–1880* (1935; reprint, New York: Atheneum, 1992), 30; see also W. E. B. Du Bois, *The Souls of Black Folk* (Chicago: A. C. McClurg, 1903).

11. Oliver C. Cox, *Caste, Class and Race: A Study in Social Dynamics* (New York: Doubleday, 1948), 317–44.

12. I am not trying to reduce race to a simple reflection of historical circumstances. My formulation of race does not view the material forms and necessities of society as an explanation. Here I agree with Émile Durkheim's formulation regarding religion. Durkheim argued: "I do indeed take it to be obvious that social life depends on and bears the mark of its material base, just as the mental life of the individual depends on the brain and indeed on the whole body. But collective consciousness is something other than a mere epiphenomenon of its morphological base, just as individual consciousness is something other than a mere product of the nervous system. If collective consciousness is to appear, a sui generis synthesis of individual consciousnesses must occur. The product of this synthesis is a whole world of feelings, ideas, and images that follow their own laws once they are born. They mutually attract one another, repel one another, fuse together, subdivide, and proliferate; and none of these combinations is directly commanded and necessitated by the state of the underlying reality. Indeed, the life thus unleashed enjoys such great independence that it sometimes plays about in forms that have no aim or utility of any kind, but only for the pleasure of affirming itself" (Émile Durkheim, *The Elementary Forms of Religious Life*, trans. Karen E. Fields [1912; New York: Free Press, 1995], 426). Although Durkheim did not write directly about the problems of racial stratification or white racism, the idea of the "social fact" provides a deep intellectual and theoretical line of connection to many contemporary issues.

13. Social statistics are either deductive or inductive. Deductive social statistics are the focus of demographers. Demographic analysis focuses on estimating population processes. Inductive social statistics are the focus of inferential statisticians. Inferential statistics are based on empirical induction. Statistical induction is the process of reasoning from a part to a whole, from the particular to the general, from the individual to the universal, from the sample to the population.

14. See Alain Desrosières, *The Politics of Large Numbers: A History of Statistical Reasoning*, trans. Camille Naish (1993; Cambridge, Mass.: Harvard University Press, 1998), 324–37.

15. Ibid, 337.

16. John H. Stanfield II notes, "Few social scientists realize that the mundane racial categories they use in their research are actually grounded in folk beliefs derived from precolonial era thinking about the inherent superiority and inferiority of populations along phenotypic and genetic lines" (John H. Stanfield II, "Epistemological Considerations," in *Race and Ethnicity in Research Methods*, ed. John H.

Stanfield II and Rutledge M. Dennis [Newbury Park: Sage Publications, 1993], 17).
Also see: Allan Chase, *The Legacy of Malthus: The Social Costs of the New Scientific Racism* (Urbana: University of Illinois Press, 1980); William H. Tucker, *The Science and Politics of Racial Research* (Urbana: University of Illinois Press, 1994); Milton Terris, "Desegregating Health Statistics," *American Journal of Public Health* 63 (1973): 477–80; Nancy D. Fortney, "The Anthropological Concept of Race," *Journal of Black Studies* 8 (1977): 35–74; Richard Cooper, "A Note on the Biologic Concept of Race and Its Application in Epidemiologic Research," *American Heart Journal* 108, no. 3, part 2 (1984): 715–23; Doris Y. Wilkinson and Gary King, "Conceptual and Methodological Issues in the Use of Race as a Variable: Policy Implications," *Milbank Quarterly* 65 (1987), suppl. 1: 56–71; Albert H. Yee, Halford H. Fairchild, Fredric Weizmann, and Gail E. Wyatt, "Addressing Psychology's Problems with Race," *American Psychologist* 48 (1993): 1132–40; Norman B. Anderson and Cheryl A. Armstead, "Toward Understanding the Association of Socioeconomic Status and Health: A New Challenge for the Biopsychosocial Approach," *Psychosomatic Medicine* 57 (1995): 213–25; David R. Williams "Racism and Health: A Research Agenda," *Ethnicity and Disease* 6 (1996): 1–6; and Nobles, *Shades of Citizenship*.

17. My formulation of the relations of domination follows Orlando Patterson's conceptualization of slavery as a parasitic relationship: "Parasitism emphasizes the asymmetry of all such unequal relations: the degree to which the parasite depends on the host is not necessarily a direct measure of the extent to which the host is exploited in supporting the parasite. A parasite may be only partially dependent on its host, but this partial dependence may entail the destruction of the host. Or the host may be totally dependent on the parasite, but the parasitism may only partially influence the host—or may have no effects beyond being a minor nuisance, in which case the relation approaches what biologists call commensalism" (Orlando Patterson, *Slavery and Social Death: A Comparative Study* [Cambridge, Mass.: Harvard University Press, 1982], 335).

Patterson's definition allows us to place slave systems on a continuum from societies in which the enslaved populations face genocide to those in which the enslaved have access to social power. An implcation of this continuum is that African-origin populations may not have experienced the "most extreme" form of domination in the Americas.

18. For a recent example, see William Petersen, *Ethnicity Counts* (New Brunswick, N.J.: Transaction Publishers, 1997), 11–49.

19. For an interesting example of this issue as it relates to the underclass debate, see Stephen Steinberg, *Turning Back: The Retreat from Racial Justice in American Thought and Policy* (Boston: Beacon Press, 1995), chapter 6.

20. By African diaspora, I mean "the global dispersion (voluntary and involuntary) of Africans throughout history; the emergence of a cultural identity abroad based on origin and social condition; and the psychological or physical return to the homeland, Africa" (Joseph E. Harris, "Introduction," in *Global Dimensions of the African Diaspora*, ed. Joseph E. Harris [Washington, D.C.: Howard University Press, 1982], 3). My focus is on the African diaspora created by the European slave trade to the Americas.

21. W. E. B. Du Bois, *Black Folks: Then and Now* (1939; reprint, Millwood, N.Y.: Kraus-Thomson Organization, 1975), 92.

## 1.  Racial Domination

1.  Oliver C. Cox, *Caste, Class and Race: A Study in Social Dynamics* (New York: Doubleday, 1948), 322–45.

2.  Orlando Patterson, *Slavery and Social Death: A Comparative Study* (Cambridge, Mass.: Harvard University Press, 1982), vii.

3.  St. Clair Drake, *Black Folk Here and There: An Essay in History and Anthropology* (Los Angeles: University of California, Center for Afro-American Studies, 1987), vol. 2, chapter 7; also see Robert William Fogel, *Without Consent or Contract: The Rise and Fall of American Slavery* (New York: W. W. Norton, 1989), 22.

4.  Abdul Sheriff, *Slaves, Spices and Ivory in Zanzibar: Integration of an East African Commercial Empire into the World Economy, 1770–1873* (Dar es Salaam: Tanzania Publishing House, 1987), chapters 1, 2, and 3; Patterson, *Slavery and Social Death*; I. Hrbek, "Africa in the Context of World History," in *Africa from the Seventh to the Eleventh Century*, ed. M. El Fasi and I. Hbrek, vol. 3 of *General History of Africa* (Paris: UNESCO, 1988), 1–30. In fact, both Africans and Arabs brought large numbers of Europeans into the North African cities of Tangier, Algiers, Tunis, Tripoli, and Fez for purposes of enslavement. For a more detailed analysis of the transition from a multinational and "multiracial" to an exclusively African source of slaves, see Drake, *Black Folk Here and There*, vol. 2, chapter 7, esp. 232–36.

5.  Robin Blackburn, *The Making of New World Slavery: From the Baroque to the Modern, 1492–1800* (London: Verso, 1997), 77–78.

6.  "The Emperor Justinian drew up a late Roman legal code which was to have enduring authority. It summarily announced: 'Slaves are in the power of their masters; for we find that among all nations slaveowners have the power of life and death over their slaves, and whatever a slave earns belongs to his master.' If it was true—or nearly true—that 'all nations' had a conception of slavery, the specificity of Roman law was, on the one hand, the thoroughness with which it codified slaves as private property or chattels and, on the other, its formal lack of interest in the slave's ethnic or racial provenance. The Roman slave became part of the household of the owner; while slaves might be thought of as Greeks, Syrians, Britons or Germans, the institutions of slavery and manumission produced such a mingling of nations that after a generation or two, and sometimes less, the resulting population was comprised of Roman slaves and Roman freedmen or women. The combination of slavery and imperial rule fostered a distinctive Roman cosmopolitanism" (Blackburn, *The Making of New World Slavery*, 35).

7.  Ibid., 103–12.

8.  Ibid., 99–100.

9.  Ibid., 100.

10.  Drake, *Black Folk Here and There*, 2:234–36; Blackburn, *The Making of New World Slavery*, 111.

11.  Walter Rodney, *How Europe Underdeveloped Africa* (Washington, D.C.: Howard University Press, 1981); and Immanuel Wallerstein, *The Modern World-System I: Capitalist Agriculture and the Origins of the European World-Economy in the Sixteenth Century* (New York: Academic Press, 1974), chapter 5.

12.  Bernard Makhosezwe Magubane, *The Political Economy of Race and Class in South Africa,* (New York: Monthly Review Press, 1990), 29.

13. Eric Williams has noted that "[u]nder certain circumstances slavery has some obvious advantages. In the cultivation of crops like sugar, cotton and tobacco, where the cost of production is appreciably reduced on larger units, the slave owner, with his large-scale production and his organized slave gang, can make more profitable use of the land than the small farmer or peasant proprietor. For such staple crops, the vast profits can well stand the greater expense of inefficient slave labor. Where all the knowledge required is simple and a matter of routine, constancy and coop-eration in labor—slavery—is essential, until, by importation of new recruits and breeding, the population has reached the point of density and the land available for appropriation has been already apportioned. When the stage is reached, and only then, the expenses of slavery, in the form of the cost and maintenance of slaves, pro-ductive and unproductive, exceed the cost of hired laborers" (Eric Williams, *Capitalism and Slavery* [Chapel Hill: University of North Carolina Press, 1944], 6–7). See also Magubane, *The Political Economy of Race and Class in South Africa*, 4–5.

14. Drake, *Black Folk Here and There*, 2:232–36; Drake's thesis has been strongly supported by Robin Blackburn's research. See Blackburn, *The Making of New World Slavery*, 33, 62–64, 77–79, 97, 100.

15. For an excellent summary and discussion of the difference between direct and indirect rule, see Mahmood Mamdani, *Citizen and Subject: Contemporary Africa and the Legacy of Late Colonialism* (Princeton: Princeton University Press, 1996), 16–18.

16. Rodney, *How Europe Underdeveloped Africa*, 75. The arrival of Africans in the Americas may well have begun before the arrival of Europeans. Recent research, such as on the Olmec stone heads of Mexico, is suggestive of the pre-Columbus contact of Africans and Americans. However, if African boats did reach America and American boats did reach Africa, research has yet to establish that they developed two-way links. Africans and Native Americans did not develop international trade. See: Leo Wiener, *Africa and the Discovery of America* (Philadelphia: Innes and Sons, 1920); and Ivan Van Sertima, *They Came before Columbus* (New York: Random House, 1977); also see Jack D. Forbes, *Africans and Native Americans: The Language of Race and the Evolution of Red-Black Peoples* (Urbana: University of Illinois Press, 1993).

17. Rodney, *How Europe Underdeveloped Africa*, 75–82.

18. J. D. Fage, *A History of Africa*, 3d ed. (New York: Routledge, 1995), 244–47; Herbert S. Klein, *African Slavery in Latin America and the Caribbean* (Oxford: Oxford University Press, 1986), 45–50.

19. Williams, *Capitalism and Slavery*, 7–9; Blackburn, *The Making of New World Slavery*, 166–67; Forbes, *Africans and Native Americans*, 26–64.

20. Russell Thornton, *American Indian Holocaust and Survival: A Population History since 1492* (Norman: University of Oklahoma Press, 1987), 44–56.

21. The existence and nature of slavery in Africa before and during the European slave trade continues to be a debated issue. See the classic article by Walter Rodney, "African Slavery and Other Forms of Social Oppression on the Upper Guinea Coast in the Context of the Atlantic Slave Trade," *Journal of African History* 7 (1966): 431–43. To follow the debate, also see John D. Fage, "Slaves and Society in Western Africa," *Journal of African History* 21 (1980): 289–310; John Thornton, *Africa and Africans in the Making of the Atlantic World, 1400–1680* (Cambridge: Cambridge University Press, 1992), 72–97; and Joseph E. Inikori, "Slavery in Africa and the Transatlantic Slave Trade," in *The African Diaspora*, ed. Alusine Jalloh and Stephen E. Maizlish (College Station: Texas A&M University Press, 1996), 39–72; Joseph C. Miller, *Way of Death:*

*Merchant Capitalism and the Angolan Slave Trade, 1730–1830* (Madison: University of Wisconsin Press, 1988), 105–39; Klein, *African Slavery in Latin America and the Caribbean*, 10–16.

22. Klein, *African Slavery in Latin America and the Caribbean*, 38–39.

23. Fage, *A History of Africa*, 244–52; Klein, *African Slavery in Latin America and the Caribbean*, 45–50.

24. Klein, *African Slavery in Latin America and the Caribbean*, 49.

25. Fogel, *Without Consent or Contract*, 23–25; Klein, *African Slavery in Latin America and the Caribbean*, 66.

26. See Thomas C. Holt, "'An Empire over the Mind': Emancipation, Race, and Ideology in the British West Indies and the American South," in *Region, Race, and Reconstruction: Essays in Honor of C. Vann Woodward*, ed. J. Morgan Kousser and James M. McPherson (New York: Oxford University Press, 1982), 283–313.

27. See Leon Higginbotham, Jr., *In the Matter of Color: Race and the American Legal Process: The Colonial Period* (Oxford: Oxford University Press, 1978), 371–89; Miller, *Way of Death*, 526–30; and Magubane, *The Political Economy of Race and Class in South Africa*, 53–54, 81–86.

28. Higginbotham, *In the Matter of Color*, 371.

29. See C. L. R. James, *The Black Jacobins: Toussaint l'Ouverture and the San Domingo Revolution* (New York: Random House, 1963).

30. Jay R. Mandle, "Black Economic Entrapment after Emancipation in the United States," in *The Meaning of Freedom: Economics, Politics, and Culture after Slavery*, ed. Frank McGlynn and Seymour Dreshler (Pittsburgh: University of Pittsburgh Press, 1992), 69.

31. Thomas C. Holt, *The Problem of Freedom, Race, Labor, and Politics in Jamaica and Britain, 1832–1938* (Baltimore: Johns Hopkins University Press, 1992), 56–57.

32. Holt, "'An Empire over the Mind,'" 304.

33. Prior to this date several northern states in the United States abolished slavery as a legal institution: Vermont in 1777, Pennsylvania and Massachusetts in 1780; also, in 1784 Rhode Island and Connecticut began to dismantle their systems of slavery.

34. W. E. B. Du Bois, *Black Reconstruction in America, 1860–1880* (1935; reprint, New York: Atheneum, 1992), 670.

35. João José Reis, *Slave Rebellion in Brazil: The Muslim Uprising of 1835 in Bahia*, trans. Arthur Brakel (Baltimore: Johns Hopkins University Press, 1993), chapter 2.

36. George Reid Andrews, *Blacks and Whites in São Paulo, Brazil, 1888–1988* (Madison: University of Wisconsin Press, 1991), 32–42; David Eltis, *Economic Growth and the Ending of the Transatlantic Slave Trade* (New York: Oxford University Press, 1987), 214–16.

37. Andrews, *Blacks and Whites in São Paulo, Brazil*, 42–53.

38. Ibid., 52.

39. H. L. Wesseling, *Divide and Rule: The Partition of Africa, 1880–1914*, trans. Arnold J. Pomerans (1991; Westport, Conn.: Praeger, 1996), 330.

## 2. The Evolution of Racial Classification

1. For a classic description of this, see Winthrop D. Jordan, *White over Black: American Attitudes towards the Negro, 1550–1812* (Chapel Hill: University of North Carolina Press, 1968), 216–28.

2. As Jordan observes, "Though other people, most notably the Indians, were enslaved by Europeans, slavery was typically a Negro-white relationship. This fact in itself inevitably meant that the Negro would not be accorded a high place when Europeans set about arranging the varieties of men on a grand scale. No one thought of the Great Chain of Being as originating in differences in power or social status between human groups; to do so would have been to blaspheme the Creator. However, this did not prevent the idea of the Chain of Being from being applied to social relationships" (ibid., 227).

3. Leonard Thompson, *A History of South Africa* (New Haven: Yale University Press, 1995), 58; Wesseling *Divide and Rule*, 264.

4. For some examples of how the term *Hottentot* was used in speech and writing, see the quotations in Bernard M. Magubane, *The Making of a Racist State: British Imperialism and the Union of South Africa, 1875–1910* (Trenton, N.J.: Africa World Press, 1996), 13, 41–42, 44, 144, 211–12, 330–31, 386; also see Saul Dubow, *Scientific Racism in Modern South Africa* (Cambridge: Cambridge University Press, 1995), 20–22.

5. See St. Clair Drake, *Black Folk Here and There: An Essay in History and Anthropology* (Los Angeles: University of California, Center for Afro-American Studies, 1987), vol. 2, chapters 4, 6, and 7.

6. Eric Williams, *Capitalism and Slavery* (Chapel Hill: University of North Carolina Press, 1944), 3–4; Mahmood Mudimbe, *The Invention of Africa: Gnosis, Philosophy, and the Order of Knowledge* (Bloomington: Indiana University Press, 1988), 20, 51–54; Robin Blackburn, *The Making of New World Slavery: From the Baroque to the Modern, 1492–1800* (London: Verso, 1997), 103.

7. See Clark Spencer Larsen, Christopher B. Ruff, Margaret J. Schoeninger, and Dale L. Hutchinson, "Population Decline and Extinction in La Florida," in *Disease and Demography in the Americas,* ed. John W. Verano and Douglas H. Ubelaker (Washington, D.C.: Smithsonian Institution Press, 1992), 25–39; and Russell Thornton *Holocaust and Survival: A Population History since 1492* (Norman: University of Oklahoma Press, 1987), chapter 3.

8. Some of the others include the Count de Buffon. See Jonathan Marks, *Human Biodiversity: Genes, Race, and History* (New York: Aldine de Gruyter, 1995), chapter 1.

9. Charles Darwin, *On the Origin of Species by Means of Natural Selection, or the Preservation of Favored Races in the Struggle for Life* (1859; reprint, New York: Modern Library, 1995), 3.

10. He did so in the anonymously published *An Essay on the Principle of Population as It Affects the Future Improvement of Society, with Remarks on the Speculations of Mr. Goodwin, M. Condorcet and Other Writers* (London: J. Johnson, 1798). Malthus's work served three related purposes: it elaborated a theory of natural selection; it disputed the radical progressivism of Godwin and Condorcet; and it presented a systematic opposition to legislative changes (then proposed) in the Poor Laws in Great Britain that would make welfare payments proportional to family size. After admitting that he wrote the essay, Malthus responded to his critics by publishing a revised version of it, entitled *An Essay on the Principle of Population; or, a View of Its Past and Present Effects on Human Happiness; with an Inquiry into Our Prospects Respecting the Future Removal or Mitigation of the Evils Which It Occasions,* ed. Donald Winch (1826; Cambridge: Cambridge University Press, 1992). (All quotations come from this revised version.) Malthus went on to publish seven editions of the *Essay on the Principle of Population.* Other writers, such as Antoine-Nicolas de Condorcet

and William Godwin, had addressed the issue of the social consequences of population growth. However, Malthus's *Essay* was the most influential book to systematically connect population growth to its social consequences.

11. However, he doubted the efficacy of attempts at selective breeding. For example, Malthus doubted Condorcet's idea of "organic perfectibility": "The foundations therefore, on which the arguments for the organic perfectibility of man rest, are unusually weak, and can only be considered as mere conjectures. It does not, however, by any means, seem impossible, that by an attention to breed, a certain degree of improvement, similar to that among animals, might take place among men. . . . As the human race however could not be improved in this way, without condemning all the bad specimens to celibacy, it is not probable that any attention to breed should ever become general . . ." (Malthus, *An Essay on the Principle of Population,* 170–71).

12. Jordan, *White over Black,* chapters 1 and 2; and Drake, *Black Folk Here and There,* chapter 7.

13. Charles Darwin, *Autobiography and Selected Letters,* ed. Francis Darwin (1887; reprint, New York: Dover Press, 1958), 42–43.

14. For a more detailed description and contrast among the early evolutionary theorists, see Marks, *Human Biodiversity,* chapter 1.

15. Richard Hofstadter, *Social Darwinism in American Thought* (Boston: Beacon Press, 1944), 143–69. In this important chapter Hofstadter demonstrates how evolutionary theory had a profound impact upon psychology, anthropology, sociology, and ethics. He argues that evolutionary theory was not as successful in economics. However, economists of the time and immediately following the period he observed argued differently.

16. John Maynard Keynes, *The Collected Writings of John Maynard Keynes* (London: Macmillan, 1972), 9:276–77.

17. Herbert Spencer, *Essays: Scientific, Political, and Speculative* (New York: D. Appleton, 1896), 10.

18. Herbert Spencer, *Principles of Sociology* (1885; reprint, New York: D. Appleton, 1901–1907), 1:95, 432–34, 550–56, 614–22, 757, 764; 2:242–43; 3:331.

19. J. S. Haller, *Outcasts from Evolution: Scientific Attitudes of Racial Inferiority, 1859–1900* (Urbana: University of Illinois Press, 1971), 128, 153.

20. W. E. B. Du Bois, *Black Reconstruction in America, 1860–1880* (1935; reprint, New York: Atheneum, 1992), 139.

21. See William Darity Jr., "Many Roads to Extinction: Early AEA Economists and the Black Disappearance Hypothesis," *History of Economics Review* 21 (1994): 47–64.

22. Francis Amasa Walker, "The Colored Race in the United States," *Forum* 11 (1891): 501–9.

23. Hoffman's conclusions spoke to the racial prejudices of Social Darwinists: "Nothing is more clearly shown from this investigation than that the southern black man at the time of emancipation was healthy in body and cheerful in mind. He neither suffered inordinately from disease nor from impaired bodily vigor. His industrial capacities as a laborer were not of a low order, nor was the condition of servitude such as to produce in him morbid conditions favorable to mental disease, suicide, or intemperance. What are the conditions thirty years after? The pages of this work give but one answer, an answer which is a most severe condemnation of modern

attempts of superior races to lift inferior races to their own elevated position.... In the plain language of the facts brought together, the colored race is shown to be the downward grade tending toward a condition . . . when disease will be more destructive, vital resistance still lower, when the number of births will fall below the deaths, and gradual extinction of the race take place" (Frederick L. Hoffman, "Race Traits and Tendencies of the American Negro," *Publications of the American Economic Association* 11, nos. 1, 2, and 3 (1896): 311–12).

24. For a prominent example, see Charles Horton Cooley, *Social Organization: A Study of the Larger Mind* (1909; reprint, New York: Schocken Books, 1962), 295.

25. Darity, "Many Roads to Extinction."

26. The same could be said about some European social scientists as well. For example, see the Max Weber and Karl Marx quotations above in the introduction.

27. Hofstadter, *Social Darwinism in American Thought,* 157.

28. Charles Horton Cooley, *Human Nature and the Social Order* (1902; reprint, New York: Schocken Books, 1964), 12–13. In his later work Cooley was more critical of eugenic research (see Charles Horton Cooley, *Social Process* [New York: Charles Scribner's Sons, 1918], 206). In *Social Process,* Cooley criticizes the eugenicists for not learning from Darwin.

29. For an example of Cooley's Darwinist research, see Cooley, *Human Nature and Social Order,* 35–80. Cooley's ideas were more consistent with the ideas stressed by John Dewey regarding the social conditioning of an individual's reaction patterns (compare Cooley's work with John Dewey, *Human Nature and Conduct* [New York: Modern Library, 1930], 21–22).

## Part II.  Racial Statistics

1. For an excellent review of this history see: Richard A. Soloway, *Demography and Degeneration: Eugenics and the Declining Birthrate in Twentieth-Century Britain* (Chapel Hill: University of North Carolina Press, 1990), 3–17, 22, 24, 28, 38–39. On page 149 the author notes: "The problem of evaluating the role of biological determinism and social and economic opportunity had been implicit in Victorian ideas of individualistic self-interest and laissez-faire which reinforced the assumption that success or failure was a consequence of individual, even innate characteristics rather than environmental conditions. Victorian positivists, seeking the science of society, were, for example, divided over the relative contributions of nature and nurture to individual accomplishment, and their differing estimates provoked a significant disagreement between August Comte himself and John Stuart Mill, among others."

2. George Reid Andrews, *Blacks and Whites in São Paulo, Brazil, 1888–1988* (Madison: University of Wisconsin Press, 1991), 249–58; George Reid Andrews, *The Afro-Argentines of Buenos Aires, 1800–1900* (Madison: University of Wisconsin Press, 1980), 8–9; Peter Wade, *Blackness and Race Mixture: The Dynamics of Racial Identity in Colombia* (Baltimore: Johns Hopkins University Press, 1993), 21–22; Thomas E. Skidmore, "Race and Class in Brazil: Historical Perspectives," in *Race, Class, and Power in Brazil,* ed. Pierre-Michel Fontaine (Los Angeles: Center for Afro-American Studies, University of California), 17.

3. Soloway, *Demography and Degeneration,* chapter 1.

4. Charles Horton Cooley, *Social Organization: A Study of the Larger Mind* (1909; reprint, New York: Schocken Books, 1962), 219.

5. In addition to the examples mentioned in the text, see: Stefan Kühl, *The Nazi Connection: Eugenics, American Racism, and German National Socialism* (New York: Oxford University Press, 1994); Carl N. Degler, *In Search of Human Nature: The Decline and Revival of Darwinism in American Social Thought* (New York: Oxford University Press, 1991); Daniel Kevles, *In the Name of Eugenics: Genetics and the Uses of Human Heredity* (Berkeley: University of California Press, 1985); Stephen Jay Gould, *The Mismeasure of Man* (New York: W. W. Norton, 1981); William Darity Jr., "Many Roads to Extinction: Early AEA Economists and the Black Disappearance Hypothesis," *History of Economics Review* 21 (1994): 47–64; Soloway, *Demography and Degeneration;* Thomas M. Shapiro, *Population Control Politics: Women, Sterilization, and Reproductive Choice* (Philadelphia: Temple University Press, 1985). *The Bell Curve* makes extensive use of the research of demography and population genetics to support their European eugenic ideas (Richard J. Hernnstein and Charles Murray, *The Bell Curve: Intelligence and Class Structure in American Life* [New York: Free Press, 1994]).

6. Carl Degler has documented the revival of Darwinism in the social sciences in his recent book *In Search of Human Nature*.

7. See Elazar Barkan, *The Retreat of Scientific Racism: Changing Concepts of Race in Britain and the United States between the World Wars* (Cambridge: Cambridge University Press, 1992), 260–66.

8. Quoted in Daniel J. Kevles, "Out of Eugenics: The Historical Politics of the Human Genome," in *The Code of Codes: Scientific and Social Issues in the Human Genome Project,* ed. Daniel J. Kevles and Leroy Hood (Cambridge, Mass.: Harvard University Press, 1992), 16.

## 3. Eugenics and the Birth of Racial Statistics

1. Roland Pressat, ed., *The Dictionary of Demography,* ed. Christopher Wilson (New York: Basil Blackwell, 1985), 72; emphasis added.

2. I am aware of what might be referred to as the movement for better hygiene within the eugenics movement. This part of the movement consisted of popular films and books. This aspect of the movement did not have a significant impact on social statistics or the quantification of race and so does not play an important role in my story. However, it is not difficult to see how the notion of hygiene was extended to "racial hygiene" within the eugenics movement.

3. Francis Galton wrote in the preface to his classic work *Hereditary Genius: An Inquiry into Its Laws and Consequences* (1869; 2d ed., 1892; reprint of 2d ed., Gloucester, Mass.: Peter Smith, 1972): "The idea of investigating the subject of hereditary genius occurred to me during the course of a purely ethnological inquiry, into the mental peculiarities of different races; when the fact, that characteristics cling to families, was so frequently forced on my notice as to induce me to pay especial attention to that branch of the subject" (23).

4. Francis Galton, *Inquiries into the Human Faculty* (New York: Macmillan, 1883), 25.

5. My definitions of these two fallacies are similar to those used in Stephen Jay Gould's argument. Gould defines reification as the tendency to convert abstract

concepts into things, and ranking as the "propensity to ordering complex variation as a gradual ascending scale" (Stephen Jay Gould, *The Mismeasure of Man* [New York: W. W. Norton, 1981], 24).

6. My narrative of the history of social statistics follows that of traditional statistical history. My contribution is to look more closely at the use of race and population difference in this history. For examples of the literature on the history of social statistics see: Paul F. Lazarsfeld, "Notes on the History of Quantification in Sociology— Trends, Sources and Problems," *Isis* 52 (1960): 277–333; Stephen M. Stigler, *The History of Statistics: The Measurement of Uncertainty before 1900* (Cambridge, Mass.: Belknap Press of Harvard University, 1986), 161–220, 265–361; Theodore M. Porter, *The Rise of Statistical Thinking, 1820–1900* (Princeton: Princeton University Press, 1986), 23–39, 41–92, 128–46, 270–314; Anders Hald, *A History of Probability and Statistics and Their Applications before 1750* (New York: John Wiley and Sons, 1990); and Anders Hald, *A History of Mathematical Statistics from 1750 to 1930* (New York: John Wiley and Sons, 1998).

7. The word *statistics* originated in eighteenth-century Germany. In Germany *Staatwissenschaft* referred to "science of the state." For more on Germany's unique history with regard to statistical debates and analysis, see Alain Desrosières, *The Politics of Large Numbers: A History of Statistical Reasoning* (Cambridge, Mass.: Harvard University Press, 1998), 178–88; and Harald Westergaard, *Contributions to the History of Statistics* (London: P. W. King and Son, 1932), 4–15. As Westergaard notes, "In conclusion, summing up the results of the whole evolution, it may perhaps be said that the system, which Conring, Achenwall and their disciples had cultivated, had in the long run been more influenced by political arithmetic than the reverse" (14).

8. John Graunt, *Natural and Political Observations Mentioned in a Following Index and Made upon the Bills of Mortality* (1662; reprint, New York: Arno Press, 1975). For a general discussion of Graunt's place in statistical history, see Hald, *A History of Probability and Statistics,* 81–105; and Karl Pearson, *The History of Statistics in the 17th and 18th Centuries against the Changing Background of Intellectual, Scientific and Religious Thought* (New York: Macmillan, 1920), 10–73.

9. Porter, *The Rise of Statistical Thinking,* 27.

10. Thomas Robert Malthus, *An Essay on the Principle of Population,* ed. Donald Winch (1826; Cambridge: Cambridge University Press, 1992), 20. Malthus played a key role in the development of social statistics in Europe (see Porter, *The Rise of Statistical Thinking,* 26–27).

11. Pierre-Simon Laplace, *Philosophical Essay on Probabilities,* trans. Andrew I. Dale (1825; New York: Springer-Verlag, 1995), 3.

12. Immanuel Kant, *On History,* trans. Lewis White Beck, Robert E. Anchor, and Emil L. Fackenheim (1784; Indianapolis: Bobbs-Merrill, 1963), 12.

13. If I say I am uncertain whether Jesse L. Jackson will be elected president of the United States, I am stating that I cannot predict if he will be elected. If I give a probability for his election in the year 2000 or some future date, I express my limited knowledge and ability to predict his election.

14. See Hald, *A History of Mathematical Statistics,* 2.

15. Quetelet's major contribution to social science research was in his fitting of probability distributions to social phenomena. In 1846, he published *Lettres à S.A.R. Le Duc Régnant de Saxe-Cobourg et Gotha sur la théorie des probabilitiés appliquée*

*aux sciences morales et politiques* (translated in 1849 as *Letters Addressed to H.R.H. the Grand Duke of Saxe Coburg and Gotha, on the Theory of Probabilities as Applied to the Moral and Political Sciences*), a treatise on the application to social statistics of probability theory.

16. See Hald, *A History of Probability and Statistics*, 223–25; 375–96; and Hald, *A History of Mathematical Statistics*, 567–87.

17. For example, he estimated that the number of "dead letters" in Paris's post office was constant from year to year (Laplace, *Philosophical Essay on Probabilities*, 37).

18. Demography is the study of births, deaths, and migration among human populations. The processes of birth and death have both biological and social aspects. While the events of birth and death are biological, all social influences work through these to affect rates. Demographers have attempted to understand both the biological and social factors of mortality and fertility.

19. Auguste Comte outlined a hierarchy of the sciences and discouraged the use of mathematics and numbers in the physiological and social disciplines. Like Comte, Adolphe Quetelet thought that society followed certain laws that could not be impeded by the arbitrary acts of political actors. Yet, Quetelet's methodological orientation was not consistent with the positivistic ideas of Comte (see Auguste Comte, *Cours de philosophie positive*, vol. 4 [1839; Paris: Baillière, 1877], 7, 511–16).

20. In 1835, Quetelet established his international reputation as a social statistician with the publication of *Sur l'homme et le développment de ses facultés, ou essai de physique sociale* (translated in 1842 as *A Treatise on Man and the Development of His Faculties*). In this work he developed the idea of the "average man" (*l'homme moyen*). The initial idea resulted from his efforts to analyze morphological differences among groups of people. Measurable aspects of a population produced an estimate for that population's average man. He wrote, for example, of crime within a specific community or class rather than moralizing about wicked acts of a group of deviant persons. Yet, his idea of the average man was more than a statistical abstraction; it was also a measure of morality.

Quetelet argued that deviations from the average man were imperfections or errors. He believed that social science should look to celestial science by employing the techniques of astronomy to solve the methodological problems of social statistics in understanding this law of society. His formulation of social statistics was based on his application of probability theory to social data. He thought there was a true average height of man, to which every man was an imperfect replication. He demonstrated this by measuring the chest circumferences of Scottish soldiers. He argued that if one calculated the average chest of a miscellaneous assortment of soldiers, the result would be an arithmetic mean of their circumferences, because the underlying distribution would not be systematic. However, if one measured 5,738 Scottish soldiers, each measurement would approximate the astronomical law of errors. As the measuring process continued, a uniform pattern of the average man would emerge from the data.

The concept of the average man does not allow us to see the importance of individual variation. Quetelet assumed that all other things are equal. That is, he ignored the potential complexity of multiple causes and variation that prevent everything from being equal. For example, extremely wealthy individuals would increase the average wealth while extremely poor individuals would lower the average wealth in a population. The idea of the average man does not allow us to see differences in wealth or to understand these differences. The "average man" did not actually exist in society as Quetelet thought.

Quetelet's notion of the average man was not foreign to social science and can be seen in some of the classics of sociology. For example, the average man and society as a social entity can be seen in the work of Émile Durkheim. In his classic study *Suicide: A Study in Sociology*, Durkheim embraces Quetelet's average man: "The conclusion from all these facts is that the social suicide rate can be explained only sociologically. At any given moment the moral constitution of society establishes the contingent of voluntary deaths. There is, therefore, for each people a collective force of a definite amount of energy, impelling men to self-destruction. The victim's acts which at first seem to express only his personal temperament are really the supplement and prolongation of a social condition which they express externally" (Émile Durkheim, *Suicide: A Study in Sociology*, trans. John A. Spaulding and George Simpson [original French publication, 1897; New York: Free Press, 1951], 299). Though Quetelet's moral perspective had parallels with the Durkheimian conceptualization of social inquiry, the Durkheimians openly criticized his use of averages (Paul Lazarsfeld, *Quantification of Measurement in the Natural and Social Sciences* [Indianapolis: Bobbs-Merrill, 1961], 147–203).

21. In 1738, Abraham de Moivre introduced the exponential function.

$$\int_{-a}^{a} \frac{1}{\sqrt{2\pi}} e^{-x^2/2} dx$$

This function became known variously as probable error, the astronomer's error law, the normal distribution, the *normal curve*, or simply the bell curve. Quetelet used the curve in the construction of histograms in the comparisons of data.

Quetelet's concept of the average man was an essential step in separating fixed from random individualistic determinants of behavior. He provided the foundation now used in most behavioral models in modern social statistics. However, he also mistakenly thought that homogeneity followed necessarily from the fact that observations are normally distributed.

22. Stigler, *The History of Statistics*, 219.

23. For example, poor families do not all have a single parent. Whether a poor family has a single parent depends on various social circumstances; this is best understood as a tendency of poor families to be single-parented and should be measured by the probability of poor families to be single-parent households. As the statistician Glenn Shafer points out, "different causal explanations serve different purposes" (Glenn Shafer, *The Art of Causal Conjecture* [Cambridge, Mass.: MIT Press], 304). Thus, different causal explanations of poverty among poor families serve different purposes. It is probably better to say that single parentage explains family poverty and then spell out how it does so and for what purpose. Early social statisticians did not contextualize their findings, nor has it been the practice among most modern social statisticians.

24. European eugenics is partly responsible for the casting of "the light of science upon superstitions concerning conception, pregnancy, and childbirth, notably the law of maternal impressions . . . that the characteristics of offspring were shaped by the experiences of the pregnant mother" (Daniel J. Kevles, *In the Name of Eugenics: Genetics and the Uses of Human Heredity* [Berkeley: University of California Press, 1985], 66).

25. Charles Darwin, *The Descent of Man and Selection in Relation to Sex* (1871; reprint, New York: Modern Library, 1995), 414; emphasis added.

26. Anders Hald summarizes Quetelet's social statistics as follows: "In analogy with the mechanical physical universe Quetelet looks upon society as a mechanical machine turning out human beings with a multitude of characteristics. In *Physique sociale* his aim is to find the laws for these physical and moral characteristics as they depend on the social conditions and as they develop over time. Because of the variability of the characteristics, the laws must be statistical laws, that is, based on the average of a large number of observations. Hence the main object of his study is the average man" (Hald, *A History of Mathematical Statistics,* 588).

27. Stigler, *The History of Statistics,* chapter 8; Kevles, *In the Name of Eugenics,* chapter 1.

28. Francis Galton, *The Narrative of an Explorer in Tropical South Africa* (London: John Murray, 1853).

29. Galton, *Hereditary Genius,* 69.

30. The midparent is imagined to have a stature equal to the average of the paternal and "adjusted" maternal statures. Galton expressed this relationship by a linear regression equation:

$$x = \left(\frac{2}{3}\right)y$$

where $x = X - \overline{X}$ and $y = Y - \overline{Y}$. Where $X$ = filial stature, $\overline{X}$ = mean filial stature, $Y$ = midparent stature, and $\overline{Y}$ = mean midparent stature. Galton first developed this argument in his 1885 presidential address at the meeting of the anthropological section of the British Association for the Advancement of Sciences. It was published in 1886 as "Regression towards Mediocrity in Hereditary Stature," in the *Journal of the Anthropological Institute* 15: 246–63. In this article he argued that the stature of a person is equal, on average, to one-third of the sum of the height of the father, the mother, and the average height of their race.

31. Darwin, *The Descent of Man,* 584.

32. In fact, Galton's research up to this point suggested a "linear reversion relationship," in which each generation moved toward the mean. He noted that successive generations resemble each other in their general features.

33. Correlation allowed social scientists to measure the extent of association between two variables. Prior to this development social statisticians could observe that height and "race" seemed to vary together, but they could not measure how the two variables were associated. With Galton's and later Pearson's development, social statisticians could specify the magnitude of association. For example, Pearson's correlation coefficient, $r$, allowed the measurement of association on a scale ranging from a perfectly inverse relationship ($-1$) to a perfectly direct relationship ($+1$), with 0 meaning no association. The correlation coefficient, or Pearson product-moment correlation coefficient, $r$ = average of ($x$ in standard units) $\times$ ($y$ in standard units). More formally,

$$r_{xy} = \frac{\sum_i z_{xi}z_{yi}}{N}$$

34. Francis Galton, "Statistics by Intercomparison, with Remarks on the Law of Frequency of Error," *Philosophical Magazine,* 4th series, 49 (1875): 33–46.

35.  See Karl Pearson, *The Life, Letters and Labours of Francis Galton,* vol. 3 (Cambridge: Cambridge University Press, 1930), 56–57. Francis Galton, "Co-relations and Their Measurement, Chiefly from Anthropometric Data," *Proceedings of the Royal Society of London* 45 (1889): 134–145.

36.  Galton, "Co-relations and Their Measurement," 135.

37.  Galton, *Hereditary Genius,* 27.

38.  Francis Ysidro Edgeworth, "Methods of Statistics," *Jubilee Volume of the Statistical Society* (1885): 181–217.

39.  In the 1890s, Edgeworth extended his statistical interest from correlation to regression analysis. Francis Ysidro Edgeworth: "Correlated Averages," *Philosophical Magazine and Journal of Science* 34 (July–December 1892): 190–205; "A New Method of Treating Correlated Averages," *Philosophical Magazine and Journal of Science* 35 (January–June 1893): 63–64; and "Note on the Calculation of Correlation between Organs," *Philosophical Magazine and Journal of Science* 36 (July–December 1893): 350–51.

40.  Stigler, *The History of Statistics,* 319–25.

41.  The long series of memoirs entitled Mathematical Contributions to the Theory of Evolution was reissued by the trustees of Biometrika in 1948 in a single volume. The selected papers consist of articles published in the *Philosophical Transactions of the Royal Society,* in the *Drapers' Company Research Memoirs,* and in *Philosophical Magazine.* Most of these papers cover Pearson's Mathematical Contributions to the Theory of Evolution series. The article published in *Philosophical Magazine,* "On the Criterion That a Given System of Deviations from the Probable in the Case of a Correlated System of Variables Is Such That It Can Be Reasonably Supposed to Have Arisen from Random Sampling," presents the first derivation of the distribution referred to as the chi-square. The chi-square test, a goodness-of-fit test, is considered Pearson's most significant contribution to statistical theory. The chi-square is calculated from

$$x^2 = \sum \frac{[f(observed) - f(expected)]^2}{f(expected)}$$

where $f(observed)$ stands for the empirically observed and $f(expected)$ stands for the frequency expected under the theory being examined. In this work Pearson greatly expanded social statistics. He also expanded on Edgeworth's significance test by measuring difference in terms of standard deviations. (See: Karl Pearson, *Early Statistical Papers* [Cambridge: Cambridge University Press, 1948]; Stigler, *The History of Statistics,* 310–28; and B. Norton, "Metaphysics and Population Genetics: Karl Pearson and the Background to Fisher's Multi-factorial Theory of Inheritance," *Annals of Science* 32 [1975]: 537–53.)

42.  Pearson's correlation coefficient, *r*, continues to be the most commonly used measure of correlation. When people use the term *correlation* without any other specification, this is what they mean. Pearson's new approach produced an approximation for the probable error of a coefficient of correlation, *r*, as

$$(1 - r^2)/\sqrt{n}$$

Edgeworth had presented an equivalent formula for estimating a correlation coefficient (for example, compare Francis Ysidro Edgeworth, "Exercises in the Calculation of Errors," *Philosophical Magazine and Journal of Science* 36 [July–December

1893]: 98–111; and Pearson and Filon's paper, "Mathematical Contributions to the Theory of Evolution. IV. On the Probable Errors of Frequency Constants and on the Influence of Random Selection on Variation and Correlation," in Karl Pearson, *Early Statistical Papers* [Cambridge: Cambridge University Press, 1948], 179–261). Pearson and Filon made a much more significant contribution. They considered the general issue of determining the standard deviations of the "best" values of the coefficients of a bivariate normal distribution and of the coefficients in several skewed curves (for a discussion of the relative contributions of these two important papers, see Stigler, *The History of Statistics*, 343). Fisher called this later contribution into question on the basis of the criterion used in finding the coefficients for the skewed curves. As I have generally argued these important statistical discussions took place within the context of eugenic research.

43. Pearson, *Early Statistical Papers*, 121.

44. The traditional beginnings of path models lie in the 1920s with the population geneticist Sewall Wright's "Correlation and Causation," *Journal of Agricultural Research* 20 (1921): 557–85. Wright played a leading role in the "new synthesis," which bridged Darwinian evolution and Mendelian genetics. Wright did not participate in the racial statistics debate. The first and most influential application of the path model in the social sciences was by Peter Blau and Otis Duncan in their classic study of education and social stratification, *The American Occupational Structure* (New York: Wiley, 1967).

45. Yule's paper "On the Theory of Correlation" reconciled the theory of correlation with the method of least squares from the traditional theory of errors (see George Udny Yule, "On the Theory of Correlation," *Journal of the Royal Statistical Society* 60 [1897]: 812–54). Also see Stigler, *The History of Statistics*, 348–58, for an excellent discussion of the importance of this paper for social statistics. Linking least squares and regression made the developments in simplifying the solutions of normal equations and the calculation of the probable errors of coefficients by astronomers and geodesists available for regression analysis among social statisticians.

46. In the paper "On the General Theory of Skew Correlation and Non-linear Regression," Pearson summarized his intent: "In a series of Memoirs presented to the Royal Society I have endeavored to show that the Gaussian-Laplace normal distribution is very far from being a general law of frequency distribution either for errors of observation or for the distribution of deviations from type such as occur in organic populations. It is quite true that the normal distribution applies within certain fields with a remarkable degree of accuracy, notably in a whole series of anthropometric, particularly craniometric observations. In other fields it is not even approximately correct, for example in the distribution of barometric variations, of grades of fertility and incidence of disease. For such cases I have introduced a series of skew frequency curves which serve the purpose of describing the frequency of innumerable skew distributions well within the errors of random sampling. An exact test for 'goodness of fit' in the case of frequency distributions has also been now provided" (Karl Pearson, "Mathematical Contributions to the Theory of Evolution. XIV. On the General Theory of Skew Correlation and Non-linear Regression," *Drapers' Company Research Memoirs*, Biometric Series II, [1905] 1956; reprinted in Pearson, *Early Statistical Papers*, 477–78).

47. Yule, "On the Theory of Correlation," 812.

48. David A. Freedman, "Statistical Models and Shoe Leather," *Sociological Methodology* 21 (1991): 292.

49. George Udny Yule, "An Investigation into the Causes of Changes in Pauperism in England, Chiefly during the Last Two-Intercensal Decades, I," *Journal of the Royal Statistical Society* 62 (1899): 249–95. Stephen M. Stigler argues that Yule's conservative perspective was questioned and criticized by his contemporaries (*The History of Statistics*, 355–57).

50. Stigler, *The History of Statistics*, 359.

51. On this point see Mary S. Morgan, "Searching for Causal Relations in Economic Statistics: Reflections from History," in *Causality in Crisis? Statistical Methods and the Search for Causal Knowledge in the Social Sciences*, ed. Vaughn R. McKim and Stephen P. Turner (Notre Dame: University of Notre Dame Press, 1997), 47–80.

52. As cited in Morgan, "Searching for Causal Relations in Economic Statistics," 69.

53. I will return to this issue in chapter 7.

54. R. A. Fisher, "On the Mathematical Foundations of Theoretical Statistics," *Philosophical Transactions, Royal Society of London*, series A, 222A (1922): 309–68; R. A. Fisher, "Theory of Statistical Estimation," *Proceedings of the Cambridge Philosophical Society* 22 (1925): 700–725.

55. As Fisher notes: "The solution of the problems of calculating from a sample the parameters of the hypothetical population, which we have put forward in the method of maximum likelihood, consists, then, simply of choosing such values of these parameters as have the maximum likelihood. Formally, therefore, it resembles the calculation of the mode of an inverse frequency distribution. . . . Likelihood also differs from probability in that it is not a differential element, and is incapable of being integrated: it is assigned to a particular point of the range of variation, not to a particular element of it" (Fisher, "On the Mathematical Foundations of Theoretical Statistics," 328).

56. Ronald A. Fisher, *Statistical Methods for Research Workers* (London: Oliver and Boyd, 1925); and Ronald A. Fisher, *The Design of Experiments* (London: Oliver and Boyd, 1935).

57. Ronald A. Fisher, *Statistical Methods for Research Workers*, 2.

58. Mendel's research found that each plant parent contributed one of a pair of factors to determine each character in the makeup of its offspring. If a plant was hybrid for a particular character, one of those factors being *recessive* (the latent trait), then in the character the plant would look like the *dominating* (the visible character) form but would pass the factors to its own offspring at random—half dominant and half recessive. These findings have led to a statistical view of heredity, where investigators look at a "large" number of offspring over successive generations to observe patterns.

Gregor Mendel maintained that characters were determined by hereditarily transmitted elements. The process of transmission was characterized by segregation and independent assortment. Mendel maintained that "in his pea plants, there were two elements for every character—e.g., height. According to the segregation law, they were separated from each other in the formation of gametes, i.e., sperm or eggs. According to the law of independent assortment, the elements for one character recombined independently of those for another. The recombination of the various elements which was made possible by the sexual union of the sperm and egg cells was thus determined by the laws of combinatorial probability" (quoted in Kevles, *In the Name of Eugenics*, 41–43).

59. According to Norton, "Pearson's biometric approach to heredity was, therefore, purely phenotypic and theory-free. His laws of ancestral heredity were instruments of prediction. They simply *described* the routines of experience, and did not fall into what Pearson saw as the metaphysical trap of trying to *explain* these routines, by postulating 'theoretical entities' whose unseen operation was held responsible for the behavior of the visible realm. For Pearson, one either described the flow of appearances in one's science, or, one fell into the trap of postulating 'shadowy unknowables' reminiscent of the Kantian *Ding an sich*, in a misguided attempt to explain what could only be described. Thus, one could if one wished, employ theoretical terms such as 'gene' or 'atom' in one's science, but only so long as they were not taken to refer to unseen existents" (Norton, "Metaphysics and Population Genetic," 540).

60. Gregor Mendel, "Versuche über Pflanzen-Hybriden," *Verhandlungen des Naturforschenden Vereines in Brunn* 4 (1865): 3–47.

61. Daniel J. Kevles, "Out of Eugenics: The Historical Politics of the Human Genome," in *The Code of Codes: Scientific and Social Issues in the Human Genome Project*, ed. Daniel J. Kevles and Leroy Hood (Cambridge, Mass.: Harvard University Press, 1992), 11.

62. Ronald A. Fisher, "Some Hopes of a Eugenist," *Eugenics Review* 5 (1914): 311.

63. Ronald A. Fisher, "Positive Eugenics," *Eugenics Review* 9 (1917): 206.

64. George Udny Yule's 1902 paper, "Mendel's Laws and Their Probable Relation to Intraracial Heredity," *New Phytologist* 1: 193–207, 222–38, was the first to suggest reconciliation between ancestral heredity and Mendelism. However, Fisher is credited with synthesizing the biometric and Mendelian approaches to the study of heredity in his classic article "The Correlation between Relatives on the Supposition of Mendelian Inheritance," *Transactions of the Royal Society of Edinburgh* 52 (1918): 399–433. Fisher had worked out the essentials of the synthesis of biometry and Mendelian theory as early as 1911. See B. Norton and E. S. Pearson, "A Note on the Background to and Refereeing of R. A. Fisher's 1918 Paper 'The Correlation between Relatives on the Supposition of Mendelian Inheritance,'" *Notes and Records of the Royal Society of London* 31 (1976): 151–62.

65. Ronald A. Fisher, "The Causes of Human Variability," *Eugenics Review* 10 (1918): 213.

66. Ronald A. Fisher, *The Genetical Theory of Natural Selection* (Oxford: Clarendon, 1930).

67. Kevles, *In the Name of Eugenics*, chapter 3.

68. C. B. Davenport and M. Steggerda, *Race Crossing in Jamaica* (Washington, D.C.: Carnegie Institution of Washington, 1929), 469–71.

69. Kevles, "Out of Eugenics," 3–36.

70. For a historical account of this line of genetic research, see Horace Freeland Judson, "A History of the Science and Technology behind Gene Mapping and Sequencing," in *The Code of Codes: Scientific and Social Issues in the Human Genome Project*, ed. Kevles and Hood, 37–80.

71. Ibid., 37.

72. Judson notes: "The technology of genetic experiment and analysis has done more than facilitate research and theory. It has driven research and theory—nowhere

more obviously than in the changing concepts of the gene, the sequence of genes, and the map of genes" (ibid., 78).

73. *Morphology* refers to the form and structure of an organism; *physiology* refers to its functions and activities.

74. Joan Fisher Box, *R. A. Fisher: The Life of a Scientist* (New York: John Wiley and Sons, 1978), 338–50; Kevles, "Out of Eugenics," 11–12.

75. These expansions hit a new high with the publication of *Blood Groups in Man* (in 1950) by Robert Russell Race and Ruth Sanger; and *The Distribution of the Human Blood Groups* (in 1954) by Arthur Ernest Mourant. In the foreword to *Blood Groups in Man,* Fisher observed: "The need for an exact and comprehensive textbook has been increasingly evident during the rapid progress of the last decade, and no authors could be better qualified for the task" (Robert Russell Race and Ruth Sanger, *Blood Groups in Man* [Oxford: Blackwell Scientific Publications, 1950], v). Also see A. E. Mourant, A. C. Kopec, and K. Domaniewska-Sobczak, *The Distribution of the Human Blood Groups and Other Polymorphisms,* 2d ed. (London: Oxford University Press, 1976).

76. Several population geneticists have commented on this process. For examples, see L. Luca Cavalli-Sforza, Paolo Menozzi, and Alberto Piazza, *The History and Geography of Human Genes* (Princeton: Princeton University Press, 1994), 19–20; and for a perspective more sympathetic to the actual existence of race, see Phillip V. Tobias, "Race," in *The Social Science Encyclopedia,* ed. Adam Kuper and Jessica Kuper (London: Routledge and Kegan Paul, 1985), 678–82.

77. We should keep in mind that there has never been a universal consensus to reject the idea of race among scientists. For examples of some important early arguments for the usefulness of the race concept in understanding population genetics and human evolution, see William Boyd, *Genetics and the Races of Man* (Boston: Little, Brown, 1950); C. S. Coon, S. M. Garn, and J. B. Birdsell, *Races* (Springfield, Illinois: C. C. Thomas, 1950); and Theodosius Bobzhansky, *Mankind Evolving: The Evolution of the Human Species* (New Haven: Yale University Press, 1965).

78. Charles Spearman, "'General Intelligence,' Objectively Determined and Measured," *American Journal of Psychology* 159 (1904): 201–93.

79. Factor analysis is a complicated statistical procedure for estimating the underlying structure in large matrices of data. In statistical analysis, latent variables are constructed or hypothesized to be the parents for variables that are empirically observed. Latent variables are used in causal models but are not directly measured. Such variables are thought to provide a description of aspects of nature we do not observe.

80. Spearman's rank-correlation coefficient uses ranks as the numerical values for the computation of the correlation coefficient, and can be given the following computation form when no ties in rank exist:

$$r_s = 1 - \left[ \frac{6\left(\sum_i D_i^2\right)}{N(N^2 - 1)} \right]$$

where $D_i$ is the difference between ranks associated with the particular individual, $i$, and $N$ is the number of individuals observed.

81. For an excellent account of the mismeasurement of intelligence, see Gould, *The Mismeasure of Man,* chap. 6.

82. Charles Spearman, "The Measurement of Intelligence," *Eugenics Review* 6 (1914): 312–13.

83. Relying heavily on research by Pearson and on eugenic notions of population quality, Spearman presented a two-factor theory of intelligence. Spearman produced *g* by the *first principal component* method. He used this factor analysis technique to produce a grand average of all tests in matrices of positive correlation coefficients where the vectors pointed in the same general direction. See Gould, *The Mismeasure of Man*, 296–316.

84. In place of Spearman's principal component solution, Thurston took the principal components and rotated them to different positions that maximized their closeness to clusters of vectors. This rotation process produced high positive projections for vectors clustered near it and close to zero or zero projections for all others. See Gould, *The Mismeasure of Man*, 296–316.

85. Asa. G. Hillard III, "Back to Binet: The Case against the Use of IQ Test in the Schools," *Contemporary Education* 4 (1990): 184–89. Recent research suggests that "[w]hile SAT scores have a modest effect on earnings, school selectivity and rank in class have a more lasting impact" (William G. Bowen and Derek Bok, *The Shape of the River: Long-Term Consequences of Considering Race in College and University Admissions* [Princeton: Princeton University Press, 1998], 154).

86. Degler, *In Search of Human Nature*, 230.

87. Kevles, *In the Name of Eugenics*, 169–70.

88. Norton, "Metaphysics and Population Genetics," 538.

89. Gould, *The Mismeasure of Man*, 234–39.

90. Otto Klineberg, *Negro Intelligence and Selective Migration* (New York: Columbia University Press, 1935).

91. Arnold Rose and Caroline Rose, *America Divided: Minority Group Relations in the United States* (New York: Knopf, 1948), 267–68.


## 4. Eugenics and Racial Demography

1. For comments regarding the importance of Graunt's demographic analysis, see: D. V. Glass, "John Graunt and His Natural and Political Observations," *Proceedings of the Royal Society*, series B, 159 (1963): 2–32; I. Sutherland, "John Graunt: A Tercentenary Tribute," *Journal of the Royal Statistical Society*, series A, 126 (1963): 537–56; Philip Kreager, "New Light on Graunt," *Population Studies* 42 (1988): 129–40; and Philip Kreager, "Histories of Demography: A Review Article," *Population Studies* 47 (1993): 519–39.

2. *Life expectancy* refers to the average duration of life after any given age is reached, as calculated from a life table. Life tables are the classic method of evaluating the mortality experience of a population. The life table shows the implications for longevity of a set of age-specific death rates. Death rates vary by age. Life tables summarize age-specific death rates independently of the age structure of the population. Life expectancy is an example of such standardization.

3. Benjamin Gompertz, "On the Nature of the Function Expressive of the Law of Human Mortality," *Philosophical Transcripts of the Royal Society* 115 (1825): 513–93.

4. W. E. B. Du Bois, *Black Reconstruction* (1935; New York: Atheneum, 1992), 580–636.

5. A. Leon Higginbotham, *Shades of Freedom: Racial Politics and Presumptions of the American Legal Process* (New York: Oxford University Press, 1996), chapter 9.

6. Charles Spearman, *The Abilities of Man* (New York: Macmillan, 1927), 8. As William H. Tucker notes, "the mental test replaced the anthropometrists' techniques and quickly became accepted as a convincing measure of human worth" (*The Science and Politics of Racial Research* [Urbana: University of Illinois Press, 1994], 73).

7. Compare the work by J. L. Sadie and the American demographers cited below in notes 12–17 (for examples of some of Sadie's work, see J. L. Sadie: "Differential Mortality in South Africa," *South African Journal of Economics* 19 (1951): 361–96; and "The Cost of Population Growth in South Africa," *South African Journal of Economics* 40 (1972): 107–18.

8. Michael S. Teitelbaum and Jay M. Winter, *The Fear of Population Decline* (Orlando: Academic Press, 1985), chap. 3; Thomas M. Shapiro, *Population Control Politics: Women, Sterilization, and Reproductive Choice* (Philadelphia: Temple University Press, 1985), 40–62; Richard A. Soloway, *Demography and Degeneration: Eugenics and the Declining Birthrate in Twentieth-Century Britain* (Chapel Hill: University of North Carolina Press, 1990), 86–109, chapters 8 and 9.

9. I say this with caution and do not want to overemphasize the role of Nazism in the decline of overt eugenics in the 1940s. As Richard A. Soloway notes: "Confronted with changing scientific evidence coming out of the genetic laboratories about the nature of heredity and its uncertain relationship to environment reform, eugenicists in the 1930s had begun to retreat, reconsider, and regroup. But they were prodded to do so as much by the social and political environment of the interwar years as they were by the lessons of Huxley, Fisher, Haldane, Muller, Hogben, and the other architects of modern genetics who were themselves stimulated to varying degrees by this environment. The often stormy process of reevaluation and reformulation of eugenic principles and policies was not forced by the rise of Nazism but paralleled it. It would have happened without Hitler, or, for that matter, without Stalin, whom some left-wing scientists and social scientists regarded for a while as their eugenic 'man on horseback'" (Soloway, *Demography and Degeneration,* 353).

10. Daniel J. Kevles, *In the Name of Eugenics: Genetics and the Uses of Human Heredity* (Berkeley: University of California Press, 1985), 175.

11. Dennis Hodgson identifies four factions involved in the foundation of population studies: groups concerned with immigration restriction, eugenicists, those concerned with neo-Malthusian birth controls, and demographers (Dennis Hodgson, "The Ideological Origins of the Population Association of America," *Population and Development Review* 17, no. 1 [1991]: 1–34). My intent is to explore the intersections of these different factions, such that the distinctions among them are less important. For example, the immigration-restriction group is, in my view, a faction within the eugenics movement.

12. Louis Dublin was the president of the Population Association of America (PAA) for 1935–1936; Warren S. Thompson was PAA president for 1936–1938; P. K. Whelpton was PAA president for 1941–1942; and Frederick Osborn was PAA president for 1949–1950.

13. P. K. Whelpton, "An Empirical Method of Calculating Future Population," *Journal of the American Statistical Association* 31 (1936): 457–73. It is quite interesting that P. H. Leslie would mathematically formalize Whelpton's early use of matrix-based population projections in the British statistical journal *Biometrika* (P. H.

Leslie, "On the Use of Matrices in Certain Population Mathematics," *Biometrika* 33 [1945]: 183–212). W. F. R. Weldon, Francis Galton, and Karl Pearson founded *Biometrika* in 1906. The journal had been edited by Weldon, Pearson, and Davenport and was being edited by Pearson's son E. S. Pearson when Leslie's article appeared.

14. P. K. Whelpton, *Needed Population Research* (Lancaster, Penn.: Science Press Printing, 1938), 183.

15. Louis I. Dublin, "The Significance of the Declining Birth Rate," *Science* 47 1209 (1918): 201–10, quotation from 209. This paper was first delivered as Dublin's retirement address as a vice-president of the American Association for Advancement of Science in 1917.

16. Warren S. Thompson, "Race Suicide in the United States," *American Journal of Physical Anthropology* 3, no. 1 (1920): 145–46; emphasis added.

17. Frederick Osborn, *Preface to Eugenics* (New York: Harper Brothers, 1940); Frederick Osborn, *The Future of Human Heredity: An Introduction to Eugenics in Modern Society* (New York: Weybright and Talley, 1968).

18. See: Robert B. Zajonc and Gregory B. Markus, "Birth Order and Intellectual Development," *Psychological Review* 82 (1975): 74–88; Robert B. Zajonc, Gregory B. Markus, Michael L. Berbaum, John A. Bargh, and Richard L. Moreland, "One Justified Criticism plus Three Flawed Analyses Equals Two Unwarranted Conclusions: A Reply to Retherford and Sewell," *American Sociological Review* 56, no. 1 (1991): 159–65.

19. R. D. Retherford and W. H. Sewell, "Intelligence and Family Size Reconsidered," *Social Biology* 35 (1988): 1–40; Robert D. Retherford and W. H. Sewell, "Birth Order and Intelligence: Further Tests of the Confluence Model," *American Sociological Review* 56, no. 2 (1991): 141–58; Judith Blake, *Family Size and Achievement* (Berkeley: University of California Press, 1989), chapters 4 and 5.

20. For examples of this work in the United States, see: Dublin, "The Significance of the Declining Birth Rate"; Thompson, "Race Suicide in the United States," 97–146; and Walter F. Willcox, "Fewer Births and Deaths: What Do They Mean?" *Journal of Heredity* 7, no. 3 (March 1920): 119–27. For a description of this work in Britain, see Soloway, *Demography and Degeneration,* 86–109, 193–225, 312–62.

21. For a discussion of the context of this paper, see Allan Chase, *The Legacy of Malthus: The Social Costs of the New Scientific Racism* (Urbana: University of Illinois Press, 1980), 9, 308–10, 491.

22. For a more detailed treatment of Paul Ehrlich's role, see Allan Chase's *The Legacy of Malthus,* 397–405.

23. For example, on the impact of reproductive differentials on population intelligence, some researchers find a dysgenic trend. See: W. J. Andrews, "Eugenics Revisited," *Mankind Quarterly* 30 (1990): 235–302; M. VanCourt and F. D. Bean, "Intelligence and Fertility in the United States: 1912–1982," *Intelligence* 9 (1985): 23–32; D. R. Vining, "On the Possibility of the Reemergence of a Dysgenic Trend with Respect to Intelligence in American Fertility Differentials," *Intelligence* 6 (1982): 241–64; D. R. Vining, "Social versus Reproductive Success: The Central Theoretical Problem of Human Sociobiology," *Behavioral and Brain Sciences* 9 (1986): 167–216; M. J. Ree and J. A. Earles, "The Stability of $g$ across Different Methods of Estimation," *Intelligence* 15 (1991): 271–78; Retherford and Sewell, "Intelligence and Family Size Reconsidered"; Richard J. Herrnstein and Charles Murray, *The Bell Curve: Intelligence and Class Structure in American Life* (New York: Free Press, 1994). Other population scientists find

no evidence of any dysgenic trend in the United States. See: J. V. Higgins, E. W. Reed, and S. C. Reed, "Intelligence and Family Size: A Paradox Resolved," *Social Biology* 9 (1962): 84–90; M. R. Olneck, B. L. Wolfe, and C. Dean, "Intelligence and Family Size: Another Look," *Review of Economic and Statistics* 62 (1980): 241–47.

24.  Daniel Kevles, *In the Name of Eugenics: Genetics and the Uses of Human Heredity* (Berkeley: University of California Press, 1985); Richard A. Soloway, *Demography and Degeneration: Eugenics and the Declining Birthrate in Twentieth-Century Britain* (Chapel Hill: University of North Carolina Press, 1990); and Degler, *In Search of Human Nature.*

25.  For more information on the individuals and personalities who crossed both lines in the early part of the twentieth century, see Shapiro, *Population Control Politics,* 45–47; and Kevles, *In the Name of Eugenics,* 59–60; see also Soloway, *Demography and Degeneration.*

26.  "A New Name—Society for the Study of Social Biology" (formerly the American Eugenics Society). This "note" was listed in the contents, and I assume it contained an editor's comments (see *Social Biology* 20 (1973): 1).

27.  Ibid.

28.  "Society for the Study of Social Biology: Descriptions and Goals," *Social Biology* 40 (1993): 158.

29.  Ibid.; and Antonio McDaniel, "Fertility and Racial Stratification," *Population and Development Review* S22 (1996): 134–50.

30.  Several excellent books have attempted to explain various aspects of these developments. See: Daniel J. Kevles, *In The Name of Eugenics: Genetics and the Uses of Human Heredity* (Berkeley: University of California Press, 1985); Saul Dubow, *Scientific Racism in Modern South Africa* (Cambridge: Cambridge University Press, 1995); Stefan Kühl, *The Nazi Connection: Eugenics, American Racism, and German National Socialism* (New York: Oxford University Press, 1994); Nancy Leys Stepan, *"The Hour of Eugenics": Race, Gender, and Nation in Latin America* (Ithaca: Cornell University Press, 1991); Soloway, *Demography and Degeneration;* and Du Bois, *Black Reconstruction.*

31.  Stepan, *"The Hour of Eugenics,"* 46–64.

32.  Shapiro, *Population Control Politics,* 37.

33.  Shapiro, *Population Control Politics,* 36; and Robert V. Guthrie, *Even the Rat Was White* (New York: Harper & Row, 1976), 86–88.

34.  Kühl, *The Nazi Connection,* 32–35. In 1947, the IUSSPP dropped "Problems" from its name.

35.  Ibid., 32.

36.  Francis Galton, *Hereditary Genius: An Inquiry into Its Laws and Consequences* (1892, 2d ed.; reprint, Gloucester, Mass.: Peter Smith, 1972), 86.

37.  Davenport was a leading individual in the eugenics movement between 1900 and 1935. He was active in bringing eugenicists in the United States and Germany closer together (Kühl, *The Nazi Connection,* 67–69).

38.  Ibid., 42–44.

39.  E. S. Gosney and Paul Popenoe, *Sterilization for Human Betterment: A Summary of Results of 6,000 Operations in California, 1909–1929* (New York: Macmillan, 1931). Earlier, in 1918, Paul Popenoe, a student of Charles Davenport, also wrote (with Roswell Hill Johnson) *Applied Genetics,* a major genetics text (Paul Popenoe

and Roswell Hill Johnson, *Applied Genetics* [New York: Macmillan, 1918]). In this text the authors argue that Africans are inferior to Europeans and that the color line is not only necessary but also natural.

40. Gosney and Popenoe, *Sterilization for Human Betterment,* 135.

41. Compare Dubow, *Scientific Racism in Modern South Africa;* Stepan, "*The Hour of Eugenics*"; Kühl, *The Nazi Connection;* and Soloway, *Demography and Degeneration.*

42. Stepan, "*The Hour of Eugenics*"; Kevles, *In the Name of Eugenics.*

43. Stepan, "*The Hour of Eugenics.*"

44. Dubow, *Scientific Racism in Modern South Africa,* 128–32, 135, chapter 5.

45. Kühl, *The Nazi Connection,* 78–79.

46. For an excellent discussion of the past influence of the eugenics movement, see Kühl, *The Nazi Connection,* 65–76. For some examples of contemporary influences, see R. A. Gordon, "SES Versus IQ in the Race-IQ Delinquency Model," *International Journal of Sociology and Social Policy* 7 (1987): 30–96; Edward O. Wilson, *On Human Nature* (Cambridge, Mass.: Harvard University Press, 1978), esp. 195–209; James Q. Wilson and Richard J. Herrnstein, *Crime and Human Nature* (New York: Simon and Schuster, 1985); Herrnstein and Murray, *The Bell Curve.*

47. James S. Coleman, E. Q. Campbell, C. J. Hobson, J. McPartland, A. M. Mood, F. D. Weinfeld, and R. L. York, *Equality of Educational Opportunity* (Washington, D.C.: U.S. Government Printing Office, 1966).

48. Nicholas Lemann, *The Big Test: The Secret History of the American Meritocracy* (New York: Farrar, Straus, Giroux, 1999), 161.

49. See William H. Tucker, *The Science and Politics of Racial Research* (Urbana: University of Illinois Press, 1994), chapter 5, for a detailed discussion of Shockley and Jensen.

50. Arthur Jensen, "The Culturally Disadvantaged: Psychological and Educational Aspects," *Educational Research* 10 (1967): 10.

51. Arthur R. Jensen, "How Much Can We Boost IQ and Scholastic Achievement?" *Harvard Educational Review* 39, no. 1 (1969): 1–123.

52. Tucker, *The Science and Politics of Racial Research,* 260–64.

53. See Ashley Montagu, ed., *Race and IQ* (New York: Oxford University Press, 1975).

54. Arthur R. Jensen, *Bias in Mental Testing* (New York: Free Press, 1979). Jensen dedicated this volume "to the memory of the great pioneers: Sir Francis Galton (1822–1911), Alfred Binet (1857–1911), Charles Spearman (1863–1945)." Herrnstein and Murray, *The Bell Curve.*

55. For example, both Herrnstein and Murray's *The Bell Curve* and Dinesh D'Souza's *The End of Racism* (New York: Free Press, 1995) received wide coverage in the media.

56. Herrnstein and Murray, *The Bell Curve,* chapter 13; D'Souza, *The End of Racism,* chapter 11; J. Philippe Rushton, *Race, Evolution, and Behavior: A Life History Perspective* (New Brunswick, N.J.: Transaction Publishers, 1995), chapter 6; Michael Levin, *Why Race Matters: Race Differences and What They Mean* (Westport, Conn.: Praeger, 1997), chapter 3.

57. Herrnstein and Murray, *The Bell Curve,* 275. Even Jensen was aware of the potential for confounding "biological" aspects of race and other factors. He noted, "Thus, the term 'race' here is not exclusively a biological factor but some combina-

tion of all the factors associated with the racial classification except whatever socio-economic factors are measured by the SES index" (Jensen, *Bias in Mental Testing*, 43).

58. Herrnstein and Murray, *The Bell Curve*, 360–61.

59. Ibid., chapters 13–16.

60. For examples of this research, see Frances Cress Welsing, *The Isis Papers: The Keys to the Colors* (Chicago: Third World Press, 1991); Richard King, *African Origin of Biological Psychiatry* (Germantown, Tenn.: Seymour-Smith, 1990); Carol Barnes, *Melanin: The Chemical Key to Black Greatness* (n.p., 1988); Richard D. King, "The Symbolism of the Crown in Ancient Egypt," *Journal of African Civilization* 6, no. 2 (1985): 133–52; T. Owens Moore, *The Science of Melanin: Dispelling the Myths* (Silver Spring, Md.: Venture Books/Beckham House Publishers, 1995).

61. Welsing, *The Isis Papers*, vi.

62. Ibid., 6.

63. St. Clair Drake, *Black Folk Here and There: An Essay in History and Anthropology* (Los Angeles: University of California, Center for Afro-American Studies, 1987) 1:99–101.

64. King, *African Origin of Biological Psychiatry*, 24.

65. Welsing, *The Isis Papers*, chap. 1; King, *African Origin of Biological Psychiatry*, chap. 1.

66. Welsing, *The Isis Papers*, 12–13.

67. For a summary of the scientific literature on African and African American biological diversity, see Fatimah Linda Collier Jackson, "Evolutionary and Political Economic Influences on Biological Diversity in African Americans," *Journal of Black Studies* 23, no. 4 (1993): 539–60.

68. For the latest scientific evidence of the African population being the original, see R. L. Cann, M. Stoneking, and A. C. Wilson, "Mitochondrial DNA and Human Evolution," *Nature* 325 (1995): 31–36. For an introduction to this subject, see: Roger Lewin, *Human Evolution: An Illustrated Introduction* (Boston: Blackwell Scientific, 1993), chapters 25 and 26; Cheikh Anta Diop, *Civilization or Barbarism: An Authentic Anthropology* (Chicago: Lawrence Hill Books, 1991), pt. 1; and Christopher Stringer and Robin McKie, *African Exodus: The Origins of Modern Humanity* (New York: Henry Holt, 1996), chapter 5. For an opposing view to the monogenetic origins of humanity in Africa, see Milford Wolpoff and Rachel Caspari, *Race and Human Evolution* (New York: Simon and Schuster, 1997). For the discussions of the paleontological evidence for the monogenetic origins of humanity, see Diop, *Civilization or Barbarism*, chapters 1 and 2; and Stringer and McKie, *African Exodus*, chapters 1 and 7. For a discussion of the genetic evidence, see Luca Cavalli-Sforza, Paolo Menozzi, and Alberto Piazza, *The History and Geography of Human Genes* (Princeton: Princeton University Press, 1994), chapter 2.

69. As the geneticist Fatima Jackson notes, Africans are the most biologically diverse population in the world (see Jackson, "Evolutionary and Political Economic Influences").

70. For a review of the scientific literature on this subject, see Rick Kittles, "Nature, Origin, and Variation of Human Pigmentation," *Journal of Black Studies* 26, no. 1 (1995): 36–61; see also Diop, *Civilization or Barbarism*, chapter 2.

71. Diop, *Civilization or Barbarism*, 15–16.

72. Ibid., 16.

73. Ibid., 63.

74. Herrnstein and Murray, *The Bell Curve*, chapter 13; D'Souza, *The End of Racism*, chapter 11; Rushton, *Race, Evolution, and Behavior*, chap. 6; Levin, *Why Race Matters*, chapter 3.

75. For recent examples, see Herrnstein and Murray, *The Bell Curve*; D'Souza, *The End of Racism*.

76. D'Souza, *The End of Racism*, 437.

77. Ibid., 422.

78. Glenn C. Loury, *One by One from the Inside Out: Essays and Reviews on Race and Responsibility in America* (New York: Free Press, 1995), 304.

## 5. Noneugenic Racial Statistics

1. On Laplace, see Anders Hald, *A History of Mathematical Statistics from 1750 to 1930* (New York: John Wiley and Sons, 1998), 286–89. On Weber, see Alain Desrosières, *The Politics of Large Numbers: A History of Statistical Reasoning* (Cambridge, Mass.: Harvard University Press, 1998), 185.

2. Martin Bulmer, Kevin Bales, and Kathryn Kish Sklar, "The Social Survey in Historical Perspective," in *The Social Survey in Historical Perspective, 1880–1940*, ed. Martin Bulmer, Kevin Bales, and Kathryn Kish Sklar (New York: Cambridge University Press, 1991), 19.

3. Charles Booth, *The Aged Poor in England and Wales: Conditions* (London: Macmillan, 1894).

4. George Udny Yule, "On the Correlation of Total Pauperism with Proportion of Out-Relief, I: All Ages," *Economic Journal* 5 (1895): 603–11.

5. George Udny Yule, "An Investigation into the Causes of Changes in Pauperism in England, Chiefly during the Last Two Intercensal Decades," *Journal of the Royal Statistical Society* 62 (1899): 249–95. In modern notation his regression equation could be rewritten as follows: $\Delta Pauperism = a + b \cdot \Delta O + c \cdot \Delta P + d \cdot \Delta A + error$. Here, $\Delta$ stands for percentage difference, $O$ for the out-of-doors relief ratio, $P$ for population size, and $A$ for the proportion of the population over age sixty-five (for an analysis of this regression, see David A. Freedman, "From Association to Causation via Regression," in *Causality in Crisis? Statistical Methods and the Search for Causal Knowledge in Social Science*, ed. Vaughn R. McKim and Stephen P. Turner [Notre Dame: University of Notre Dame Press, 1997], 114–18).

6. W. E. B. Du Bois, *The Philadelphia Negro: A Social Study* (Philadelphia: University of Pennsylvania Press, 1899), 3.

7. W. E. B. Du Bois, *The Autobiography of W. E. B. Du Bois: A Soliloquy on Viewing My Life from the Last Decades of Its First Century* (New York: International Publishers, 1968), 198.

8. Ibid.

9. Émile Durkheim, *Suicide: A Study in Sociology*, trans. John A. Spaulding and George Simpson (original French publication, 1897; New York: Free Press, 1951).

10. For a more extensive discussion of this distinction, see Desrosières, *The Politics of Large Numbers*, 96–101.

11. Durkheim, *Suicide*, 318.

12. Du Bois, *The Philadelphia Negro*, especially chapter. 2 and appendix A.

13. A. L. Bowley, "Measurement of the Precision Attained in Sampling," *Bulletin of the International Statistical Institute* 22, Suppl. to Book 1 (1926): 1–62; also see

Bowley's first use of this method in a sampling of a list of bonds and interest rates in 1906 (A. L. Bowley, "Address to the Economic Science and Statistics Section," *Journal of the Royal Statistical Society* 69 [1906]: 540–57). He used the final digits in one of the tables in the *Nautical Almanac* to make the random selection. J. Neyman, "On Two Different Aspects of the Representative Method: The Method of Stratified Sampling and the Method of Purposive Selection," *Journal of the Royal Statistical Society* 97 (1934): 558–625.

14. Bulmer, Bales, and Sklar, "The Social Survey in Historical Perspective," 39.

15. For an excellent summary of the history of the conversion of the informal social survey into the formal social survey, see Peter H. Rossi, James D. Wright, and Andy B. Anderson, eds., *Handbook of Survey Research* (Orlando: Academic Press, 1983), 2–8.

16. For Du Bois on the empirical observation of human action, see W. E. B. Du Bois, "The Study of the Negro Problems," *Annals of the American Academy of Political and Social Science* 11, no. 1 (1898): 1–23. For the influence of the positivist school in economic history on Du Bois's work, see Dan S. Green and Edwin O. Driver, "W. E. B. Du Bois: A Case in the Sociology of Sociological Negation," *Phylon* 37 (1976): 309–33. On the influence of DuBois's professors, see Francis L. Broderick, "German Influence on the Scholarship of W. E. B. Du Bois," *Phylon* 19, no. 3 (1958): 367–71. On the influence of Charles Booth, see Bulmer, Bales, and Sklar, "The Social Survey in Historical Perspective," 1–48; and Martin Bulmer, "W. E. B. Du Bois as a Social Investigator: *The Philadelphia Negro* 1899," in *The Social Survey in Historical Perspective*, ed. Bulmer, Bales, and Sklar, 170–88.

17. Du Bois, "The Study of the Negro Problems," 3.

18. Ibid., 3.

19. Du Bois, *The Autobiography of W. E. B. Du Bois*, 198.

20. Du Bois, *The Philadelphia Negro*, 2–3.

21. Earlier "empirical" studies were found in Benjamin C. Bacon, *Statistics of the Colored People of Philadelphia* (Philadelphia, 1856); *The Present State and Condition of the Free People of Colour of the City of Philadelphia and Adjoining Districts, as Exhibited by the Report of a Committee of the Pennsylvania Society Promoting the Abolition of Slavery, etc.* (Philadelphia: by the society, 1838); Benjamin C. Bacon, *A Statistical Inquiry into the Condition of the People of Color of the City and Districts of Philadelphia* (Philadelphia: Kite and Walton, 1849); and Edward Needles, *Ten Years' Progress: or a Comparison of the State and Condition of the Colored People in the City and County of Philadelphia from 1837 to 1847* (Philadelphia: Merrihew and Thompson, 1849). None of these studies was a social survey, nor was any comparable to the breadth and depth of Du Bois's study.

22. Du Bois, *The Autobiography of W. E. B. Du Bois*, 198–99.

23. The Department of Labor studies were: W. E. B. Du Bois, *The Negroes of Farmville, Virginia: A Social Study*, U.S. Department of Labor, Bulletin 3, No. 14 (Washington, D.C.: Government Printing Office, 1898); W. E. B. Du Bois, *The Negro in the Black Belt: Some Social Sketches*, U.S. Department of Labor, Bulletin 4, No. 22 (Washington, D.C.: Government Printing Office, 1899) (while Du Bois was listed as the author of this volume, several of his students assisted him with the collection of data and reports on the conditions of the various areas studied; this method was used most successfully in the Atlanta University studies); W. E. B. Du Bois, *The Negro*

*Landholder of Georgia,* U.S. Department of Labor, Bulletin 6, No. 35 (Washington, D.C.: Government Printing Office, 1901); W. E. B. Du Bois, *The Negro Farmer,* U.S. Department of Labor, Bulletin 8 (Washington, D.C.: Government Printing Office, 1904). *The Negro Farmer* was reissued with supplementary material in *Special Reports: Supplementary Analysis and Derivative Tables, Twelfth Census of the United States, 1900* (Washington, D.C.: Government Printing Office, 1906).

In addition to these government-commissioned studies, Du Bois created a laboratory for the continuation of the Philadelphia project at Atlanta University. He hoped through these studies to investigate broadly and systematically all the topics in the field of race. He may not have accomplished this task in full; however, what he did do was impressive. Aided by his students and colleagues from around the country, he was the senior author of nineteen studies and reports as part of his Atlanta University research on the American Negro (for a listing of these studies, see Ernest Kaiser, "A Selected Bibliography of the Published Writings of W. E. B. Du Bois," in *Black Titan: W. E. B. Du Bois, an Anthology by the Editors of Freedomways,* ed. John Henrik Clarke, Esther Jackson, Ernest Kaiser, and J. H. O'Dell (Boston: Beacon Press, 1970), 313–14.

24. For examples of his early work see, Franz Boas, "Human Faculty as Determined by Race," *Proceedings of the American Association for the Advancement of Science* 43 (August 1894): 301–7; and Franz Boas, "The Mind of Primitive Men," *Journal of American Folklore* 14 (January–March 1901): 1–11.

25. Franz Boas, *The Mind of Primitive Man* (New York: Macmillan, 1911), 115.

26. Du Bois, *The Philadelphia Negro,* 388.

27. David Levering Lewis, *W. E. B. Du Bois: Biography of a Race, 1868–1916* (New York: Henry Holt, 1993), 179–80, 206–7.

28. Some, like Pitirim Sorokin and Frank H. Hankins, took a Social Darwinist perspective and held the new eugenic research in high esteem. See Pitirim Sorokin, *Contemporary Sociological Theories* (New York: Harper and Brothers, 1928); Frank H. Hankins, *The Racial Basis of Civilization: A Critique of the Nordic Doctrine* (New York: Alfred A. Knopf, 1926). Others, like Edward B. Reuter and Robert E. Park, took a Eurocentric perspective that emphasized European cultural superiority. Eurocentric refers to the tradition of assuming that Europe and European peoples should be the point of departure for understanding social behavior. The Eurocentric perspective that has dominated the American and European academy views Europe as the exclusive birthplace of "high civilization." The remainder of humanity is judged on the basis of their closeness to the European model of behavior and achievements. For examples of this perspective, see: Robert E. Park, *Race and Culture* (Chicago: Free Press, 1950); and Edward Byron Reuter, *The American Race Problem: A Study of the Negro* (New York: Thomas Y. Crowell, 1927).

29. Park, *Race and Culture;* E. Franklin Frazier, *Race and Culture Contacts in the Modern World* (Boston: Beacon Press, 1957). Park eventually called his assimilationist model into question; however, the impact of the model continues to be substantial (see John H. Stanfield, "Methodological Reflections: An Introduction," in *Race and Ethnicity in Research Methods,* ed. John H. Stanfield and Rutledge M. Dennis [Newbury Park: Sage Publications, 1993], 3–15).

30. Park, *Race and Culture,* 211.

31. Ibid.; Frazier, *Race and Culture Contacts in the Modern World.*

32. Park, *Race and Culture*, 118.

33. Du Bois's classic effort has not been replicated. Early-twentieth-century sociology was dominated by the Chicago School tradition of using the city as a laboratory for studying immigrant assimilation, and racial isolation became a special case of the problems of assimilation. For some classic examples of the Chicago School tradition, see: Robert E. Park and Ernest W. Burgess, *The City* (Chicago: University of Chicago Press, 1925); Louis Wirth, *The Ghetto* (Chicago: University of Chicago Press, 1928); and Franklin Frazier, *The Negro Family in Chicago* (Chicago: University of Chicago Press, 1932).

34. Du Bois, *The Philadelphia Negro*, 11.

35. St. Clair Drake and Horace R. Cayton, *Black Metropolis: A Study of Negro Life in a Northern City* (1945; Chicago: University of Chicago Press, 1993), 551.

36. Allison Davis, Burleigh B. Gardner, and Mary R. Gardner, *Deep South: A Social Anthropological Study of Caste and Class* (1941; Los Angeles: University of California, Center for Afro-American Studies, 1988), 15–58. For a critique of the caste aspect of Davis and colleagues' argument, see Oliver C. Cox, *Caste, Class, and Race* (New York: Doubleday, 1948), 423–524.

37. For a detailed description and discussion of the intellectual world and racial views of sociologists, see: James B. McKee, *Sociology and the Race Problem: The Failure of a Perspective* (Urbana: University of Illinois Press, 1993); and Stephen Steinberg, *Turning Back: The Retreat from Racial Justice in American Thought and Policy* (Boston: Beacon Press, 1995).

38. Du Bois, *The Philadelphia Negro*, 390. "Nevertheless the Negro problems are not more hopelessly complex than many others have been. Their elements despite their bewildering complication can be kept clearly in view: they are after all the same difficulties over which the world has grown gray: the question as to how far human intelligence can be trusted and trained; as to whether we must always have the poor with us; as to whether it is possible for the mass of men to attain righteousness on earth; and then to this is added that question of questions: after all who are Men? Is every featherless biped to be counted a man and brother? Are all races and types to be joint heirs of the new earth that men have striven to raise in thirty centuries and more? Shall we not swamp civilization in barbarism and drown genius in indulgence if we seek a mythical Humanity which shall shadow all men?" (Du Bois, *The Philadelphia Negro*, 385–86).

39. Du Bois, *The Philadelphia Negro*; William Julius Wilson, *The Truly Disadvantaged: The Inner City, the Underclass, and Public Policy* (Chicago: University of Chicago Press, 1987).

40. William Julius Wilson concludes his manuscript with the following suggestion: "In the final analysis, therefore, the challenge of economic dislocation in modern industrial society calls for public policy programs to attack inequality on a broad class front, policy programs, in other words, that go beyond the limits of ethnic and racial discrimination by directly confronting the pervasive and destructive features of class subordination" (William Julius Wilson, *The Declining Significance of Race: Blacks and Changing American Institutions* [Chicago: University of Chicago Press, 1978], 154).

On the other hand, Charles Murray concludes his manuscript with the following suggestion: "There is no shortage of institutions to provide the rewards. Our schools know how to educate students who want to be educated. Our industries know how to find productive people and reward them. Our police know how to protect people who are ready to cooperate in their own protection. Our system of justice knows how to protect the rights of individuals who know what their rights are. Our philanthropic institutions know how to multiply the effectiveness of people who are already trying to help themselves. In short, American society is very good at reinforcing the investment of an individual in himself. For the affluent and for the middle class, these mechanisms continue to work about as well as they ever have, and we enjoy their benefits. Not so for the poor. American government, in its recent social policy, has been ineffectual in trying to stage-manage their decision to invest, and it has been unintentionally punitive toward those who would make the decision on their own. It is time to get out of their way" (Charles Murray, *Losing Ground: American Social Policy, 1950–1980* [New York: Basic Books, 1984], 234–35).

In addition to these conclusive statements contrast how they examine employment in chapter 5 of both books (for example, compare Wilson's *The Declining Significance of Race*, tables 5 and 6, with Murray's *Losing Ground*, figures 5.2 and 5.3).

41. For examples of this type of model, see H. M. Blalock, "Four-Variable Causal Models and Partial Correlations," *American Journal of Sociology* 68 (1962): 182–94; O. D. Duncan, *Introduction to Structural Equation Models* (New York: Academic Press, 1975); and K. A. Bollen, *Structural Equations with Latent Variables* (New York: John Wiley and Sons, 1989).

42. For a more formal definition and discussion of experimental designs and randomization, see Leslie Kish, *Statistical Design for Research* (New York: John Wiley and Sons, 1987), 11–17.

43. Experiments do not identify causes, but they measure the effects of given causes or the effects of the experimental manipulations. Experimental results produce statements like "An effect of racism is higher rates of poverty," not "Racism is a cause of poverty," unless we mean by the theoretical language of the latter no more than is meant in the experimental language of the former. While theories are superseded, experiments are reinterpreted and replicated. See Paul W. Holland, "Statistics and Causal Inference," *Journal of the American Statistical Association* 81, no. 396 (1986): 945–70; and Michael E. Sobel, "Causal Inference in the Social and Behavioral Sciences," in *Handbook of Statistical Modeling for the Social and Behavioral Sciences*, ed. Gerhard Arminger, Clifford C. Clogg, and Michael E. Sobel (New York: Plenum Press, 1995), 1–38; and Paul W. Holland, "Causal Inference, Path Analysis, and Recursive Structural Equations Models," *Sociological Methodology* 18 (1988): 449–484. For another view supportive of the attribution of causation in social science research, see Margaret Mooney Marini and Burton Singer, "Causality in the Social Sciences," *Sociological Methodology* 18 (1988): 347–409.

44. Richard G. Rogers, "Living and Dying in the U.S.A.: Sociodemographic Determinants of Death among Blacks and Whites," *Demography* 29, no. 2 (1992): 287–303; Daniel A. Powers and James Cherng-Tay Hsueh, "Sibling Models of Socioeconomic Effects on the Timing of First Premarital Birth," *Demography* 34, no. 4 (1997): 493–511; Arthur Sakamoto, Huei-Hsia Wu, and Jessie M. Tzeng, "The Declining Significance of Race among American Men during the Latter Half of the Twentieth Century," *Demography* 37, no. 1 (2000): 41–51.

45. Paul L. Menchik, "Economic Status as a Determinant of Mortality among Black and White Older Men: Does Poverty Kill?" *Population Studies* 47 (1993): 427–36, quotation from 435; emphasis added.

46. Timothy J. Biblarz and Adrian E. Raftery, "Family Structure, Educational Attainment, and Socioeconomic Success: Rethinking the 'Pathology of Matriarchy,'" *American Journal of Sociology* 105 (1999): 349; emphasis added.

47. Michael Hughes and Melvin E. Thomas, "The Continuing Significance of Race Revisited: A Study of Race, Class, and Quality of Life in America, 1972 to 1996," *American Sociological Review* 63 (1998): 787; emphasis added.

48. Clifford C. Clogg and Adamantios Haritou, "The Regression Method of Causal Inference and a Dilemma Confronting This Method," in *Causality in Crisis? Statistical Methods and the Search for Causal Knowledge in the Social Sciences,* ed. Vaughn R. McKim and Stephen P. Turner (Notre Dame: University of Notre Dame Press, 1997), 83–112; Freedman, "From Association to Causation via Regression," 113–62.

49. See Sakamoto, Wu, and Tzeng, "The Declining Significance of Race among American Men," 50.

50. Menchik, "Economic Status as a Determinant of Mortality among Black and White Older Men," 435.


## Part III. Beyond Racial Statistics

1. For an example of this research, see William Petersen, *Ethnicity Counts* (New Brunswick, N.J.: Transaction Publishers, 1997). This important contribution does not cover the issue of how we will deal with racial stratification without collecting racial data. It also lacks a critique of the methodology that has accompanied the debates among geneticists, statisticians, and other social scientists.

2. For some examples, see: Lee D. Baker, *From Savage to Negro: Anthropology and the Construction of Race, 1896–1954* (Berkeley: University of California Press, 1998); Patricia Hill Collins, *Fighting Words: Black Women and the Search for Justice* (Minneapolis: University of Minnesota Press, 1998); Lewis R. Gordon, *Bad Faith and Antiblack Racism* (Atlantic Highlands, N.J.: Humanities Press, 1995); Lewis R. Gordon, *Fanon and the Crisis of European Man: An Essay on Philosophy and the Human Sciences* (New York: Routledge, 1995); James B. McKee, *Sociology and the Race Problem: The Failure of a Perspective* (Urbana: University of Illinois Press, 1993); and Charles W. Mills, *The Racial Contract* (Ithaca: Cornell University Press, 1997).

3. For examples, see: Paul W. Holland, "Statistics and Causal Inference," *Journal of the American Statistical Association* 81, no. 396 (1986): 945–60; Michael E. Sobel, "Causal Inference in the Social and Behavioral Sciences," in *Handbook of Statistical Modeling for Social and Behavioral Science,* ed. Gerhard Arminger, Clifford C. Clogg, and Michael E. Sobel (New York: Plenum Press, 1995), 1–38; David R. Cox, "Causality: Some Statistical Aspects," *Journal of the Royal Statistical Society,* Series A, 155 (1992): part 2, 291–301; and Paul R. Rosenbaum, "From Association to Causation in Observational Studies: The Role of Tests of Strongly Ignorable Treatment Assignment," *Journal of the American Statistical Association* 79, no. 385 (1984): 41–47.

4. Other studies have focused on the conceptualization of race. This important line of research has not focused on the methodological implication of the use of race as a variable in social statistics. See n. 16 to the introduction.

5. Clifford Clogg and Adamantios Haritou argue that "without assumptions or knowledge that cannot be determined from or validated with the data in hand, we cannot tell whether a given model gives a biased estimator of the causal effect of X

or Y due to omitted variables or due to included variables, or whether any partial regression coefficient is unbiased, or indeed whether any of the possible models permit unbiased estimation to any of the causal effects" (Clifford Clogg and Adamantios Haritou, "The Regression Method of Causal Inference and a Dilemma Confronting This Method," in *Causality in Crisis? Statistical Methods and the Search for Causal Knowledge in the Social Sciences*, ed. Vaughn R. McKim and Stephen P. Turner [Notre Dame: University of Notre Dame Press, 1997], 104). David Freedman asks, "[C]an quantitative social scientists infer causality by applying statistical technology to correlation matrices?" And he answers, "That is not a mathematical question, because the answer turns on the way the world is put together. As I read the record, correlational methods have not delivered the goods. We need to work on measurement, design and theory. Fancier statistics are not likely to help much" (David A. Freedman, "From Association to Causation via Regression," in *Causality in Crisis?* ed. McKim and Turner, 157; also see David A. Freedman, "As Others See Us: A Case Study in Path Analysis," *Journal of Education Statistics* 12, no. 2 [1987]: 101–28.

## 6. Challenging Race as a Variable

1. Lucius T. Outlaw, Jr., *On Race and Philosophy* (New York: Routledge, 1996), 169.

2. Patricia Hill Collins, *Fighting Words: Black Women and the Search for Justice* (Minneapolis: University of Minnesota Press, 1998), 123.

3. Lewis R. Gordon, *Bad Faith and Antiblack Racism* (Atlantic Highlands, N.J.: Humanities Press, 1995), 136.

4. European eugenic arguments assumed a single best homozygous type of human as their objective. In general, populations provide one another with genetic material, adding diversity and heterogeneity to the gene pool. Genetic diversity is an advantage for any particular gene pool. It provides individual heterozygosity, which is more beneficial than homozygosity in individuals. (*Heterozygosity* refers to the proportion of diploid organisms that have inherited different alleles [of any particular gene] from each parent for a given locus in a population. *Homozygosity* refers to the proportion of diploid organisms that have inherited the same allele from both parents for a given locus in a population.) From a genetic perspective the eugenic ideal is dysgenic.

5. James E. Bowman and Robert F. Murray, *Genetic Variation and Disorders in Peoples of African Origin* (Baltimore: Johns Hopkins University Press, 1990), 76–77; also see Edward O. Wilson, *Consilience: The Unity of Knowledge* (New York: Alfred A. Knopf, 1998), 146.

6. Julian Adams, "Introduction: Genetics and Demography and Historical Information," in *Convergent Issues in Genetics and Demography,* ed. Julian Adams et al. (New York: Oxford University Press, 1990), 3–13. Humans are a community with the potential for random mating despite race.

7. James C. King, *The Biology of Race* (Berkeley: University of California Press, 1981), 156–57.

8. Luca Cavalli-Sforza, Paolo Menozzi, and Alberto Piazza, *The History and Geography of Human Genes* (Princeton: Princeton University Press, 1994), 19.

9. Bowman and Murray, *Genetic Variation and Disorders in Peoples of African Origin,* ix.

10. In chapter 1 of *The Biology of Race,* King provides an informative discussion on the concept of race as understood by conventional biology. See also Phyllis B. Eveleth and James M. Tanner, *Worldwide Variation in Human Growth,* 2d ed. (Cambridge: Cambridge University Press, 1990) for the authoritative discussion of population differences in stature and growth; and Bowman and Murray, *Genetic Variation and Disorders in Peoples of African Origin.*

11. Cavalli-Sforza, Menozzi, and Piazza, *The History and Geography of Human Genes,* 4.

12. *Genotype* refers to the genetic constitution of an organism, which acting together with environmental factors determines phenotype. *Phenotype* refers to the visible or otherwise measurable physical and biochemical characteristics of an organism. *Phenotype* also refers to a group of individuals exhibiting the same phenotypic characters. *Morphology* refers to the form and structure of an organism as distinct from its physiology. See Eleanor Lawrence, ed., *Henderson's Dictionary of Biological Terms,* 11th ed. (New York: John Wiley and Sons, 1995), 225, 362, 432.

13. Eveleth and Tanner, *Worldwide Variation in Human Growth,* chapters 8–10.

14. Geoffrey Dean, *The Porphyrias* (London: Pitman, 1963); Phillip V. Tobias, "History of Physical Anthropology in Southern Africa," *Yearbook of Physical Anthropology* 28 (1985): 1–52. *Henderson's Dictionary of Biological Terms* defines a "founder effect" as the genetic differences between an original population and an isolated offshoot due to alleles in the founder members of the new population being unrepresentative of the alleles in the original population as a whole.

15. Jonathan Marks, *Human Biodiversity: Genes, Race, and History* (New York: Aldine de Gruyter, 1995), 164–65.

16. Marks, *Human Biodiversity,* 157–82; Cavalli-Sforza, Menozzi, and Piazza, *The History and Geography of Human Genes,* especially chapters 3, 4, and 5.

17. The spread of AIDS is an excellent example of how culture influences biology and has an impact on the demographic composition of the population. There is some evidence to suggest that resistance to HIV is higher among European-origin populations than among African-origin populations as a result of genetic differences. Population geneticist Stephen O'Brien and his colleagues at the National Cancer Institute offer strong evidence that persons with two mutant copies of the CKRS gene (the chemokine receptor that HIV uses when it initially affects white cells) are resistant to HIV infection and that persons who get infected with HIV, but have a mutant copy of the CKRS gene, progress to AIDS more slowly than persons without the mutation. O'Brien's team saw the mutant allele much more frequently in people of European descent (11 percent) than in people of African descent (1.7 percent). AIDS is characterized by the deterioration of the immune system and is triggered by a virus known as the human immunodeficiency virus (HIV). HIV is contracted by sexual contact, by the transfer of blood, or by being born to a mother with the disease. Other ways of contracting the disease have been suggested but not conclusively established to date. See Michael Dean et al., "Genetic Restrictions of HIV-1 Infection and Progression to AIDS by a deletion allele of the CKRS Structural Gene," *Science* 273, no. 5283 (1996): 1856–63.

18. Richard S. Cooper and Charles N. Rotimi, "Hypertension in Populations of West African Origin: Is There a Genetic Predisposition?" *Journal of Hypertension* 12, no. 3 (1994): 215–27; Richard S. Cooper, Charles N. Rotimi, Susan L. Ataman, Daniel L. McGee, Babatunde Osotimehin, Solomon Kadiri, Walinjon Muna, Samuel Kingue,

Henry Fraser, Terrence Forrester, Franklyn Bennett, and Rainford Wilks, "Hypertension Prevalence in Seven Populations of African Origin," *American Journal of Public Health* 87, no. 2 (1997): 160–68; and Richard S. Cooper, Charles N. Rotimi, and Ryk Ward, "The Puzzle of Hypertension in African-Americans" *Scientific American* 280, no. 2 (1999): 56–63.

19. Cooper and Rotimi, "Hypertension in Populations of West African Origin," 23.

20. See Sherman A. James, "John Henryism and the Health of African-Americans," *Culture, Medicine and Psychiatry* 18, no. 2 (1994): 163–82; Sherman A. James, "Racial and Ethnic Differences in Infant Mortality and Low Birth Weight: A Psychosocial Critique," *Annals of Epidemiology* 3, no. 2 (1993): 130–36; S. A. James, N. L. Keenan, D. S. Strogatz, S. R. Browning, and J. M. Garrett, "Socioeconomic Status, John Henryism, and Blood Pressure in Black Adults: The Pitt County Study," *American Journal of Epidemiology* 35, no. 1 (1992): 59–67; K. C. Light, P. A. Obrist, A. Sherwood, S. A. James, and D. S. Strogatz, "Effects of Race and Marginally Elevated Blood Pressure on Responses to Stress," *Hypertension* 10, no. 6 (1987): 555–63; S. A. James, D. S. Strogatz, S. B. Wing, and D. L. Ramsey, "Socioeconomic Status, John Henryism, and Hypertension in Blacks and Whites," *American Journal of Epidemiology* 126, no. 4 (1987): 664–73; and S. A. James, "Psychosocial Precursors of Hypertension: A Review of the Epidemiologic Evidence," *Circulation* 76 (1987): 160–66.

21. See Fatimah Jackson, "Anthropological Measurement: The Mismeasure of African Americans," *Annals of the American Academy of Political and Social Science* 568 (2000): 154–71, quotation from 156.

22. Cavalli-Sforza, Menozzi, and Piazza, *The History and Geography of Human Genes,* xii.

23. For a more systematic examination of these differences and an integration of the two different perspectives, see: Kingsley Davis and Judith Blake, "Social Structure and Fertility: An Analytic Framework," *Economic Development and Cultural Change,* no. 4 (1956): 211–35; Mendel C. Sheps and Jane A. Menken, *Mathematical Models of Conception and Birth* (Chicago: University of Chicago Press, 1973); and John Bongaarts and Robert G. Potter, *Fertility, Biology, and Behavior: An Analysis of the Proximate Determinants* (San Diego: Academic Press, 1983).

24. Edwin J. C. G. Van Den Oord and David C. Rowe, "Racial Differences in Birth Health Risk: A Quantitative Genetic Approach," *Demography* 37, no. 3 (2000): 286.

25. For an estimation of the magnitude of interracial reproduction, see Roderick J. Harrison and Claudette E. Bennett, "Racial and Ethnic Diversity," in *State of the Union: America in the 1990s,* vol. 2: *Social Trends,* ed. Reynolds Farley (New York: Russell Sage Foundation, 1995), 164–69. For an empirical illustration of the impact of interracial births on estimates of infant mortality, see Robert A. Hahn, Joseph Mulinare, and Steven M. Teutsch, "Inconsistencies in Coding of Race and Ethnicity between Birth and Death in US Infants: A New Look at Infant Mortality, 1983 through 1985," *Journal of the American Medical Association* 267, no. 2 (1992): 259–63.

26. For examples of the explication of multigroup demography, see Robert Schoen, *Modeling Multigroup Populations* (New York: Plenum Press, 1988), chap. 10.

27. For examples of this research, see Kenneth M. Weiss, "The Biodemography of Variation in Human Frailty," *Demography* 27, no. 2 (1990): 185–206; Harriet B. Presser, "Age at Menarche, Socio-Sexual Behavior, and Fertility," *Social Biology* 25, no. 2 (1978): 94–101; J. Richard Udry, "The Nature of Gender," *Demography* 31, no. 4 (1986): 561–73; and Kenneth W. Wachter and Caleb E. Finch, eds., *Between Zeus and the*

*Salmon: The Biodemography of Longevity* (Washington, D.C.: National Academy Press, 1997); Julian Adams, Albert Hermalin, David Lam, and Peter Smouse, eds., *Convergent Issues in Genetics and Demography* (New York: Oxford University Press, 1990); and Linda G. Martin and Beth J. Soldo, eds., *Racial and Ethnic Differences in the Health of Older Americans* (Washington, D.C.: National Academy Press, 1997), esp. chapters 2, 3, 4, and 8.

28.  Mary Water, *Ethnic Options: Choosing Identities in America* (Berkeley: University of California Press, 1990).

29.  Mario T. Garcia, *Mexican Americans: Leadership, Ideology, and Identity, 1930–1960* (New Haven: Yale University Press, 1989), 46–49.

30.  Paul Starr, "Social Categories and Claims in the Liberal State," *Social Research* 59, no. 2 (1992): 263–95.

31.  Statistical Council, "Minutes of a meeting of the Statistical Council held at Pretoria on Monday the 14th November," 1921, State Archives, Transvaal Depot, Ref no. SES, 5/10/5.

32.  Dr. D. F. Malan, cited in Hermann Giliomee, "The Growth of Afrikaner Identity," in *Segregation and Apartheid: In Twentieth Century South Africa,* ed. William Beinart and Saul Du Bow (New York: Routledge, 1995), 192. Dr. Malan, along with General Hertzog, was one of the original Afrikaner nationalists at the beginning of the century.

33.  J. L. Sadie, "The Political Arithmetic of the S.A. Population," *Journal of Racial Affairs* 1 (1949): 3.

34.  Sadie, "The Political Arithmetic of the S.A. Population," 3–8; C. W. Cousins, 1921, cited in *Census of the Union of South Africa,* vol. 1, no. 15 (Pretoria: Union Government, 1923), vi.

35.  For a general discussion of race and social justice, see Bernard Boxill, *Blacks and Social Justice* (Lenhan, N.J.: Rowman and Littlefield, 1984).

36.  In an insightful moment of reflection on the meanings of measurement of statistical observations in *Statistical Methods for Research Workers,* Ronald A. Fisher states: "Indeed, since no observational record can completely specify a human being, the populations studied are always to some extent abstractions. If we have records of the stature of 10,000 recruits, it is rather the population of statures than the population of recruits that is open to study. Nevertheless, in a real sense, statistics is the study of populations, or aggregates of individuals, rather than individuals" (Ronald A. Fisher, *Statistical Methods for Research Workers* [London: Oliver and Boyd, 1925], 2).

## 7.  Deracializing the Logic of Social Statistics

1.  See chapter 3. Also, several statisticians have brought the issue of causation into clearer focus. See David A. Freedman, "Statistical Models and Shoe Leather," *Sociological Methodology* 21 (1991): 291–358; David R. Cox, "Causality: Some Statistical Aspects," *Journal of the Royal Statistical Society,* Series A, 135 (1992): part 2, 291–301; Michael E. Sobel, "Causal Inference in the Social and Behavioral Sciences," in *Handbook of Statistical Modeling for the Social and Behavioral Sciences,* ed. Gerhard Arminger, Clifford C. Clogg, and Michael E. Sobel (New York: Plenum Press, 1995), 1–38; Clifford C. Clogg and Adamantios Haritou, "The Regression Method of Causal Inference and a Dilemma Confronting This Method," in *Causality in Crisis? Statisti-*

*cal Methods and the Search for Causal Knowledge in the Social Sciences* ed. Vaughn R. McKim and Stephen P. Turner (Notre Dame: University of Notre Dame Press, 1997), 83–112; and David A. Freedman "From Association to Causation via Regression," in *Causality in Crisis?* ed. McKim and Turner, 113–62.

2. Otis D. Duncan, "Path Analysis: Sociological Examples," *American Journal of Sociology* 72 (1966): 1–16. Path analysis was introduced by the geneticist S. Wright in "Correlation and Causation," *Journal of Agricultural Research* 20 (1921): 557–85. Also see Otis D. Duncan, *Introduction to Simultaneous Equation Models* (New York: Academic Press, 1975).

3. This point is very clearly made by Stuart Hall in his classic article on racial theory. Hall emphasizes "the non-reductive approach to questions concerning the interrelationship between class and race. This has proved to be one of the most complex and difficult theoretical problems to address, and it has frequently led to the adoption of one or another extreme positions. Either one 'privileges' the underlying class relationships, emphasizing that all ethnically and racially differentiated labour forces are subject to the same exploitative relationships within capital; or one emphasizes the centrality of ethnic and racial categories and divisions at the expense of the fundamental class structuring of society. Though these two extremes appear to be the polar opposites of one another, in fact, they are inverse, mirror-images of each other, in the sense that, both feel required to produce a single and exclusive determining principle of articulation—class or race—even if they disagree as to which should be accorded the privileged sign" (Stuart Hall, "Gramsci's Relevance for the Study of Race and Ethnicity," *Journal of Communication Inquiry* 10 [1986]: 5–27).

4. I use the term *regression* in a broad sense to include logistic regression, regression analysis, regression analysis of survival data, ordinary least-squares regression, and so on.

5. Otis Duncan refers to this process as *statisticism* (see Otis Dudley Duncan, *Notes on Social Measurement: Historical and Critical* [New York: Russell Sage Foundation, 1984], 226–27).

6. Cox, "Causality," 297.

7. Compare R. A. Fisher, "The Correlation between Relatives on the Supposition of Mendelian Inheritance," *Transactions of the Royal Society of Edinburgh* 52 (1918): 399–433; and Francis Galton's two articles: "Regression towards Mediocrity in Hereditary Stature," *Journal of the Anthropological Institute* 15 (1886): 246–63, and "Correlations and Their Measurement, Chiefly from Anthropometric Data," *Proceeding of the Royal Society of London* 45 (1889): 135.

8. See Herbert L. Smith, "Specification Problems in Experimental and Non-Experimental Social Research," *Sociological Methodology* 20 (1990): 59–91; Paul R. Rosenbaum, "From Association to Causation in Observational Studies: The Role of Tests of Strongly Ignorable Treatment Assignment," *Journal of the American Statistical Association* 79, no. 385 (1984): 41–47; and Cox, "Causality."

9. Rosenbaum, "From Association to Causation in Observational Studies," 42.

10. For example, the methodological assumptions of independence of the treatment and the response variable and the positive probability of receiving each treatment are referred to as the assumption that treatment assignment is strongly ignorable. See Rosenbaum, "From Association to Causation in Observational Studies," 23. For a more general discussion of the assignment mechanism, see Donald B. Rubin,

"Practical Implications of Modes of Statistical Inference for Causal Effects and the Critical Role of the Assignment Mechanism," *Biometrics* 47 (1991): 1213–34.

11. See Stanley Lieberson, "Einstein, Renoir, and Greeley: Some Thoughts about Evidence in Sociology," *American Sociological Review* 57 (1992): 1–15.

12. Ibid., 7.

13. Paul W. Holland, "Statistics and Causal Inference," *Journal of the American Statistical Association* 81, no. 396 (1986): 945–70. Also see the discussion of Yule in chapter 3 above.

14. Ibid., 946.

15. An unbiased estimator of the average effect of public school in the population is $E(Y_t u - Y_c u) = T$, where $T$ is the average causal effect. In probabilistic terms, $T = E(Y_t u) - (Y_c u)$, where $E(\cdot)$ is the expectation in the population. For an estimate of the average effect of $t$, we would calculate $E(Y_t u)$, that is, $\overline{Y_t} u$, as the sample mean among individuals receiving treatment $t$; in our example this would refer to individuals attending private school. Likewise we would use data on individuals receiving treatment $c$, public school, to estimate $E(Y_c u)$. In practice, these are estimates of $E(Y_t u \mid T = t)$ and $E(Y_c u \mid T = c)$. Yet, these quantities are not equal to the respective unconditional expectations unless our sample is random and the population is randomly divided into treatment and control groups. Randomization allows the assumption that $Y_1, \ldots, Y_t \amalg T$ is statistically reasonable and allows us to estimate the average effect of attending private school, $t$, versus $c$ by $\overline{Y_t} u - \overline{Y_c} u$.

16. See James J. Heckman, "The Common Structure of Statistical Models of Truncation, Sample Selection and Limited Dependent Variables and a Simple Estimator for Such Models," *Annals of Economic and Social Measurement* 5 (1976): 475–92. For example, selection bias arises in evaluating the impact of private school attendance on test scores when the mean test scores of private school students differ from the mean test scores of comparison-group members even in the absence of private school attendance.

17. Holland, "Statistics and Causal Inference"; Cox, "Causality"; Sobel, "Causal Inference in the Social and Behavioral Sciences"; and Rosenbaum, "From Association to Causation in Observational Studies."

18. For a more general presentation of the model of associational inference, see Holland, "Statistical and Causal Inference"; and Rosenbaum, "From Association to Causation in Observational Studies."

19. Note the similarity between my examples and those presented by Holland, "Statistics and Causal Inference," 954–55.

20. Ronald A. Fisher, *The Design of Experiments* (New York: Hafner Publishing, 1971), 16.

21. Ronald A. Fisher, *Statistical Methods and Scientific Inference* (New York: Hafner Publishing, 1973), 37–38.

22. Social statisticians have made substantial progress in developing methods that recognize this commitment, and they have begun the task of formalizing the process. For some examples, see James J. Heckman and V. Joseph Hotz, "Choosing among Alternative Nonexperimental Methods for Estimating the Impact of Social Programs: The Case of Manpower Training," *Journal of the American Statistical Association* 84, no. 2 (1989): 862–74; and James J. Heckman and Jeffrey A. Smith, "Assessing the Case for Social Experiments," *Journal of Economic Perspectives* 9, no. 2 (1995): 85–110.

23. Holland, "Statistics and Causal Inference"; Cox, "Causality"; Sobel, "Causal Inference in the Social and Behavioral Sciences"; Smith, "Specification Problems in Experimental and Non-Experimental Social Research."

24. Lieberson, "Einstein, Renoir, and Greeley," 9.

25. See Paul Meier, Jerome Sacks, and Sandy L. Zabell, "What Happened in Hazelwood: Statistics, Employment Discrimination and the 80% Rule," in *Statistics and the Law*, ed. Morris H. DeGroot, Stephen E. Fienberg, and Joseph B. Kadane (New York: John Wiley and Sons, 1986), 1–40; Delores A. Conway and Harry V. Roberts, "Regression Analyses in Employment Discrimination Cases," in *Statistics and the Law*, ed. DeGroot, Fienberg, and Kadane, 107–68; Arthur P. Dempster, "Employment Discrimination and Statistical Science," *Statistical Science* 3, no. 2 (1988): 149–95; Stephen E. Fienberg and Miron L. Straf, "Statistical Evidence in the US Courts: An Appraisal," *Journal of the Royal Statistical Society* 154 (1991): part 1, 49–59.

26. Meier, Sacks, and Zabell, "What Happened in Hazelwood."

27. *Castaneda v. Partida*, 430 U.S. 482 (1977), section 4.2, notes.

28. Imagine a simple regression model of racial discrimination of the form: $Y_i = R_i\alpha + X_i\beta + e_i$, where $i$ denotes values for a particular employee: $Y_i$ stands for the salary of the *ith* employee, $R_i$ for the race of the *ith* employee (1 for black and 0 for white), and $X_i$ is a vector of observed characteristics of the *ith* employee (education, experience, etc.). The error term, $e_i$, is conventionally said to vary randomly and independently from the values of $R_i$ and $X_i$, whereas $\alpha$ and $\beta$ are said to be the parameters of the model.

29. See Arthur P. Dempster "Employment Discrimination and Statistical Science."

30. More formally employers are thought to determine employee productivity as $Y^* = E(Y^{**} \mid R, X^*)$, where $X^*$ denotes a vector of employee characteristics known to the employer (but not necessarily known by the social statistician), $Y^{**}$ denotes the "true worth measures" of employee productivity (unknown to both the employer and the social statistician), and $Y^*$ is employee productivity as estimated by the employer. It is implicitly assumed that the sums and differences of $Y$, $Y_i^*$, and $Y_i^{**}$ are meaningful. In the case of overt racial discrimination, the employer hires or rewards "white" employees while "black" employees are not hired or rewarded, $Y^*$, such that $Y_i = R_i\alpha' + Y^*$.

31. Edmund S. Phelps, "The Statistical Theory of Racism and Sexism," *American Economic Review* 62, no. 4 (1972): 659–61; Kenneth J. Arrow, "The Theory of Discrimination," in *Discrimination in Labor Markets*, ed. Orley Ashenfelter and Albert Rees (Princeton: Princeton University Press, 1973), 3–33. This analysis has been extended to the examination of the impact of affirmative action on employer beliefs and worker productivity (see Shelly J. Lundberg, "The Enforcement of Equal Opportunity Laws under Imperfect Information: Affirmative Action and Alternatives," *Quartile Journal of Economics* 106, no. 1 [1991]: 309–26; and Stephen Coate and Glenn C. Loury, "Will Affirmative-Action Policies Eliminate Negative Stereotypes?" *American Economic Review* 83, no. 5 [1993]: 1220–40).

32. See R. D. Bullard, *Dumping in Dixie: Race, Class, and Environmental Quality* (Boulder: Westview Press, 1990); Douglass L. Anderton, Andy B. Anderson, John Michael Oakes, and Michael R. Fraser, "Environmental Equity: The Demographics of Dumping," *Demography* 31, no. 2 (1994): 229–48.

33. Howard Schuman, Charlotte Steeh, Lawrence Bobo, and Maria Krysan, *Racial Attitudes in America: Trends and Interpretations* (Cambridge, Mass.: Harvard Univer-

sity Press, 1998); Lawrence D. Bobo, "Reclaiming a Du Boisian Perspective on Racial Attitudes," *Annals of the American Academy of Political and Social Science* 568 (2000): 186–202.

34. Lawrence D. Bobo, "Reclaiming a Du Boisian Perspective on Racial Attitudes."

## Epilogue

1. For some examples of this research, see: William H. Tucker, *The Science and Politics of Racial Research* (Urbana: University of Illinois Press, 1994); Oscar H. Gandy Jr., *Communication and Race: A Structural Perspective* (New York and Oxford: Arnold, 1998), chapter 6; Michael C. Dawson, *Behind the Mule: Race and Class in African-American Politics* (Princeton: Princeton University Press, 1994), esp. chapter 8; Hayward Derrick Horton, "Rethinking American Diversity: Conceptual and Theoretical Challenges for Racial and Ethnic Demography," forthcoming in *American Diversity: A Demographic Challenge for the Twenty-First Century,* ed. Stewart Tolnay and Nancy Denton; Lawrence D. Bobo, "Reclaiming a Du Boisian Perspective on Racial Attitudes," *Annals of the American Academy of Political and Social Science* 568 (2000): 186–202; Lee D. Baker, *From Savage to Negro: Anthropology and the Construction of Race, 1896–1954* (Berkeley: University of California Press, 1998); Patricia Hill Collins, *Fighting Words: Black Women and the Search for Justice* (Minneapolis: University of Minnesota Press, 1998); Lewis R. Gordon, *Bad Faith and Antiblack Racism* (Atlantic Highlands, N.J.: Humanities Press, 1995); Lewis R. Gordon, *Fanon and the Crisis of European Man: An Essay on Philosophy and the Human Sciences* (New York: Routledge, 1995); James B. McKee, *Sociology and the Race Problem: The Failure of a Perspective* (Urbana: University of Illinois Press, 1993); and Charles W. Mills, *The Racial Contract* (Ithaca: Cornell University Press, 1997).

2. Awareness of these limits of racial thinking by critical thinkers such as Frantz Fanon led to his rejection of the ontological and fixed existence of racial identity. See Frantz Fanon, *Black Skin, White Masks* (New York: Grove Press, 1967); and Frantz Fanon, *The Wretched of the Earth* (New York: Grove Press, 1963). As Lewis R. Gordon notes, "persons of color," unlike the Jews, have no identity before their pejorative conceptualization by post-Columbus Europeans (see Gordon, *Fanon and the Crisis of European Man,* 38–66).

# Index

created by Eileen Quam

**Tukufu Zuberi** is professor of sociology at the University of Pennsylvania. He is author of *Swing Low, Sweet Chariot: The Mortality Cost of Colonizing Liberia in the Nineteenth Century* (published under the name Antonio McDaniel). His interests in the sociology of race and the demography of Africa and the African diaspora are reflected in his current work with the African Census Analysis Project and the Interracial Contact and Social Stratification Project.